MW00522773

COLLABORATIVE FINANCE

KATHERINE L. JACKSON
Indiana University - South Bend

South-Western College Publishing
Thomson Learning™

Australia • Canada • Denmark • Japan • Mexico • New Zealand • Philippines
Puerto Rico • Singapore • South Africa • Spain • United Kingdom • United States

Collaborative Finance, by Katherine L. Jackson

Vice President/Publisher: Jack W. Calhoun
Acquisitions Editor: Michael B. Mercier
Senior Developmental Editor: Susanna C. Smart
Production Editor: Amy S. Gabriel
Marketing Manager: Julie Lindsay
Media Technology Editor: Kurt Gerdenich
Media Production Editor: Vicky True
Manufacturing Coordinator: Charlene Taylor
Cover Design: A Small Design Studio/Ann Small
Cover Illustration: Warren Gebert
Printer: Webcom

COPYRIGHT ©2000 by South-Western College Publishing, a division of Thomson Learning.
The Thomson Learning logo is a registered trademark used herein under license.

All Rights Reserved. No part of this work covered by the copyright hereon may be reproduced or
used in any form or by any means – graphic, electronic, or mechanical, including photocopying,
recording, taping, or information storage and retrieval systems – without the written permission of
the publisher.

Printed in Canada
1 2 3 4 5 02 01 00 99

For more information contact South-Western College Publishing, 5101 Madison Road,
Cincinnati, Ohio, 45227 or find us on the Internet at http://www.swcollege.com

For permission to use material from this text or product, contact us by
• telephone: 1-800-730-2214
• fax: 1-800-730-2215
• web: http://www.thomsonrights.com

Library of Congress Cataloging-in-Publication Data
ISBN: 0-538-89070-3

This book is printed on acid-free paper.

BRIEF CONTENTS

SECTION ONE:
CASH FLOWS AND FINANCIAL STATEMENTS

SECTION TWO:
TIME VALUE OF MONEY

SECTION THREE:
RISK AND RETURN

SECTION FOUR:
SECURITY VALUATION

SECTION FIVE:
CAPITAL BUDGETING

CONTENTS

SECTION TWO:
TIME VALUE OF MONEY

SECTION THREE:
RISK AND RETURN

SECTION FOUR:
SECURITY VALUATION

SECTION FIVE:
CAPITAL BUDGETING

Preface

For the past several years, there has been heightened awareness of the benefits of teamwork. Businesses widely employ teams, which are an essential component to remaining competitive in a global marketplace. Indeed, the effective use of teams has been the standard—not the exception—for success.

More recently, collaborative learning approaches and student teamwork have received an increased following among university and college educators as a technique for improving the learning process in their classes. The results have been remarkably positive. Research shows that teams promote greater retention and more productivity, and advance higher-order learning skills that students will need to solve complex problems.

The goal of *Collaborative Finance* is to share the knowledge and ignite a sense of enthusiasm for collaborative learning, as well as a better understanding of why and when it is appropriate and beneficial.

How Collaborative Learning Works

Collaborative learning is active learning. It allows students to practice in a hands-on manner with other students in small groups, so that they work together to maximize their own and each other's learning. The more students work in collaborative groups, the more they learn, the better they understand, and the easier it is for them to remember the subject matter. As an added bonus, students tend to feel better about themselves, their team members, and the course.

The basic elements of collaborative learning are positive interdependence, face-to-face interaction individual accountability and personal responsibility, social skills, and group processing. The first of these, positive interdependence, highlights the fact that the group's success requires the indispensable efforts of each participant, so that the success of one depends on the success of the other. Each group member has a distinctive contribution to make to the joint endeavor because of her resources or role responsibilities. Positive interdependence can include positive goal interdependence, joint reward, shared resources, and assigned roles.

Face-to-face interaction allows students to talk through each element of the assignment in a group discussion. This helps bolster decision-making skills and leads to insights into the problem the group is deliberating, giving every member the ability to influence each other's efforts and move the team towards completion of the group's goals.

Individual accountability and personal responsibility require that students be assessed individually, as well as together as a group. Not only the instructor, but also the group must know which members need assistance. Group processing helps the team reflect on how well they are functioning by describing what was helpful and what was ineffectual for the group, and then deciding what actions to continue or change. The purpose of group processing is to improve the members' contributions to the collaborative efforts towards achieving the team's goals.

Social skills are also a vital part of collaborative learning. Students need to use appropriate interpersonal and small-group skills and must possess leadership and decision-making abilities. Members need to be willing to get to know and trust each other. They should communicate accurately and unambiguously, accept and support each other, and resolve conflicts constructively. These talents do not magically appear; rather, they arise through practice. Collaborative learning provides that practice and prepares students for future team efforts in their business careers.

Features and Supplements

One of the best features of this book is that it contains no notation and thus does not compete with, but complements, the textbook already in use. Students won't find "SV" for stock value in their textbook and then "P_0" for stock value in this book; they will simply find the words "stock value."

Collaborative learning works especially well in finance because the course is very *problem-oriented*. Thus, another important feature of the text is the number, variety, and level of problems included in the Practice Sets throughout the book. In addition, Challenge Problems are included to further stimulate students or to serve as term projects. Solutions to all Practice Sets are provided at the end of each section; short answers are provided for Challenge Problems and their full solutions are included in the instructor's manual.

The text Web site at **http://jackson.swcollege.com** provides links to relevant finance sites and to the resources available on the South-Western finance site, which include Finance Online, the Student Center, the Faculty Center, and more.

Thomson Investors Network is the leading provider of Internet-based, online financial information, offering individual investors a wealth of information and tools needed to make informed investment decisions. A portfolio tracker, live stock quotes, business news, a variety of company and industry reports, market analysis and commentary, and more are available at the site. Instructors using this text receive a complimentary subscription, and their students can subscribe at a deeply discounted rate. Contact your South-Western representative for details. Meanwhile, visit **http://www.thomsoninvest.net** for a preview.

An **Instructor's Manual** by the text author provides tips on teaching with the collaborative method, as well as full solutions for challenge problems.

Acknowledgements

The following reviewers were extremely helpful in the preparation of the final text:

Elizabeth Booth
Michigan State University

Paul Bursik
St. Norbert's College

David Durst
University of Akron

Peppi M. Kenny
Western Illinois University

Morris Knapp
Miami-Dade Community College

Thomas Krueger
University of Wisconsin at La Crosse

Deryl W. Martin
Tennessee Tech University

Lee McClain
Western Washington University

Kathleen S. McNichol
LaSalle University

Charles R. Rayhorn
Northern Michigan University

Emery A. Trahan
Northeastern University

Sarah S. Wells
Columbia College

Shirley Zaragoza
Borough of Manhattan Community College

I would like to thank my editors at South-Western College Publishing—Jack Calhoun, Mike Mercier, Susan Smart, and Amy Gabriel—who all had faith in my ideas for this book and were there to help put together the pieces to produce this final product. Also deserving of my thanks is Tracy Stuart, who first put me in contact with the South-Western group to get this project going. In addition, I thank the many students who have passed through my classes and seemed to enjoy and learn from my method of teaching; I've learned from and enjoyed teaching them as well.

Finally, I would like to thank my husband Keith and daughter Sarah for not only tolerating my distracted mind, long hours, and cranky moments, but for encouraging me and for loving me despite the time spent away from them while writing this book.

Katherine L. Jackson
Indiana University at South Bend

SECTION 1:
Cash Flows and
Financial Statements

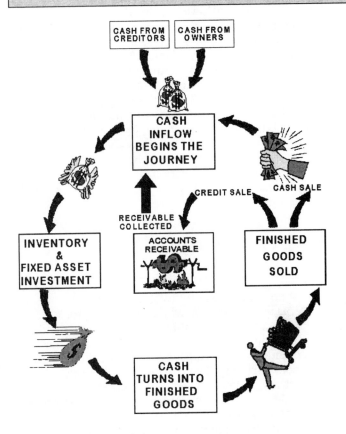

I. CASH FLOWS

Financial managers fill most of their working hours with thoughts of cash flows. Cash flows are a company's lifeblood. How much profit or loss a firm may have is merely a reporting function of the firm's accountant. Numbers on financial statements do not represent the pulsation of the firm's cash inflows and outflows. For instance, most sales are credit transactions, so while the accountant reports a profit on the firm's financial statements, the firm may not have collected any cash. Therefore, sales are celebrations of mere physical occurrences (the trading of goods for promises to pay) and do not always have the delicious aroma of cash.

Waiting patiently for your cash can be trying at times. Suppose you build up too much inventory. Your cash will now spend too long clogged up in inventory before it gets converted to cash again. Time is money and having to wait longer to receive your cash reduces the return on your investment. Alternatively, suppose you get overly ambitious to increase sales and extend credit to anyone who wanders in off the street and has a pulse. Soon your receivables start to grow. True, your accountant is happily reporting profits. You, however, are growing yourself out of business because your potential cash flows are down there in receivables. Your firm has no money. Your creditors begin to grumble, your workers get rebellious; a cash-strapped firm makes everyone cranky.

To be a successful firm you have to do more than make your accountant happy (although that's a start). You have to have an ongoing cash inflow. Financial managers must evaluate everything they do in terms of the cash flow implications.

To figure out cash inflows and outflows we need to have a firm's financial statements (i.e., balance sheet, income statement, statement of cash flows). We will use financial statements in just about everything because it is the one set of information that is available from all companies. Financial statements are so coveted because accounting rules force standardization. While there are different rules that companies can throw in just to complicate our lives (e.g., LIFO versus FIFO), the financial statements remain, for the most part, extremely useful. For our current purposes (we'll have more later) we want to construct a cash flow statement to tell us where the inflows came from and where the outflows went. To put together the statement of cash flows we first need to construct the firm's balance sheet and income statement. The following sections give a brief review of accounting statement construction. If it has been a while since you had your accounting courses you may want to use this as a quick refresher.

II.   FINANCIAL STATEMENTS

No doubt you had at least one, and probably two, accounting courses as a prerequisite for this class. Perhaps it's been a while since you took those courses or maybe you weren't paying as much attention as you wish you had. In any event, before we go any further and dazzle you with the wonders of finance we need to have you up to speed on accounting statements. Thus, the next item of business is to learn how to construct the basic financial statements. We're going to construct a balance sheet and income statement. Then we'll use those financial statements to construct the cash flow statement. If you need further review, refer to your text or dust off those accounting books and get busy.

Financial statements are wonderful innovations. Not only do they give us the data to construct our cash flow statement, but we also use them to conduct the financial analysis (via financial ratios) that management and investors alike use to gauge a firm's relative strengths and weaknesses. Financial ratios, as we'll see later, help us ascertain how well a firm has performed. We also use existing financial statements to help forecast the firm's future financial well-being under differing (investment and financing) scenarios. This information helps management make the best investment and financing decisions possible.

A. Balance Sheet

Remember a balance sheet is a financial statement that lists what a firm owns on the left-hand side (assets) and on the right-hand side lists how they paid for it (liabilities and equity). As with your own asset purchases, you either borrowed the money, used your own money or some combination. Firms operate the same way. When a firm buys an asset they either borrow the money producing a liability, the owners of the firm supplied the funds (shareholder's equity) or some combination of the two occurred.

A balance sheet is a snapshot of a company's finances at a particular moment. If you took another picture ten minutes later, the two photos may differ. For example, consider the balance sheet for Weiler Corporation below.

Suppose during that ten-minute interval the accountant for Weiler sent a check for $500 to pay a company supplier for goods purchased on credit. The cash account would decrease by $500 to $2,500 and accounts payable would decrease by $500 to $1,000 (remember a balance sheet has to balance). The balance sheet depicted in the second photo would look different from the first photo, emphasizing that the balance sheet shows what the firm owns and owes at a specific point in time.

WEILER CORPORATION
BALANCE SHEET
FOR THE YEAR ENDED DECEMBER 31, 2000
(Thousands of Dollars, Except Per Share Data)

ASSETS		LIABILITIES	
Cash	$3,000	Accounts Payable	$1,500
Marketable Securities	$3,000	Accrued Salaries & Wages	$1,200
Accounts Receivable	$8,000	Accrued Taxes	$2,000
Inventory	$10,000	Total Current Liabilities	$4,700
Total Current Assets	$24,000	Notes Payable	$5,300
Gross Fixed Assets	$98,000	Mortgage Bonds	$37,000
Accumulated Depreciation	$14,000	Debentures	$10,000
Net Fixed Assets	$84,000	Total Long-Term Debt	$52,300
		Total Liabilities	$57,000
		SHAREHOLDER'S EQUITY	
		Common Stock (par value)	$1,000
		Additional Paid-In Capital	$15,000
		Retained Earnings	$35,000
		Total Shareholder's Equity	$51,000
Total Assets	$108,000	Total Claims	$108,000

1 Million Shares Outstanding
Book value per share = Total shareholder equity/Shares outstanding
Book value per share = $51,000,000/1,000,000 = $51
Current market value per share = $85

We can't leave the balance sheet until we discuss the various accounts. If you need further explanations of the various individual asset, liability and equity accounts refer to either your textbook or drag those accounting books off the shelf. Assets are items a company owns such as inventory, receivables, fixed assets, etc. Accountants list the items on the balance sheet in order of liquidity, listing the most liquid assets (e.g., cash and marketable securities) first and the least liquid assets (e.g., fixed assets) last.

Capital refers to the funds a firm uses to purchase/finance their assets. Capital comes in two forms: liabilities and equity. Liabilities represent borrowed funds. Equity is owner-supplied capital. Borrowed funds can be short term or long term depending on the type of asset being financed. Firms typically use long-term financing for more permanent (fixed) assets and short-term liabilities to fund their working capital assets (e.g., inventory and receivables). Liabilities are listed in order of maturity with the debts coming due the soonest (e.g., accounts payable and accruals) listed first and long-term debt (e.g., bonds) listed last. Equity accounts typically consist of common equity and retained earnings. Common equity is the money your firm raises selling shares of common stock. In contrast, retained earnings are the portion of net income that management retains (i.e., the portion of net income that the company does not pay out as dividends) and reinvests into the firm. The retained earnings account on the balance sheet represents the amount of capital the owners have reinvested into the firm over its life. Don't get confused, retained earnings are not a pool of funds waiting for some creative spender. The retained earnings account reported on the balance sheet represents the cumulative portion of net income the owners have put toward the acquisition of more assets and/or repayment of liabilities.

Note one more important item about balance sheets. Because accountants are who they are and professional standards say so, all asset, liability and equity accounts are recorded at cost (a.k.a. book value). Thus, a computer manufacturer might have a warehouse chock-full of Commodore 64 computers listed in the inventory account on the balance sheet at $2,000,000. Yet, the firm would probably have to pay precious dollars to have a plastic recycler cart these obsolete computers off the premises.

Now that we've used the balance sheet to determine what a firm owns and owes at a given moment in time, let's turn our attention to the income statement. The income statement documents the movement of accounting income over a period of time.

B. Income Statement

The income statement shows what inflows and outflows have taken place over a period. The income statement, like a motion picture, shows what has occurred over a period of time. Below is the income statement for Weiler Corporation.

WEILER CORPORATION
INCOME STATEMENT
FOR THE YEAR ENDED DECEMBER 31, 2000
(Thousands of Dollars, Except Per Share Data)

Sales	$120,000
Cost of Goods Sold	$73,000
Salaries and Wages	$34,000
Depreciation Expense (DEP)	$3,000
Total Operating Costs	$110,000
Earnings Before Interest & Taxes (EBIT)	$10,000
Interest Expense	$4,700
Earnings Before Taxes (EBT)	$5,300
Taxes	$1,802
Net Income (NI)	$3,498
Common Dividends	$1,796
Additions to Retained Earnings	$1,702

Earnings per share = Net income/Shares outstanding
Earnings per share = $3,498,000/1,000,000 = $3.50
Dividends per share = Dividends paid to stockholders/Shares outstanding
Dividends per share = $1,796,000/1,000,000 = $1.80

A firm starts with sales revenues and subtracts the cost of making their product (cost of goods sold). The IRS also allows them to deduct the cost of doing business. For example, Weiler Corporation deducts advertising, interest, and depreciation expenses before calculating taxable income. These deductible expenses lower Weiler's taxable income and hence their tax liability. Note that while the cost of debt (interest expense) is tax deductible, dividends paid to common and preferred shareholders are not a tax-deductible expense. The tax deductibility of interest expense makes the cost of debt financing lower than financing with equity. In effect, the government subsidizes the cost of borrowing by letting firms deduct their interest expense.

Then there's depreciation (a.k.a. the fake or noncash charge). Tax laws stipulate that firms may not write off a fixed asset such as a piece of equipment or machinery at the time of acquisition. They must deduct the expense over the asset's life in the form of depreciation. Thus, even though they may have acquired the equipment in the current year, they must expense it over a number of years. They will, in effect, deduct for an expense they didn't really have. Remember, they have already paid for (or financed) the piece of equipment so depreciation merely represents the IRS's effort to match cost with usage.

Depreciation expense is the deduction against income for the current accounting period. Accumulated deprecation reported on the balance sheet is the depreciation expenses summed up over the life of the fixed asset (i.e., literally the accumulated depreciation expenses).

We have now covered the basics for constructing the balance sheet and income statement. There is, however, no substitute for doing it yourself. On the following pages are two practice sets. These will help solidify your knowledge. Work the first problem in the practice set creating the balance sheet and income statement for Carolina Business Machines (should take you about 20-30 minutes) and then check your answers with the solutions at the end of this section.

Don't peek ➤➤➤ ➤➤➤ at the answers while you're working the problems. If you sneak a glimpse at the solutions whenever you get in a tight spot, you'll never learn from your mistakes and be doomed to repeat them on a test - where peeking is a big no no. If time permits and you need more practice then continue on to the second problem using the financial information of Dakota Corporation. Again, check your answers with the solutions.

NOTES: _____

_____

_____

_____

_____

_____

_____

_____

_____

_____

PRACTICE SET A
Financial Statement Construction

Instructions: Use the following information to construct the 2000 balance sheet and income statement for Carolina Business Machines. Forms for the balance sheet and income statement are provided on the following page. Round all numbers to the nearest whole dollar. All numbers are in thousands of dollars. Unless you have a really big eraser, be sure to read the whole problem before you jump in and get started.

1. At the end of 1999 the firm had $43,000 in gross fixed assets. In 2000 they purchased an additional $14,000 of fixed asset equipment. Accumulated depreciation at the end of 1999 was $21,000. The depreciation expense in 2000 is $4,620. At the end of 2000 the firm had $3,000 in cash and $3,000 in accounts payable. In 2000 the firm extended a total of $9,000 in credit to a number of their customers in the form of accounts receivable.

 The firm generated $60,000 in sales revenue in 2000. Their cost of goods sold was 60 percent of sales. They also incurred salaries and wages expense of $10,000. To date the firm has $1,000 in accrued salaries and wages. They borrowed $10,000 from their local bank to help finance the $15,000 in inventory they now have on hand. The firm also has $7,120 invested in marketable securities.

 The firm currently has $20,000 in long-term debt outstanding and paid $2,000 in interest on their outstanding debt. Over the firm's life, shareholders have put up $30,000. Eighty percent of the shareholder's funds are in the form of retained earnings. The par value per share of Carolina Business Machines stock is $1.00. To date, the firm has accrued $1,500 in taxes owed.

 For simplicity assume that all taxable income is taxed at a flat rate of 34 percent. The firm has consistently paid out 40 percent of net income in the form of dividends.

CAROLINA BUSINESS MACHINES
BALANCE SHEET
FOR THE YEAR ENDED DECEMBER 31, 2000
(Thousands of Dollars, Except Per Share Data)

ASSETS		LIABILITIES	
		SHAREHOLDER'S EQUITY	

CAROLINA BUSINESS MACHINES
INCOME STATEMENT
FOR THE YEAR ENDED DECEMBER 31, 2000
(Thousands of Dollars, Except Per Share Data)

Instructions: Use the following information to construct the 2000 balance sheet and income statement for Dakota Corporation. Forms for the balance sheet and income statement are provided on the following page. Round all numbers to the nearest whole dollar. All numbers are in thousands of dollars.

2. At the end of 1999 Dakota Corporation had $75,000 in gross fixed assets. In 2000 they purchased an additional $7,000 of fixed asset equipment. Accumulated depreciation at the end of 1999 was $29,000. The depreciation expense in 2000 is $2,000. At the end of 2000 the firm had $10,000 in cash and $12,000 in accounts payable. In 2000 the firm extended a total of $16,000 in credit to a number of their customers in the form of accounts receivable.

    The firm generated $180,000 in sales revenue in 2000. Their cost of goods sold was 70 percent of sales. They also incurred salaries and wages expense of $34,500. To date the firm has $4,500 in accrued salaries and wages. They borrowed $7,000 from their local bank to help finance the $31,000 in inventory they now have on hand. The firm also has $2,000 invested in marketable securities.

    The firm currently has $26,000 in long-term debt outstanding and paid $4,500 in interest on their outstanding debt. Over the firm's life, shareholders have put up $59,000. Of that amount, $46,000 is in the form of retained earnings. The par value per share of Dakota Corporation stock is $1.00. To date, the firm has accrued $1,500 in taxes owed.

    For simplicity assume that all taxable income is taxed at a flat rate of 34 percent. The firm has consistently paid out 30 percent of net income in the form of dividends.

Dakota Corporation's
Top Dog

DAKOTA CORPORATION
BALANCE SHEET
FOR THE YEAR ENDED DECEMBER 31, 2000
(Thousands of Dollars, Except Per Share Data)

ASSETS		LIABILITIES	
		SHAREHOLDER'S EQUITY	

DAKOTA CORPORATION
INCOME STATEMENT
FOR THE YEAR ENDED DECEMBER 31, 2000
(Thousands of Dollars, Except Per Share Data)

C. Cash Flow Statement

We now have a working knowledge of how to put together a balance sheet and income statement. Next, we need to move on to the construction of the statement of cash flows. The appearance may vary from text to text and across firms so don't worry so much about format as content (i.e., showing the points of arrival and departure for the firm's cash flows). Put simply, the statement of cash flows tells us what the change in the cash account was, but more importantly it explains how these changes took place. We can see on Weiler's balance sheets for 1999 and 2000 below what change occurred in the cash account.

WEILER CORPORATION BALANCE SHEETS FOR DECEMBER 1999 AND 2000 (Thousands of Dollars, Except Per Share Data)		
ASSETS	**1999**	**2000**
Cash	$5,398	$3,000
Marketable Securities	$2,000	$3,000
Accounts Receivable	$6,000	$8,000
Inventory	$8,400	$10,000
Total Current Assets	$21,798	$24,000
Gross Fixed Assets	$86,000	$98,000
Accumulated Depreciation	$11,000	$14,000
Net Fixed Assets	$75,000	$84,000
Total Assets	$96,798	$108,000
LIABILITIES		
Accounts Payable	$500	$1,500
Accrued Salaries & Wages	$1,000	$1,200
Accrued Taxes	$1,000	$2,000
Total Current Liabilities	$2,500	$4,700
Notes Payable	$4,000	$5,300
Mortgage Bonds	$30,000	$37,000
Debentures	$11,000	$10,000
Total Long-Term Debt	$45,000	$52,300
Total Liabilities	$47,500	$57,000
SHAREHOLDER'S EQUITY		
Common Stock (par value)	$1,000	$1,000
Additional Paid-In Capital	$15,000	$15,000
Retained Earnings	$33,298	$35,000
Total Shareholder's Equity	$49,298	$51,000
Total Claims	$96,798	$108,000

The cash account for Weiler decreased $2,398 between 1999 and 2000. So? What we want to know is where did those funds go? The statement of cash flows tells us where the cash inflows came from and where the cash outflows went. This is much more interesting and informative than being told by Weiler's accountant that cash decreased by $2,398.

We build the statement of cash flows from the income statement and incremental changes in the balance sheet accounts. We can't just use net income because it's not cash flow. We have all heard of firms that report negative net income, but still manage to have cash flow to pay employees, buy equipment, and the like. Alternatively, there are firms whose net income is in the triple digits yet they struggle to meet payroll.

Accounting standards require companies to classify their activities into three categories: Operating, Investing or Financing. We first recognize any change in cash flows and then enter these changes into the appropriate schedule on the statement of cash flows. Got that? You will!

Finding cash flow from operating activities requires us to examine each item on the income statement as well as both the current asset and current liability accounts on the balance sheet to see the inflows and outflows from the firm's operations. Investing activities usually result from the firm's purchase of fixed assets. Changes in the investing category may also occur because of security purchases or sales the firm made. For example, if the firm invests in the stocks or bonds (a.k.a. marketable securities) of another company, we would categorize this as a purchase and record the activity in the investment section of the cash flow statement. Finally, cash flows from financing activities come from changes in the firm's long-term liability and stockholders' equity accounts as well as any common or preferred dividends paid out to shareholders.

Sales Revenue and Accounts Receivable

Let's begin with the first item on the income statement, namely, sales. We assume that all sales began as credit transactions. We want to compare the net income figure from the income statement with the changes in the firm's accounts receivable. This allows us to determine the amount of cash the firm collected as a result of its sales efforts. Weiler had total sales in 2000 of $120,000 and their accounts receivable increased by $2,000 (from $6,000 in 1999 to $8,000 in 2000). Thus Weiler had $2,000 more in sales than it collected in cash. Therefore, the cash inflow from sales was $118,000 ($120,000 sales - $2,000 increase in accounts receivable) and this is the amount we report in the operating activities section in the statement of cash flows.

Sales	$120,000
+Beginning accounts receivable	$6,000
Potential collections	$126,000
−Ending accounts receivable	($8,000)
Cash collections from customers	$118,000

Cost of Goods Sold

The income statement reports that Weiler's cost of goods sold was $73,000. This doesn't mean the firm used this much cash to pay inventory suppliers. Why? Well, for one thing, the cost of goods sold represents the amount of inventory sold, not the amount purchased (the number of interest to us). For another thing, the amount of inventory the company purchased is not the same as cash because most companies purchase their inventory on credit. Inventory increased by $1,600 from 1999 to 2000. This means that purchases were $1,600 more than inventory sold. Recall, our interest is in how much inventory they purchased and not how much they sold.

Ending inventory	$10,000
+Cost of goods sold	$73,000
Inventory to account for	$83,000
−Beginning inventory	($8,400)
Purchases of inventory	$74,600

Thus, inventory purchases must have been $74,600 ($73,000 cost of goods sold + $1,600 increase in inventory). But remember, the company made at least some of these purchases on credit.

Note from the balance sheet that accounts payable increased $1,000 between 1999 and in 2000. This means that Weiler's purchases were $1,000 more than its cash payments.

Beginning accounts payable	$500
+Purchases	$74,600
Total amount to be paid	$75,100
−Ending accounts payable	($1,500)
Amount paid in cash	$73,600

Thus, cash outflows for inventory must have been $73,600 ($74,600 in inventory purchased - $1,000 increase in accounts payable) and we record this outflow under operating activities in the cash flow statement.

Salaries and Wages Expense and Salaries and Wages Payable
The second expense on the income statement is salaries and wages of $34,000. We have to know whether Weiler actually paid this amount (i.e., was this the actual size of the cash outflow). The accrued salary and wage account increased $200 between 1999 and 2000. This means that the amount of cash paid to employees was $200 less than the amount of salaries and wages expense recorded on the income statement.

Beginning accrued salaries and wages	$1,000
+Salaries and wages expense	$34,000
Total amount to be paid	$35,000
−Ending accrued salaries and wages	($1,200)
Cash payments to employees	$33,800

Thus, the firm would record $33,800 ($34,000 salary and wage expense - $200 increase in accrued salaries and wages) as cash payments to employees in the operating activities section of the statement of cash flows.

Depreciation Expense
The next item on the income statement is depreciation expense of $3,000. Recall that depreciation has no effect on cash flows so we don't record depreciation.

Interest Expense
The amount of interest expense reported on the income statement is $4,700. There is no accrual account for interest owed but not yet paid so we show the entire $4,700 as a cash outflow in the operating section of the statement of cash flows.

Income Tax Expense and Income Taxes Payable

The income statement reports income tax expense of $1,802. Note, however, that accrued taxes increased by $1,000 from 1999 to 2000. This means that the amount of cash paid to the government in taxes was $1,000 less than the amount of tax expense reported on the income statement.

Beginning accrued taxes	$1,000
+Income tax expense	$1,802
Total amount to be paid	$2,802
−Ending accrued taxes	($2,000)
Cash payments to IRS	$802

Thus, the firm made payments of $802 ($1,802 income tax expense - $1,000 increase in accrued taxes) and this is what we report as the firm's cash outflow.

We examined all the items on the income statement and both the current asset and current liability accounts on the balance sheet except marketable securities. Marketable securities represent the firm's investment in stocks and bonds in other companies and we will discuss this in more detail in the following section. Right now it's time to look at our completed cash flow from operations section of the statement of cash flows.

WEILER CORPORATION
PARTIAL STATEMENT OF CASH FLOWS
DECEMBER 31, 2000 (Thousands of Dollars)

CASH FLOW FROM OPERATING ACTIVITIES

Cash receipts from customers		$118,000
Cash payment for:		
Inventory	($73,600)	
Salaries & wages	($33,800)	
Interest	($4,700)	
Income taxes	($802)	
Total cash payments		($112,902)
Net cash provided by operating activities		$5,098

Determine the Cash Flows from Investing Activities

Now we'll concentrate on the long-term investments, such as property, plant and equipment as well as any purchases/sales of marketable securities. Weiler's balance sheet shows a $12,000 increase in gross fixed assets between 1999 and 2000. In addition to the purchase of fixed assets, Weiler also purchased $1,000 more in marketable securities. Our completed cash flow from investing activities is shown below.

WEILER CORPORATION
PARTIAL STATEMENT OF CASH FLOWS
DECEMBER 31, 2000 (Thousands of Dollars)

CASH FLOW FROM INVESTING ACTIVITIES

Purchase of fixed assets	($12,000)	
Purchase of marketable securities	($1,000)	
Net cash used for investing activities		($13,000)

Determine the Cash Flows from Financing Activities

To determine cash flow from financing activities we begin with the examination of the firm's long-term liability and equity accounts. What we are looking for is any "arranged" financing in which the firm engaged. This differs from cash flows that occurred in the operating activities section that were the result of the firm conducting its usual business. In the financing section, firms make formal arrangements for cash inflows either through an increase in long-term debt or through the issuance of common or preferred stock. They may also produce cash outflows through a reduction in long-term debt or by purchasing their own common stock as reflected in the firm's treasury stock account. We also include dividend payments in this section because they don't happen automatically as a result of a firm's ongoing business; dividends reflect management's decision for an arranged cash outflow.

Notes Payable

Weiler Corporation increased their notes payable by $1,300 between 1999 and 2000. They accomplished this by borrowing more from their financial institution(s). We record this cash inflow in the financing activities section of the statement of cash flows.

Mortgage Bonds

Weiler issued $7,000 more in mortgage bonds in 2000. This is a cash inflow and represents an increase in their long-term debt. We record this cash inflow in the financing activities section.

Debentures

Weiler repaid $1,000 in principal to their investors reducing their debentures outstanding from $11,000 in 1999 to $10,000 in 2000. We record this as a cash outflow.

Shareholder's Equity

Weiler made no changes in their common stock or additional paid-in capital account. If Weiler had issued common stock (a cash inflow) or had repurchased any of its common stock (a cash outflow), we would record these changes in cash flows in the financing activities section of the statement of cash flows.

Retained Earnings

Weiler had an increase in retained earnings. We don't record this amount because retained earnings are a netted figure (net income - dividends). The cash flow statement should show where the cash came from and where it went. We do, however, want to record the amount of dividends Weiler paid to their shareholders. We can either get this amount directly from the income statement, $1,796, or as the difference between net income and the increase in retained earnings ($3,498 net income – $1,702 increase in retained earnings = $1,796 dividends paid to shareholders). We record this cash outflow in the cash flows from financing activities section of the statement of cash flows.

WEILER CORPORATION PARTIAL STATEMENT OF CASH FLOWS DECEMBER 31, 2000 (Thousands of Dollars)		
CASH FLOW FROM FINANCING ACTIVITIES		
Increase in notes payable	$1,300	
Increase in mortgage bonds	$7,000	
Decrease in debentures	($1,000)	
Dividends paid	($1,796)	
Net cash provided by financing activities		$5,504

Now that we have developed the individual schedules for operating, investing and financing activities let's put the whole statement of cash flows together. The completed statement of cash flows for Weiler Corporation is on the next page.

WEILER CORPORATION		
STATEMENT OF CASH FLOWS		
DECEMBER 31, 2000 (Thousands of Dollars)		

CASH FLOW FROM OPERATING ACTIVITIES		
Cash receipts from customers		$118,000
Cash payment for:		
Inventory	($73,600)	
Salaries & wages	($33,800)	
Interest	($4,700)	
Income taxes	($802)	
Total cash payments		($112,902)
Net cash provided by operating activities		$5,098
CASH FLOW FROM INVESTING ACTIVITIES		
Purchase of fixed assets	($12,000)	
Purchase of marketable securities	($1,000)	
Net cash used for investing activities		($13,000)
CASH FLOW FROM FINANCING ACTIVITIES		
Increase in notes payable	$1,300	
Increase in mortgage bonds	$7,000	
Decrease in debentures	($1,000)	
Dividends paid	($1,796)	
Net cash provided by financing activities		$5,504
Net reduction in cash		($2,398)
Cash at the beginning of the year		$5,398
Cash at the end of the year		$3,000

Right away you'll no doubt notice that we've added a few lines to the bottom of our cash flow statement. These are where we show that the net increase/decrease in cash from operations, investments and financing activities explains the difference between the beginning cash balance and the ending cash balance. In this case Weiler had a net decrease in cash of $2,398. This is exactly the difference between their 1999 beginning balance of $5,398 and their 2000 ending balance of $3,000.

Now for the big question: What does it all mean? We see that Weiler generated $5,098 from operations. They spent $12,000 purchasing additional fixed assets and invested $1,000 more in marketable securities. The firm got the majority of their funding ($5,504) from their financing activities. The firm issued $7,000 worth of mortgage bonds and arranged for another $1,300 in financing as notes payable. They used part of these funds to retire a portion of their outstanding debentures and pay a dividend of $1,796 to shareholders.

Even with all these financing activities and income from operations, the firm had to dip into its cash account to make up for the shortfall created by the acquisition of fixed assets. The next question to ask is whether invasion of the cash account hurt the firm's liquidity position. We want to know, among other things, if the firm is still in a position to pay its current obligations in a timely manner. That will lead us into the next section where we look at ratio analysis.

Before we leave this section, let's turn to Practice Set B on the next page. This will give you a chance to create a cash flow statement and interpret the results. If time permits, and you need more practice, then continue on to the second problem.

PRACTICE SET B
Cash Flow Statement

1.   **Instructions:** Bally Gear has provided its 1999 and 2000 balance sheets and their 2000 income statement below. Construct Bally Gear's cash flow statement. In the space provided, briefly comment on your findings.

BALLY GEAR CORPORATION BALANCE SHEETS for 1999 and 2000		
ASSETS	**1999**	**2000**
Cash	$3,000	$5,000
Marketable Securities	$2,000	$5,000
Accounts Receivable	$18,000	$16,000
Inventory	$26,000	$31,000
Total Current Assets	$49,000	$57,000
Gross Fixed Assets	$86,000	$98,000
Accumulated Depreciation	$38,000	$42,000
Net Fixed Assets	$48,000	$56,000
Total Assets	$97,000	$113,000
LIABILITIES		
Accounts Payable	$9,000	$18,000
Accrued Salaries & Wages	$2,000	$7,000
Accrued Taxes	$3,000	$2,000
Total Current Liabilities	$14,000	$27,000
Notes Payable	$10,000	$9,000
Long-term debt	$20,000	$20,000
Total Liabilities	$44,000	$56,000
SHAREHOLDER'S EQUITY		
Common Stock (par value)	$15,000	$13,000
Retained Earnings	$38,000	$44,000
Total Shareholder's Equity	$53,000	$57,000
Total Claims	$97,000	$113,000

BALLY GEAR CORPORATION INCOME STATEMENT 2000	
Sales	$250,000
Cost of Goods Sold	$207,000
Salaries and Wages	$18,000
Depreciation Expense (DEP)	$4,000
Total Operating Costs	$229,000
Earnings Before Interest & Taxes (EBIT)	$21,000
Interest Expense	$3,000
Earnings Before Taxes (EBT)	$18,000
Taxes	$7,200
Net Income (NI)	$10,800
Common Dividends	$4,800
Additions to Retained Earnings	$6,000

BALLY GEAR CORPORATION
STATEMENT OF CASH FLOWS
DECEMBER 31, 2000 (Thousands of Dollars)

Summary of findings for Bally Gear's Cash Flow Statement:

_____

_____

_____

_____

_____

_____

_____

_____

_____

_____

_____

_____

_____

2. Instructions: Webster has provided its 1999 and 2000 balance sheets and their 1999 income statement below. Construct Webster's cash flow statement. In the space provided, briefly comment on your findings.

WEBSTER CORPORATION BALANCE SHEETS for 1999 and 2000 (Thousands of Dollars)		
ASSETS	**1999**	**2000**
Cash	$40,320	$38,700
Accounts Receivable	$245,840	$302,320
Inventory	$500,640	$650,754
Total Current Assets	$786,800	$991,774
Gross Fixed Assets	$343,700	$397,220
Accumulated Depreciation	$102,340	$127,340
Net Fixed Assets	$241,360	$269,880
Total Assets	$1,028,160	$1,261,654
LIABILITIES		
Accounts Payable	$101,500	$157,890
Accrued Salaries & Wages	$25,000	$35,000
Accrued Taxes	$70,200	$85,650
Total Current Liabilities	$196,700	$278,540
Notes Payable	$140,000	$183,107
Long-term debt	$226,403	$324,600
Total Liabilities	$563,103	$786,247
SHAREHOLDER'S EQUITY		
Common Stock (par value)	$322,000	$322,000
Retained Earnings	$143,057	$153,407
Total Shareholder's Equity	$465,057	$475,407
Total Claims	$1,028,160	$1,261,654

WEBSTER CORPORATION INCOME STATEMENT 2000	
Sales	$2,750,000
Cost of Goods Sold	$2,062,500
Salaries and Wages	$520,000
Depreciation Expense (DEP)	$25,000
Total Operating Costs	$2,607,500
Earnings Before Interest & Taxes (EBIT)	$142,500
Interest Expense	$85,000
Earnings Before Taxes (EBT)	$57,500
Taxes	$23,000
Net Income (NI)	$34,500
Common Dividends	$24,150
Additions to Retained Earnings	$10,350

WEBSTER CORPORATION
STATEMENT OF CASH FLOWS
DECEMBER 31, 2000 (Thousands of Dollars)

Summary of findings for Webster's Cash Flow Statement:

_____

_____

_____

_____

_____

_____

_____

_____

_____

_____

_____

_____

_____

_____

III. TAXES AND DEPRECIATION

Corporations, like the rest of us, don't like to pay taxes. While it is illegal to evade taxes, it is an American duty to defer taxes whenever legally possible. Recognizing some of the basic elements of the corporate tax code can help financial managers make value-maximizing decisions (finance jargon for "increase shareholder wealth"). The tax code can influence a firm's financing decisions because of the differences between the treatment of interest and dividend payments made to the firm's stakeholders (bondholders and stockholders).

Taxes even have implications for a firm's security investments. Whether a firm decides to invest any of their excess cash into stock or bonds the tax treatment of these different cash flows (dividend income versus interest income) may have a significant influence on which type of investment is value maximizing. In the following sections we will examine this issue as well as the debt versus equity financing decision.

A. Interest and Dividends <u>Paid</u> to Stakeholders

Recall from our discussion on financial statements that the interest expense on the firm's debt securities is tax deductible whereas the firm pays dividends out of after-tax income. What this means is that the federal government subsidizes corporate use of debt financing. How so? Because interest expense is tax deductible, a $1.00 paid out to bondholders only costs the firm $0.60 because the firm in a 40 percent tax bracket saves $0.40 in taxes. In the example below we have two firms. Firm A financed their assets with tax-deductible debt while Firm B used equity financing where the investor is paid out of after-tax income.

	Firm A with Debt Financing	Firm B with Equity Financing
EBIT	$6.00	$6.00
Interest expense	$1.00	$0
Taxable income	$5.00	$6.00
Taxes @ 40%	$2.00	$2.40
After-tax income	$3.00	$3.60
Equity financing costs	$0	$1.00
After-tax cash flows	$3.00	$2.60

By using debt financing, Firm A saved $0.40 in taxes. This is $0.40 that the government did not collect in tax revenue, so in essence the government subsidized the firm's financing costs. Thus the after-tax cost of financing with debt is not $1.00, but only $0.60. That might make any firm think twice about how they want to finance their assets. Before you start to pile on the debt, keep in mind that to save $0.40 in taxes the firm has to incur a $1.00 in expenses. A firm will go broke pretty fast if it continues to spend $1 to save $0.40. These tax implications do, however, have a significant influence on a firm's financing decisions.

What about dividends paid to shareholders? To pay a dollar of interest to a bondholder requires the firm to generate a dollar of pre-tax income because interest expense is deductible. To pay a dollar in dividends to shareholders, however, means that a firm in a 40 percent tax bracket must produce $1.67 in pre-tax income. How can that be?

$$\frac{dividend}{(1-\text{marginal tax rate})} = \frac{\$1}{(1-0.40)} = \$1.67$$

Let's test this out to show you how it works

Pre-tax income	$1.67
Tax rate	× .40
Taxes @ .40	$0.67
Pre-tax income	$1.67
Minus taxes	−$0.67
After-tax income available for dividend payment	$1.00

In summary, remember that dividends a corporation pays out to their shareholders are not a tax-deductible expense (i.e., firms pay dividends out of after-tax income). On the other hand, interest paid by a corporation to its bondholders is a tax-deductible expense. Now let's calculate some taxes:

Example #1   In 2000 Bargain Basement Bakery Incorporated (B[cubed]), a popular producer of authentic bagels, generated $20,000 in gross revenues, paid out $3,000 in dividends to their own shareholders and has $15,000 in bonds outstanding with an interest rate of 10 percent. What is Bargain Basement Bakery's tax liability? What is Bargain Basement Bakery's after-tax income? What does Bargain Basement Bakery contribute to retained earnings? Assume the firm pays a flat tax rate of 34 percent.

Gross revenues	$20,000
−Interest expense[1]	($1,500)
Taxable income	$18,500
−Taxes at 34%	($6,290)
After-tax income	$12,210
−Dividends paid	($3,000)
Addition to retained earnings	$9,210

[1]Interest expense $15,000(0.10) = $1,500

Before we add any interesting tax complications, let's take a look at the how the tax code influences a firm's investment decision because of the differences in the treatment of dividend and interest income *received*.

B. Interest and Dividends <u>Received</u> as Investment Income

If you are an individual and you receive dividend income you must pay taxes on the full amount received. If, however, Weiler Corporation owns stock of Roittec Corporation and Roittec pays a dividend, then Weiler only has to pay taxes on 30 percent of the dividend income received from Roittec. The other 70 percent the IRS excludes from taxable income.

Now, depending on whether you're an optimist or a pessimist, you could say that 70 percent of the dividends avoided triple taxation or you could say 30 percent of those dividend dollars got taxed three times. The government, in an effort to avoid the dreaded "T" word (Taxes), will adjust this exclusion as a way to "enhance" revenues. This is much more politically popular than raising taxes directly. Dividends paid by one corporation to another fall under the 70 percent exclusion rule. The IRS, however, considers interest income to be fully taxable. Let's look at the implications of this tax policy by examining Patton Corporation who received $1,000 in dividend income and Bradley Company who received a $1,000 in interest income.

	Patton Co. Received Dividend Income	Bradley Co. Received Interest Income
Income	$1,000	$1,000
Taxable income	$300	$1,000
Taxes @ 40%	($300 × 0.40) <u>$120</u>	($1,000 × 0.40) <u>$400</u>
After-tax income	$180	$600
Plus nontaxable dividends	<u>$700</u>	<u>$0</u>
After-tax cash flow	<u>$880</u>	<u>$600</u>

We see that Patton Corporation, who took advantage of the dividend exclusion, ended up with $280 more in after-tax income than Bradley. Thus, any savvy corporate investor with funds to make security investments would prefer to purchase stock that pays dividend income than bonds that pay interest income. Not too surprisingly, this is why corporations are the largest holders of preferred stock that, by definition, tend to pay large fixed dividends. On the next page we use B^{cubed} again to illustrate this point.

Example #2   In 2000, Bargain Basement Bakery Incorporated (Bcubed), a popular producer of authentic bagels, generated $20,000 in gross revenues, received $5,000 in dividends from some stock it owns in Dough Corporation, and received $2,000 in interest income from their bond investment in Steel House Mixer Corporation. What is Bargain Basement Bakery's tax liability? What is Bargain Basement Bakery's after-tax income? Assume the firm pays a flat tax rate of 34 percent.

Gross revenues	$20,000
+Taxable dividends[1]	$1,500
+Interest income	$2,000
Taxable Income	$23,500
−Taxes at 34%	($7,990)
+Nontaxable dividends[2]	$3,500
After-tax income	$19,010

[1]$5,000 minus the 70% exclusion = $1,500 in taxable dividends
[2]Have to remember to add back nontaxable dividends or we'd be understating the firm's after-tax income by $3,500.

You'll see that the first problem in Practice Set C combines the interest and dividends paid as well as received by Bargain Basement Bakery Incorporated (Bcubed) to determine after-tax income. In the next section we will examine how depreciation expense impacts a company's cash flows.

PRACTICE SET C
TAXES

1. In 2000 Bargain Basement Bakery Incorporated (Bcubed), a popular producer of authentic bagels, generated $20,000 in gross revenues and received $5,000 in dividends from some stock it owns in Dough Corporation. Bcubed paid out $3,000 in dividends to their own shareholders and received $2,000 in interest income from their bond investment in Steel House Mixer Corporation. Bcubed has $15,000 in bonds outstanding with an interest rate of 10 percent. What is Bargain Basement Bakery's tax liability? What is Bargain Basement Bakery's after-tax income? What does Bargain Basement Bakery contribute to retained earnings? Assume the firm pays a flat tax rate of 34 percent.

2. Stone Products produced $600,000 in income from operations (EBIT) in 2000. They paid out $20,000 in dividends to their shareholders and received $40,000 in interest income from some bonds they purchased a few years ago. They also received $80,000 in dividends from a stock investment made three years ago. Stone paid their bondholders $60,000 in interest payments in 2000. What is Stone's tax liability? What is Stone's after-tax income? What does Stone contribute to retained earnings? Assume the firm pays a flat tax rate of 34 percent.

C. Depreciation

Depreciation, you may recall from our cash flow and financial statement analysis discussions, is a noncash charge against income. When a firm purchases an asset it pays for that asset at the time of delivery. Recall that the federal government says the firm has to match machine usage with its useful life. Thus, most firms use the Modified Accelerated Cost Recovery System (MACRS) to determine depreciation expense for tax purposes. If you're not sure how MACRS works or you aren't familiar with some of the major quirks associated with MACRS, refer to your textbook. Only the government would think any of this makes sense, but we have to live by their rules. We'll return to B^{cubed} to illustrate the impact of depreciation on cash flows.

Example #3   Bargain Basement Bakery (B^{cubed}) recently purchased a Dough Squish machine (industry-specific jargon) that cost $25,000. The firm had to modify the equipment and pay delivery and installation charges of $5,000 making the depreciable base equal to $30,000. We now have a depreciable asset that creates a deductible expense. The asset falls into the three-year class life. To appreciate the value of a depreciation tax shield we'll also calculate the firm's after-tax income if they had had no depreciation expense.

MACRS 3-Year Class Life

1	33%
2	45%
3	15%
4	7%

	With Depreciation	*Without* Depreciation
Gross revenues	$20,000	$20,000
–Depreciation expense[1]	($9,900)	- $0 -
Taxable income	$10,100	$20,000
–Taxes at 34%	($3,434)	($6,800)
After-tax income	$6,666	$13,200

Now to truly appreciate the value of this tax shield we need to examine the firm's cash flows. We'll assume that all gross revenues are cash transactions. To get to cash flows we need to add the depreciation back to after-tax income because it was a noncash charge.

After-tax income	$6,666	$13,200
+Depreciation expense	$9,900	- $0 -
After-tax cash flows	$16,566	$13,200

---

[1]Depreciation expense in year 1 is $30,000(.33) =$9,900

The depreciation expense saved B^{cubed} $3,366 ($16,566 − $13,200) in taxes. The value of this tax shield is equal to depreciation times the tax rate that in this case is $9,900(0.34) =$3,366. Another documented math miracle! What if this company should decide to sell the asset? What, if any, are the tax implications? As you'll see in the next section, it depends.

D. Selling a Depreciable Asset

What are the tax implications when Bargain Basement Bakery (Bcubed) sells the asset (the Dough Squish machine)? The tax liability depends on the price at which they sell the asset. If Bcubed sells the asset for more than its book value (depreciable base minus depreciation taken to date) the IRS considers the amount above book value to be fully taxable income. If Bcubed sells the asset for less than its book value they suffer a loss and can charge that loss against income to produce a tax saving.

What if three years down the road (after taking three years of depreciation), Bargain Basement Bakery (Bcubed) decides to sell the Dough Squish machine to another company for $10,000? The machine's market value is $10,000. What are the tax consequences of selling the depreciable asset? What is the after-tax cash flow from the sale of the depreciable asset? The table below shows the annual depreciation expense for the Dough Squish Machine.

Year	MACRS Depreciation Expense for the Dough Squish Machine	
1	33%($30,000)	$9,900
2	45%($30,000)	$13,500
3	15%($30,000)	$4,500
4	7%($30,000)	$2,100
		$30,000

The firm has taken three years of depreciation. Recall that the book value of the asset is the depreciable base minus depreciation already taken:

Depreciable Base	$30,000
–1st year depreciation	($9,900)
–2nd year depreciation	($13,500)
–3rd year depreciation	($4,500)
Book Value	$2,100

Tax Consequences of Sale of Depreciable Asset

Market value	$10,000
–Book value	($2,100)
Taxable income	$7,900
Taxes @ 34%	$2,686

After-Tax Cash Flows

Market value	$10,000
–Taxes	($2,686)
After-Tax Cash Flows	$7,314

Now, what if instead the highest offer Bcubed received for the Dough Squish Machine was only $1,500? What would be the tax consequences of the sale of the depreciable asset? Recall the book value hasn't changed; it is still $2,100.

Tax Consequences of Sale of Depreciable Asset	
Market value	$1,500
–Book value	($2,100)
Loss on sale of asset	($600)
Tax savings on loss @ 34%	$204
After-Tax Cash Flows	
Market value	$1,500
+Add tax savings	$204
After-Tax Cash Flows	$1,704

Now remember to keep firmly in mind that any firm will go broke pretty fast losing $1 to save $0.34 in taxes. The only advantage the tax code gives is that it takes out a little bit of the sting of suffering a loss on the sale of an asset. The following practice set (Practice Set D) will give you an opportunity to work on these calculations. In the next section we will examine how to use the existing tax codes to take some of the sting out of corporate operating losses.

NOTES:
_____

_____

_____

_____

_____

_____

_____

_____

_____

_____

_____

PRACTICE SET D
DEPRECIATION

MACRS Depreciation Schedules

Year	3-Year Class Life	5-Year Class Life	7-Year Class Life
1	33%	20%	14.3%
2	45%	32%	24.5%
3	15%	19.2%	17.5%
4	7%	11.5%	12.5%
5		11.5%	8.9%
6		5.8%	8.9%
7			8.9%
8			4.5%

1. In 2000 Flamingo Laundry generated $300,000 in operating income. The firm finances all their asset acquisitions with equity. In 2000 they purchased a conveyor system for $60,000. The conveyor system has a three-year MACRS life. Assume the firm pays a flat tax rate of 34 percent.

a. What is the firm's tax liability?

b. What is the firm's after-tax income?

c. What are the firm's after-tax cash flows?

d. How much did the firm save in taxes by using their depreciation tax shield?

2. Referring to the information in problem 1, assume that after two years Flamingo Laundry decides to sell their conveyor system for $30,000. Assume that their marginal tax rate is still 34 percent.

a. What, if any, are the tax consequences of the sale?

b. What are the after-tax cash flows following the sale?

3. Again, referring to the information in problem 1, assume that after two years Flamingo Laundry decides to sell their conveyor system for $5,000. Assume that their marginal tax rate is still 34 percent.

a. What, if any, are the tax consequences of the sale?

b. What are the after-tax cash flows following the sale?

4. In 2000 Crey Seafood Company reported $275,000 in sales revenues after deducting all operating costs except depreciation. Two years ago, in 1998, the firm purchased a machine to increase their production output. The firm finances all their asset acquisitions with equity. The new machine cost $75,000 and has a five-year class life as dictated by MACRS. Assume the firm pays a flat tax rate of 34 percent.

a. What is the firm's tax liability?

b. What is the firm's after-tax income?

c. What are the firm's after-tax cash flows?

5. **Challenge Problem** In 2000 Zoom Auto Parts generated $450,000 in sales revenue after deducting all operating costs except depreciation. One year ago, in 1999, they purchased a conveyor system for $60,000. The firm financed the purchase by issuing 12 percent ten-year bonds that pay interest on an annual basis. The machine has a seven-year class life as dictated by MACRS. Assume the firm pays a flat tax rate of 34 precent.

a. What is the firm's tax liability?

b. What is the firm's after-tax income?

c. What are the firm's after-tax cash flows?

6. **Challenge Problem** Barking Dog Industries had $600,000 in sales in 2000. Cost of goods sold equals 70 percent of sales. Barking Dog received $10,000 in stock and $9,000 in interest from Hush Puppy bonds. Barking Dog paid its own shareholders $5,000 in dividends. The firm bought an electric bone-making machine for $80,000. Modifications to the bone machine and installation charges cost another $20,000. The new machine falls into the three-year MACRS class life. The firm has $500,000 in bonds outstanding with an interest rate of 8 percent. For the sake of simplicity, we will assume a 40 percent tax rate on all income.

a. What is Barking Dog's 2000 tax liability?

b. What is Barking Dog's after-tax income in 2000?

c. What does Barking Dog contribute to retained earnings in 2000?

d. What are Barking Dog's after-tax cash flows in 2000?

e. What is the value of Barking Dog's depreciation tax shield?

f. Assume Barking Dog sold their Bone machine three years later for $10,000. That is, Barking Dog has already taken three years worth of depreciation. What are the after-tax cash flows from the sale of the depreciable asset?

g. Assume <u>instead</u> that they sold their bone machine three years later for $2,000. What are the after-tax cash flows from the sale of the depreciable asset?

E. Carry-Forward and Carry-Back

What happens if the firm experiences a loss? This is not an uncommon occurrence when a firm introduces, for example, a new project. The tax laws try not to punish corporations for variability in their earnings and thus allow corporations to carry losses back three years and then forward for 15 years. Let's look at an example. Suppose instead of a positive taxable income of $19,010 in 2000, Bcubed had a loss of $15,000. Suppose also that in each of the last three years (1997, 1998, and 1999) Bcubed had taxable income of $40,000 and paid taxes in the amount of $13,600 (34 percent of $40,000). They would go back to the third year (1997) and amend their tax filing using the $15,000 loss as a charge against the $40,000 in income. Thus, their amended return from three years ago now says that instead of owing taxes on $40,000 they only owe taxes on $25,000 ($40,000 – $15,000). Their tax bill from three years ago declines from $13,600 to $8,500. Thus, the IRS owes Bcubed a refund of $5,100 ($13,600 – $8,500).

Bargain Basement Bakery's
Carry-Back of 2000 Net Loss

	1997	1998	1999	2000
Earnings Before Taxes	$40,000	$40,000	$40,000	($15,000)
Carry-Back credit 2000	($15,000)			
Adjusted Profit	$25,000			
Taxes paid on $40,000	$13,600			
Taxes due on $25,000 @34%	$8,500			
Tax refund ($13,600 – $8,500)				$5,100

Why did Bcubed go back to 1997 instead of simply writing off their losses against the income in 1999? Because they can only go back three years. What if Bcubed had another loss in 2001? They can't go back to 1997 because that is more than three years ago and they've already used up part of 1999 because of 2000's losses. Thus by not using the year that is furthest away (and the first year that will drop out of eligibility for write-offs) Bcubed may have to wait and carry their losses forward. Because time is money, the accountants at Bcubed don't want to wait. Now what if instead of losing only $15,000 in 2000 Bcubed had lost ten times that amount or $150,000.

Bargain Basement Bakery's
Carry-Back and Carry-Forward of 2000 Net Loss

	1997	1998	1999	2000
Earnings Before Taxes	$40,000	$40,000	$40,000	($150,000)
Carry-Back credit 2000	($40,000)	($40,000)	($40,000)	
Adjusted Profit	$0	$0	$0	
Taxes previously paid @ 34%	$13,600	$13,600	$13,600	
Taxes now due @34%	$0	$0	$0	
Tax refund	$13,600	$13,600	$13,600	
Amount left to write off	$110,000	$70,000	$30,000	
Total Tax Refund 2000				$40,800
Carry-Forward credit from 2000				$30,000

Bcubed would have to carry forward the remaining $30,000 in losses they were unable to write off in the carry-back period.

Work the problems in Practice Set E. Solutions are at the end of this section.

NOTES: _____

_____

_____

_____

_____

_____

_____

_____

_____

_____

_____

_____

_____

_____

_____

_____

_____

_____

_____

_____

PRACTICE SET E
CARRY-FORWARD AND CARRY-BACK

1. Silver Stone Corporation started business in 1987. Every year their reported revenues were exactly $50,000. In 2000, however, due to a change in management, the firms suffered its first loss of $70,000. Show the firms taxable income and taxes owed for the last three years (1998, 1999 and 2000). Assume the firm has a marginal tax rate of 34 percent.

2. Waterford Tile began business in 1978. Until the last few years the firm has always been profitable, earning $82,000 before taxes each year. In 1999 the firm reported a loss of $40,000, in 2000 they reported a loss of $93,000. Assume the firm has a marginal tax rate of 34 percent. What is the firm's adjusted tax liability in 1997? What is the firm's adjusted tax liability in 1998?

3. Cartwright Oil began business in 1995 and earned a before-tax profit of
    $70,000. In 1996 they earned a before-tax profits of $80,000. In 1997 and
    1998 they earned a before-tax profit of $50,000. In 1999 they earned
    $120,000 in before-tax profits. In 2000 the firm suffered several setbacks
    and reported a pre-tax loss of $300,000. Assume the firm has a marginal tax
    rate of 34 percent. What are the firm's (adjusted) tax liabilities in each year?

4. Frame Galleries Corporation began in New York City in 1994. They
    reported before-tax revenues of –$150,000 in 1994, –$120,000 in 1995,
    –$75,000 in 1996, $57,000 in 1997, $110,000 in 1998, $140,000 in 1999,
    and $175,000 in 2000. Assume the firm has a marginal tax rate of 34
    percent. What is their tax liability in 2000?

5. Challenge Problem Larry, Moe and Curly have operated Silly Stuff, Inc. since 1980. They manufacture and market various party favors. In 2000 they purchased a packaging machine for $50,000. Modifications and installation of the machine cost an additional $3,000. The machine has a three-year class life. Silly Stuff has made before taxes $30,000 in 1997, $35,000 in 1998 and $40,000 in 1999. Sales in 2000 were $20,000. Cost of goods sold amount to 60 percent of sales. Silly Stuff, Inc. received $3,000 in interest income from some corporate bonds they own. They have $60,000 in bonds outstanding with an annual interest rate of 10 percent. They have consistently paid dividends of $1.00 per share. There are 5,000 shares outstanding. They also own stock in Funny Stuff, Inc. that pays them an annual dividend of $3,000. Assume a level tax rate of 34 percent.

a. What is Silly Stuff's 2000 tax liability?

b. What is Silly Stuff's after-tax income in 2000?

c. What is Silly Stuff's after-tax cash flows in 2000?

d. Assume they sold their packaging machine two years later for $47,000. That is, Silly Stuff has already taken two years worth of depreciation. What are the after-tax cash flows from the sale of the depreciable asset?

e. Assume <u>instead</u> that they sold their packaging machine two years later for $5,000. What are the after-tax cash flows from the sale of the depreciable asset?

6. Challenge Problem Sarah and Michelle are the best of friends and in 1985 started Central Perk, Incorporated. They now have coffee shops all over Indiana and are thinking of expanding into Ohio where known coffee drinkers cluster and klatch. The last few years have been profitable, but in 1999 they had a loss of $110,000 resulting from an unprofitable foray into Illinois where coffee drinking is discouraged (except in Chicago). Sarah and Michelle (the CEO and CFO, respectively, of Central Perk, Incorporated) were even thinking of expanding into Iowa, but had trouble getting anyone to stay awake long enough to hear their ideas.

In 2000 they purchased an espresso machine for each of their five stores in Indiana at a cost of $35,000 each. Modifications and installation added $5,000 to the cost of each machine. The machines have a five-year class life. Central Perk has made earnings before taxes of $32,000 in 1996, $37,000 in 1997, $46,000 in 1998 and ($110,000) in 1999. Sales in 2000 were $80,000. Cost of goods sold amount to 65 percent of sales. Central Perk owns some marketable securities that produced the following cash flows: interest income of $1,500 and dividend income of $3,000. Central Perk financed part of its growth with 11 percent bonds totaling $35,000. Central Perk has not paid a dividend in five years. Use the corporate tax rates in your textbook for this problem.

a. What is Central Perk's 2000 tax liability?

b. What is Central Perk's after-tax income in 2000?

c. What does Central Perk contribute to retained earnings in 2000?

d. Assume they sell all their espresso machines three years later for $19,000 each to a small coffee chain in California. That is, Central Perk has already taken <u>three</u> years worth of depreciation. What are the after-tax cash flows from the sale of the depreciable assets?

e. Assume <u>instead</u> that they sold all their espresso machines <u>five</u> years later for $1,300 each to a caffeine fanatic in Florida. What are the after-tax cash flows from the sale of the depreciable assets?

IV. FINANCIAL ANALYSIS

There are many stakeholders in a firm including stockholders and bondholders (a.k.a. investors), general creditors, managers, employees, etc. Every stakeholder has an interest in how well their firm performs as measured by how the firm compares with its own historical performance and how the firm stacks up against its closest competitors and the industry.

Financial analysis examines the firm by subjecting the financial statements to various analytical tortures including ratio analysis and common size analysis. These two techniques use standardized accounting numbers from the balance sheet and income statement to determine the firm's financial strengths and weaknesses.

Perhaps management wants to know whether the firm carries too much or too little inventory. They can compare the firm's inventory on hand with the last five years of inventory levels to see if they are approaching their desired inventory investment goal. They can also compare their inventory holdings with a competitor and the industry to get a basis for comparison and evaluate their progress based on these parameters.

An investor may want to know how the firm performs with their invested dollars. Employees may want to know about the firm's profitability. This is a job for ratio analysis.

A. Analyze This!

While visions of caped crusaders may come to mind, let us caution you that although ratios are wonderful, the truth is that a ratio is only one number divided by another. We can thank the accounting profession for the usefulness that ratios provide. Because firms must follow the same rules (almost) for recording their assets, liabilities, revenues and expenses, that puts all firms on the same footing and allows us to make comparisons.

Let's look at a quick example of the information ratios can supply. Let's say we have two firms creatively named Firm A and Firm B. For simplicity and comparability lets assume that both firms are in the same industry, have the same level of sales, and both produced $1,500,000 in net income this last year. Given this data, investors might be indifferent between these two firms. Savvy investors, however, ask how many dollars did each firm invest in assets to produce these revenues. Firm A invested $5 million and Firm B invested $10 million. This news changes investors' original assessment. What rate of return do these firms earn on their asset investment (formally called Return on Assets or ROA for the acronym lover)?

Return = on Assets	Net income Total Assets	$\frac{\$1,500,000}{\$5,000,000} = 30\%$	$\frac{\$1,500,000}{\$10,000,000} = 15\%$

Now, investors' interest in Firm A exceeds their interest in Firm B. Firm A uses its assets more efficiently. From a comparative standpoint, Firm B has too many assets for the amount of revenue the firm produces. Dividing net income by total assets standardizes the information and allows investors to make meaningful comparisons.

1. Compare and Contrast

Simply dividing one number by another is not particularly impressive and really doesn't give us the whole picture. We need something to compare our numbers against. Something that will shed a little more light on our analysis. If we look up the industry averages for each of these ratios, we can compare our firm to the "average" firm in the industry. We even call this <u>comparative analysis</u>. Striving for average sounds sort of pathetic, so we might want to compare our firm's ratios with our closest competitor as we did with Firm A and Firm B.

Firm B with a return on assets of 15 percent sounds remarkable until we find out the competitor's return on assets is 30 percent. The news gets downright depressing when we discover the "average" firm in the industry earns more than 35 percent on their assets.

2. Trendsetters

Another useful way to examine a firm's ratios is to look at them over time. We call this <u>trend analysis</u>. Even though Firm B's return on assets is only 15 percent, there might yet be call for celebration if we knew this was the highest return on assets in five years and reflects a three percentage point increase over last year. We can see how this new information casts a different light on our previous conclusion. While it's true Firm B may not be anything to write home about, there is still hope, given the improvement over the last five years.

Below is a trend analysis graph of the return on assets for Firm A, Firm B and the industry.

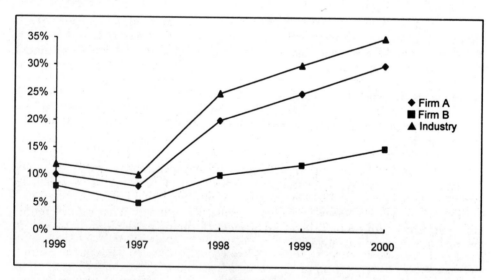

Trend analysis can also help pinpoint whether the cause of poor performance is the result of external factors (i.e., uncontrollable outside influences) such as a recession or internal factors (i.e., controllable inside influences) such as faulty management. For example, suppose you managed a firm whose return on assets had dropped by eight percentage points this year. Your shareholders' first inclination might be to put pressure on your board of directors to fire you for such an obvious fumble. Before your investors take such an action, however, they might want to consider the performance of the industry. Upon further examination, your shareholders will find this whole sector of commerce has hit hard times. In fact, your firm's closet competitor's return on assets dropped by more than 12 percentage points and the industry average declined by more than 14 percentage points.

Faced with a certain downturn in sales because of a recession, you were able to weather the worst economic slump to hit the industry in more than a decade. Given this information, your investors should reconsider their first inclination and perhaps lobby the board of directors to give you a raise. We can see from this example that a little information tells only part of the story; comparative analysis and trend analysis provide significantly more information.

3. Pigeonholing

We group ratios into five general categories. This isn't just a case of simple pigeonholing, but a way to arrange the ratios to measure the five main areas of interest to the various stakeholders. If you were to look inside all the major textbooks available for this course you would find that each might include different ratios, or different methods for calculating the same ratios. For example, one book may use sales in the numerator of the inventory turnover ratio while another book uses cost of goods sold. One book may call net income divided by sales a profit margin while another book calls this the net profit margin. Each book has a different slant on the terminology. No this is not a plot to confuse students. These authors are all trying to measure the same thing, but want to use their own lingo and preferences.

The one thing each of these books does have in common is the categorization of all these various ratios into similar categories. First we have liquidity ratios that serve to answer questions about the firm's ability to pay its upcoming debt obligations. Second on our list is asset utilization ratios that determine the impact of the firm's investment decisions. These ratios help determine whether the firm uses their assets efficiently. That is, does the firm over- or underinvest in assets and more specifically into which class of assets is the firm over- or underinvested. Third are the debt management ratios that examine the financing decisions of the firm and the implications of using borrowed funds. Fourth are the market value ratios that analyze the firm's stock price relative to other values to ascertain what value the investing public places on a firm. Last, but certainly not least are the profitability ratios that gauge the firm's control over its expenses. Profitability ratios also examine the rate of return the firm earns on its investment in assets and the rate of return provided to investors.

Because your textbook already examines each of these individual ratios we won't duplicate that effort (phew!). We will, however, spend our time looking at how these ratios fit into the grander scheme of our financial statements' analysis. Remember we get the information for the various ratios from the firm's financial statements. Thus, we use ratios to determine how well the firm is performing. Performance covers all the categories; how well they handle their liquidity position, how effective they are in the utilization of their assets, how management's financing decisions have impacted the firm's performance, how investors in the marketplace have interpreted this performance, and finally, how profitable both their investment and financing decisions have been. Did you get that? We are interested in how these ratios relate to one another and to the firm's financial statements. Again, to avoid the swamp of jargonism we won't explain each separate ratio, but instead look at the interplay of the financial statements and what impacts investor return.

Let's begin with a brief discussion of each ratio category so you understand the logic behind the ratios instead of merely memorizing the various ratios and hoping nothing falls out before you take your next exam.

4. Liquidity: The Elixir of Life

Whether someone considers a ratio satisfactory can be a function of the role in which they operate. For example, a potential creditor wants big liquidity ratios. The bigger the better because the more cushion there is against the probability of default (i.e., that the firm won't pay up). If, on the other hand, you are an investor, big liquidity ratios are a snooze because the firm could invest the money in more productive assets. More productive assets give investors greater bang for their invested buck (i.e., a higher rate of return).

5. Utilize Those Assets

We use these ratios to find out if management is putting our resources (a.k.a. money) to their best possible use. Remember we paid for these assets, we have a right to know how well they are being managed. For example, did the firm buy too much inventory? Is management keeping an "eye" on receivable traffic? And perhaps most importantly, we want to know how well are they handling our fixed asset investments.

Inventory turnover tells us how many times a firm is selling out and restocking their inventory per year. Too high a turnover as measured during the comparative analysis could lead to shortages causing back orders and ultimately lost sales revenue. Of course, it could also mean that a firm is an incredible handler of inventory because of a new computer system that monitors their goods throughout the production process and makes the management of inventory more efficient. If this were the case, the firm could argue that a high turnover does not place them in a weak position. They would point out (rather emphatically) that they are operating from a position of strength relative to the industry because of their efforts to employ high-tech means to reduce the amount of inventory needed and hence lowering their holding costs. The first scenario is the more likely one, but we can't always rule out other possibilities. This highlights some of the dilemmas of trying to make judgments about a company in which we may have little access to inside information.

The receivables turnover measures how long, on average, it takes for a firm to collect their accounts receivable. If the number is small when we conduct the comparative analysis is the firm being too efficient (blasphemy)? Without additional information, we are unable to answer this question. Our suspicion is that a firm with too small of a number is being too stingy. They need to make sure that the benefits of a strict credit policy outweigh any lost revenues. Obviously management must interpret this recommendation with caution as too liberal a credit policy (e.g., extending credit to anyone who breathes) may indeed increase our receivable turnover, but may result in an increase in the number of uncollectible accounts. Remember in such a case, the firm's accountant would report increased sales revenue and profits while firm management wouldn't see any increase in cash inflows.

The fixed asset turnover measures how much each dollar investment made in the firm's fixed assets produces in sales revenue. A large number tends to imply efficient use of fixed assets, whereas a small number implies an overinvestment in fixed assets. There are all kinds of ways to interpret a small or large number when derived at through a comparative analysis. The difference could be a function of the differences in the ages of the assets used in the measurement. An older firm that has depreciated the majority of its assets will look more efficient when compared to a relatively new firm that has yet to depreciate most of its assets. We could also come up with what looks like meaningful numbers only to find that one firm has recently purchased a number of expensive fixed assets in anticipation of future expansion, but has yet to generate the anticipated cash flows. So once again, we caution against jumping the proverbial gun in making assessments about one number divided by another. These ratios do provide meaningful information, but only if coupled with the common sense and good judgment that can only come from experience.

Total asset turnover throws in everything but the kitchen sink and should not give us any big surprises because this number is but a conglomeration of the measurements we have taken so far. Keep in mind that typically, fixed assets represent a much larger portion of a firm's asset investment. Indeed, net fixed assets represent nearly 80 percent of Weiler's total assets ($84,000/$108,000). Thus, the firm's overinvestment in fixed assets would be the dominant force when we calculate total asset turnover. If we found a problem in the fixed asset turnover it shouldn't be a shock to us if we come up with the same conclusions about the utilization of the firms total asset investment.

6. We're In Over Our Heads: Debt Management

Where the asset utilization ratios examined the firm's investment decisions, the debt management ratios look at the firm's financing decisions. We typically examine how much debt the firm used to finance their assets and then have a look at how well the firm is able to handle their debt service load. Using debt to finance assets reduces financing costs as we saw in the previous section where the firm was able to deduct the interest expense generated from their debt financing. If a firm finances, say, 60 percent of their assets with debt that means that for every dollar in assets the firm reports on their balance sheet $0.40 came from the owners and $0.60 came from borrowed funds. What does this tell us? Nothing if we don't use comparative analysis and see where our firm stands relative to others.

The times-interest-earned, cash coverage and other such ratios measure a firm's ability to service the debt they've taken on. Of particular interest is whether the firm will generate sufficient revenues and how much of a cushion there is should revenues take a dip. Is twice the amount needed going to be enough to satisfy creditors? We can really only answer that question via our comparative analysis. Remember that all kinds of interested parties are doing the same analysis and for the most part, they all have access to the same information. So if creditors find that firms similar to ours usually have three times the amount needed, our having twice the amount probably isn't going to make them particularly ecstatic and may make it more difficult for our firm to raise additional outside financing. On the other hand, if the interested parties doing the analysis are the shareholders, who tend to view cushions as underinvested resources, the answer could be quite different.

7. Everything Has Its Price

The price-earnings ratio and market-to-book ratio are ratios that investors look at to determine value. The price-earnings ratio looks at what investors are currently willing to pay for $1 in earnings. In Weiler's case, the investing public is willing to pay $24.29 dollars for every dollar in earnings. What's with these people, are they stupid? Typically, the answer is no. What they are telling us is that they feel the firm's *potential* for *future* income is worth this price. This looks as though investors are pretty optimistic about Weiler's future. When we see, however, an industry average of $30.20, this tells us that investors feel that Weiler's prospects are not as rosy (on average) as their competitors.

Some investors look at a firm's book value per share and compare it to the firm's stock price to see how much investors are willing to pay for a dollar of book value. Most firms have a market-to-book value ratio greater than one; meaning that investors value the firm's ability to produce future cash flows more than they value the mere book value of the firm's assets. If a company's book value were say $24 dollars per share and the market price of their stock were $10 per share, than management could best maximize shareholders' wealth by liquidating the firm's assets, paying off their liabilities and distributing the rest to shareholders. The moral of the story is don't let the market price of your firm's stock fall below its book value.

8. Profits Are the Name of the Game

Profitability ratios move us over to the income statement where we look at how well the firm controls expenses and what rate of return investors can expect from their invested dollars. The profit margin tells us the story of the revenue dollar. If we start our firm off with a dollar in sales revenue and then deduct expenses, how much will be left? Obviously, the better able our firm is to control expenses, the larger the amount that will be left over at the end of the journey. If our firm has a profit margin of, say, 7 percent, that means our firm was only able to squeeze out seven cents of net income from sales revenues. The better a firm can control expenses, the more that's left over at the end of the accounting cycle. Simple, right? Profits are easy to measure, but it's very difficult to rein in expenses. Have you ever tried to live on a budget? Then you know what we mean. Again, we need a comparative analysis to determine if our firm's profit margin and hence control of expenses is typical.

9. Non-Stick Ratios: The DuPont Equation

Return on assets asks how much income the firm produced relative to their asset investment (i.e., net income/total assets). We can get more information by extending this into the DuPont equation below (guess who discovered this?). The DuPont equation breaks the return on assets into two components: profit margin and total asset turnover.

Profit Margin	×	Total Asset Turnover	=	Return on Assets

$$\frac{\text{Net income}}{\text{Sales}} \times \frac{\text{Sales}}{\text{Total assets}} = \frac{\text{Net income}}{\text{Total assets}}$$

Through algebraic cancellation of Sales in both the denominator of the profit margin and the numerator of the total asset turnover gives us the original return on assets ratio: net income/total assets.

The DuPont equation answers two questions. First, how well is the firm utilizing their assets and, second, how well is the firm controlling their expenses? Better utilization of assets, all else constant, would improve the total asset turnover and hence the return on assets. More control over expenses, all else equal, would improve the profit margin and subsequently the return on assets.

We can't leave the profitability section without paying homage to the mother of all ratios—return on equity. Affectionately known as ROE, this is *the* crucial ratio to prepare. As we'll see in a moment, it measures in a somewhat crude fashion, the performance of the entire firm as inferred in their financial statements.

Let's investigate further by turning our full attention to the return on equity ratio. This ratio, as no doubt your textbook will tell you, measures shareholder's rate of return, that is, the income available to shareholders (net income) relative to their investment (common equity). If the firm had no debt, the return on assets (ROA) would be equal to the return on equity (ROE) because common equity would equal total assets. Got that?

10. DuPont

How do we explain a firm whose ROE is at an acceptable level while at the same time their asset utilization ratios are only modest and their expense ratios were meager at best? Ah, the key is debt usage. The use of debt can artificially improve performance measures. To take debt financing into account we extend our DuPont equation one step further by employing an equity multiplier. The multiplier measures the asset investment made by shareholders (i.e., total assets/common equity). If the shareholders put up the entire amount (i.e., the firm had no debt) then ROA would be equal to ROE because the equity multiplier would be one (assets = common equity). If the firm used debt financing then by definition (assets < common equity) because part of each asset dollar was borrowed.

$$\text{ROE} = \frac{\text{Net income}}{\text{Common equity}}$$

$$\text{ROE} = \text{ROA} \times \text{equity multiplier}$$

We can rewrite this equation to include the following three levers of performance:

$$\text{ROE} = \frac{\text{PROFIT}}{\text{MARGIN}} \times \frac{\text{TOTAL ASSET}}{\text{TURNOVER}} \times \frac{\text{EQUITY}}{\text{MULTIPLIER}}$$

$$\text{ROE} = \frac{\text{Net income}}{\text{Sales}} \times \frac{\text{Sales}}{\text{Total assets}} \times \frac{\text{Total Assets}}{\text{Common equity}} = \frac{\text{Net income}}{\text{Common equity}}$$

Through algebraic cancellation of Sales in both the denominator of the profit margin and the numerator of the total asset turnover and cancellation of Total assets in both the denominator of the total asset turnover ratio and the numerator of the equity multiplier gives us the original return on equity ratio: net income/common equity.

These three levers summarize the firm's financial statements. The first lever (profit margin) measures how well the firm controls their expenses and thus summarizes the firm's income statement. The second lever (total asset turnover) summarizes the left-hand side of the balance sheet by showing how well the firm utilizes their assets. This constitutes a rough measure of the firm's investment decisions. The third lever (equity multiplier) summarizes the right-hand side of the balance sheet by indicating the firm's financing decisions. At the risk of restating the obvious, remember that if the firm had no debt (i.e., financed all their assets with owner-supplied capital—equity) the equity multiplier would be equal to one because equity would equal total assets.

Let's use the financial statements for Weiler Corporation and compare them to the industry averages to show how we can use ROE as a first clue in our quest to investigate suspicious anomalies in our firm's financial performance.

PERFORMANCE LEVERS	PROFIT MARGIN	×	TOTAL ASSET TURNOVER	×	EQUITY MULTIPLIER	=	RETURN ON EQUITY
WEILER CORP.	3%	×	1.11	×	2.12	=	7%
INDUSTRY	5%	×	1.34	×	1.20	=	8%

Notice that the only reason Weiler has a competitive ROE is their use of debt. Here we see that debt provides "leverage." The firm was able to increase ROE by financing a greater portion of their assets with borrowed funds. Note that Weiler's profit margin and total asset turnover are below the industry averages. Yet the firm's return on equity is comparable with the industry average (7 percent for Weiler versus 8 percent for the industry). How can Weiler have these deficiencies and yet still show a decent return on equity?

There are three ways to attain ROE euphoria: higher profit margins, a larger total asset turnover, or use more debt financing (i.e., a larger equity multiplier). Using more debt leveraged up Weiler's ROE. Without the use of debt Weiler's return on equity would be the same as their return on assets (ROA); a little over 3 percent (profit margin 3% × total asset turnover 1.13). The use of leverage more than doubled the firm's ROE (equity multiplier of 2.12).

Industry type often dictates which lever a firm can use to obtain an acceptable ROE. For example, firms that can add value to their product enjoy larger profit margins. A good example would be manufacturers of chic women's cosmetics such as those found at upscale department stores. These firms would typically have low total asset turnovers and employ only moderate amounts of debt. Because of their perceived exclusivity and hence the accompanying price markup they are able to maintain very high profit margins.

If, however, the firm is a grocery store, there is little value that management can add to their products before they reach the consumer. Thus, profit margins will be low and they will typically work toward their ROE goal by way of a high total asset turnover and a conservative use of debt. Other firms, such as financial institutions, typically have low-to-moderate profit margins and total asset turnovers, but, by their very nature, they use a lot of debt financing. This is true because depositor's funds are considered a liability of the financial institution. Because "banks" get most of their lending dollars from depositors they have very high debt ratios. Most banks have a typical debt-to-assets ratio of over 80 percent.

By breaking down ROE into the three levers of performance we now have a clue of where to look for the problem. We see that Weiler's profit margin is low indicating that they are not controlling costs as well as other firms in the industry. We now know that we need to examine the income statement more closely and see if we can pinpoint the problem(s). We also see from our extended DuPont analysis that Weiler has a low total asset turnover implying that there is a problem(s) on the right-hand side of the balance sheet that needs their immediate attention. Before we delve further into the problems of Weiler's performance let's take a moment to note some perhaps not so obvious problems with ROE.

11. ROE: The Wise Guy

Investors should not rely solely on ROE to determine a firm's financial wellbeing. First, ROE considers only one accounting period of performance. The calculation does not consider any of the company's long-range plans. For example, perhaps Weiler Corporation had a low total asset turnover because they recently bought a large number of fixed assets for an expansion project in which the sales have yet to happen. Even if this was the brilliant project of the year,

Weiler's ROE does not even consider this long-run scenario. Second, ROE does not take into account any risks the firm took to boost ROE. Remember, we said that Weiler used debt to increase its return on equity. If we had two firms with identical ROE, an investor might feel indifferent between the two firms and not realize that one of the firms obtained its ROE as the result of extensive leverage (a.k.a. lots of debt). Therefore, the ROE says nothing about risk. Third, the basis for ROE is book value of common equity. This is rarely a close approximation of the market value of the firm's equity securities. Using a book value to determine rates of return tends to introduce an upward bias into the calculation because for most firms, market value exceeds book value.

12. Limitations of Ratio Analysis

As your textbook undoubtedly notes, it's often difficult to interpret ratios. It can also be hard to find comparative industry data. This problem is common when you consider that a lot of firms produce more than one product. In addition, some ratios may be satisfactory while others are unsatisfactory or borderline, all of which makes it more difficult to arrive at an accurate judgment of the firm's overall financial strengths and weaknesses. All these problems make it hard to get a comprehensive picture of the firm.

After performing an extensive ratio analysis we may find it beneficial to tackle the problem from another angle. Common size analysis doesn't necessarily tell us any new information, but it does present it in a different format that may give us insight into the problems you noted when examining the firm's ratios.

B. The Uncommon: Common Size Analysis

Common size analysis restates the balance sheet in terms of total assets and the income statement in terms of sales. By restating each asset category on the balance sheet as a percentage of total assets we can see what proportion of total assets each item represents. While this analysis does not supplant the ratio analysis, the results can reinforce earlier conclusions. For example, we find on Weiler's common size balance sheet (shown on next page) that more than 90 percent of their asset investment is in fixed assets. This finding strengthens our earlier conclusion: that the firm had too large of an investment in total assets as evidenced by their low total asset turnover, and by default, their low return on assets. The common size analysis results spur us to strengthen our focus on fixed assets as the underlying culprit for Weiler's poor performance. Ratio analysis would have led us to this same conclusion, but the supporting evidence helps solidify our resolve that we're on the correct path. We also confirm our findings about the firm's debt burden. Weiler has financed more than 50 percent of their assets with debt while the industry average is closer to 35 percent.

WEILER CORPORATION
COMMON SIZE BALANCE SHEET
(Thousands of Dollars)

ASSETS	2000	WEILER	INDUSTRY
Cash	$3,000	2.78%	2.85%
Marketable Securities	$3,000	2.78%	4.87%
Accounts Receivable	$8,000	7.41%	13.00%
Inventory	$10,000	9.26%	17.38%
Total Current Assets	$24,000	22.22%	38.10%
Gross Fixed Assets	$98,000	90.74%	81.90%
Accumulated Depreciation	$14,000	12.96%	20.00%
Net Fixed Assets	$84,000	77.78%	61.90%
Total Assets	$108,000	100.00%	100.00%
LIABILITIES			
Accounts Payable	$1,500	1.39%	1.50%
Accrued Salaries & Wages	$1,200	1.11%	0.25%
Accrued Taxes	$2,000	1.85%	0.75%
Total Current Liabilities	$4,700	4.35%	7.07%
Notes Payable	$5,300	4.91%	4.32%
Mortgage Bonds	$37,000	34.26%	21.00%
Debentures	$10,000	9.26%	7.21%
Total Long-Term Debt	$52,300	48.43%	28.21%
Total Liabilities	$57,000	52.78%	35.28%
SHAREHOLDER'S EQUITY			
Common Stock (par value)	$1,000	0.93%	4.61%
Additional Paid-In Capital	$15,000	13.89%	19.23%
Retained Earnings	$35,000	32.41%	40.88%
Total Shareholder's Equity	$51,000	47.22%	64.72%
Total Claims	$108,000	100.00%	100.00%

The common size income statement on the next page helps pinpoint areas in which the firm has a problem controlling expenses. For example, as we determined in the ratio analysis, the firm's profit margin is low. The benefit of this analysis is now instead of simply saying the firm's profit margin is low, we have more detail about what may be the source(s) of the problem.

WEILER CORPORATION
COMMON SIZE INCOME STATEMENT
(Thousands of Dollars)

	2000	WEILER	INDUSTRY
Sales	$120,000	100.00%	100.00%
Cost of Goods Sold	$73,000	60.83%	56.71%
Salaries and Wages	$34,000	28.33%	15.43%
Depreciation Expense (DEP)	$3,000	2.50%	2.00%
Total Operating Costs	$110,000	91.67%	74.14%
Earnings Before Interest & Taxes (EBIT)	$10,000	8.33%	25.86%
Interest Expense	$4,700	3.92%	2.00%
Earnings Before Taxes (EBT)	$5,300	4.42%	23.86%
Taxes	$1,802	1.50%	3.05%
Net Income (NI)	$3,498	2.92%	20.81%

Again, even common size analysis is not very useful if we have no means for comparison or no historical view (trend analysis). For example, on the firm's income statement we see that Weiler's Salaries and Wages expenses far exceed the industry's cost; 28.33 percent for Weiler versus 15.43 percent for the industry.

Work on the problems in Practice Set F on the next page. Solutions are at the end of this section.

NOTES:

PRACTICE SET F
Financial Analysis

1. The balance sheet and income statement for Jurassic Industries are:

JURASSIC INDUSTRIES -- INCOME STATEMENT FOR THE YEAR ENDED DECEMBER 31, 2000 (Thousands of Dollars)

ASSETS		LIABILITIES	
Cash	$7,000	Accounts Payable	$4,000
Marketable Securities	$3,000	Accrued Salaries & Wages	$5,000
Accounts Receivable	$15,000	Accrued Taxes	$2,000
Inventory	$25,000	Total Current Liabilities	$11,000
Total Current Assets	$50,000	Notes Payable	$14,000
Gross Fixed Assets	$155,000	Mortgage Bonds	$40,000
Accumulated Depreciation	$22,000	Debentures	$35,000
Net Fixed Assets	$133,000	Total Long-Term Debt	$89,000
		Total Liabilities	$100,000
		SHAREHOLDER'S EQUITY	
		Common Stock (par value)	$13,000
		Additional Paid-In Capital	$25,000
		Retained Earnings	$45,000
		Total Shareholder's Equity	$83,000
Total Assets	$183,000	Total Claims	$183,000

JURASSIC INDUSTRIES - INCOME STATEMENT FOR THE YEAR ENDED DECEMBER 31, 2000 (Thousands of Dollars)

Sales	$650,000
Cost of Goods Sold	$450,000
Salaries and Wages	$145,000
Depreciation Expense (DEP)	$12,000
Total Operating Costs	$607,000
Earnings Before Interest & Taxes (EBIT)	$43,000
Interest Expense	$8,900
Earnings Before Taxes (EBT)	$34,100
Taxes	$13,640
Net Income (NI)	$20,460

a. Use the extended DuPont equation to conduct a partial financial analysis for Jurassic Industries. The industry averages are as follows: profit margin = 5 percent, total asset turnover 2.5 and equity multiplier is 1.9.
b. What area(s) need(s) further investigation and why?
c. Prepare a common size balance sheet and income statement for Jurassic.

2. The balance sheet and income statement for Pylon Corporation are:

PYLON CORPORATION – BALANCE SHEET FOR THE YEAR ENDED DECEMBER 31, 2000

ASSETS		LIABILITIES	
Cash	$250,000	Accounts Payable	$125,000
Accounts Receivable	$125,000	Accrued Salaries & Wages	$50,000
Inventory	$175,000	Accrued Taxes	$25,000
Total Current Assets	$550,000	Total Current Liabilities	$200,000
Gross Fixed Assets	$1,100,000	Notes Payable	$50,000
Accumulated Dep.	$250,000	Mortgage Bonds	$350,000
Net Fixed Assets	$850,000	Total Long-Term Debt	$400,000
		Total Liabilities	$600,000
		SHAREHOLDER'S EQUITY	
		Common Stock (par value)	$225,000
		Additional Paid-In Capital	$375,000
		Retained Earnings	$200,000
		Total Shareholder's Equity	$800,000
Total Assets	$1,400,000	Total Claims	$1,400,000

PYLON CORPORATION – INCOME STATEMENT FOR THE YEAR ENDED DECEMBER 31, 2000

Sales	$3,000,000
Cost of Goods Sold	$2,000,000
Salaries and Wages	$450,000
Depreciation Expense (DEP)	$150,000
Total Operating Costs	$2,600,000
Earnings Before Interest & Taxes (EBIT)	$400,000
Interest Expense	$50,000
Earnings Before Taxes (EBT)	$350,000
Taxes @ 40%	$140,000
Net Income (NI)	$210,000

Additional Information

Total dividends	$100,000
Shares outstanding	80,000
Market price per share	$20

Use the financial statements for Pylon Corporation and the information below to answer the following questions. (Use the next page for your calculations.)
a. Earnings per share
b. Price-earnings ratio
c. Book value per share
d. Market to book value
e. How much of the retained earnings total was added during 2000?
f. On the next page, show Pylon's new balance sheet after the company sells 1 million new common shares in early 2001 to net $18 per share; $10 million of the proceeds go to reduce accounts payable, with the remainder deposited into the firm's bank account. The firm will eventually invest this amount in a new manufacturing process.

PYLON CORPORATION – BALANCE SHEET
FOR THE YEAR ENDED DECEMBER 31, 2001

ASSETS		LIABILITIES	
Cash		Accounts Payable	
Accounts Receivable		Accrued Salaries & Wages	
Inventory		Accrued Taxes	
Total Current Assets		Total Current Liabilities	
Gross Fixed Assets		Notes Payable	
Accumulated Dep.		Mortgage Bonds	
Net Fixed Assets		Total Long-Term Debt	
		Total Liabilities	
		SHAREHOLDER'S EQUITY	
		Common Stock (par value)	
		Additional Paid-In Capital	
		Retained Earnings	
		Total Shareholder's Equity	
Total Assets		Total Claims	

3. Using the industry average data and the information for Bad Dog, Inc., perform a trend analysis on ROA and ROE. Plot the data and discuss any trends you find that seem significant. Also indicate what you believe are the underlying causes of these trends.

Bad Dog, Inc.	1996	1997	1998	1999	2000
Profit Margin	13%	12%	11%	9%	9%
Total Asset Turnover	1.2	1.15	1.10	1.02	1.18
Equity Multiplier	1.40	1.58	1.80	2.38	2.50

Industry Data	1996	1997	1998	1999	2000
Profit Margin	11%	10%	10%	9%	9%
Total Asset Turnover	1.2	1.17	1.20	1.22	1.25
Equity Multiplier	1.50	1.55	1.57	1.60	1.63

WATERTECH ENERGY CORPORATION	

4. Assume that Watertech sells additional share of common stock and uses the proceeds raised from the sales to increase its inventories and to increase their cash balances. What is the immediate result (increase, decrease, or no change) of these transactions on the following ratios?

a. current ratio

b. quick ratio

c. debt ratio

d. total asset turnover

e. return on equity

f. return on assets

INDIANAPOLIS INDUSTRIES

5. **Challenge Problem** On the next page, fill in the balance sheet for Indianapolis Industries based on the information below. Round all numbers to the nearest whole dollar.

Sales = $250,000
Total Asset Turnover = 3.5×
Current ratio = 3.2
Quick ratio = 2
Days Sales Outstanding = 30 days
Cash on Hand = $3,000
Profit Margin = 3%
ROE = 19.1%

INDIANAPOLIS INDUSTRIES

Cash	_____	Accounts Payable	_____
Accounts Receivable	_____	Long-Term Debt	_____
Inventory	_____	Stockholders' Equity	_____
Total Current Assets	_____		_____
Fixed Assets	_____		
Total Assets	_____	Total Claims	_____

SOLUTIONS
PRACTICE SET A: Financial Statement Construction

CAROLINA BUSINESS MACHINES
BALANCE SHEET
FOR THE YEAR ENDED DECEMBER 31, 2000
(Thousands of Dollars, Except Per Share Data)

ASSETS		LIABILITIES	
Cash	$3,000	Accounts Payable	$3,000
Marketable Securities	$7,120	Accrued Salaries & Wages	$1,000
Accounts Receivable	$9,000	Accrued Taxes	$1,500
Inventory	$15,000	Total Current Liabilities	$5,500
Total Current Assets	$34,120	Notes Payable	$10,000
Gross Fixed Assets	$57,000	Debentures	$20,000
Accumulated Depreciation	$25,620	Total Liabilities	$35,500
Net Fixed Assets	$31,380	SHAREHOLDER'S EQUITY	
		Common Stock (par value)	$6,000
		Retained Earnings	$24,000
		Total Shareholder's Equity	$30,000
Total Assets	$65,500	Total Claims	$65,500

CAROLINA BUSINESS MACHINES
INCOME STATEMENT
FOR THE YEAR ENDED DECEMBER 31, 2000
(Thousands of Dollars, Except Per Share Data)

Sales	$60,000
Cost of Goods Sold	$36,000
Salaries and Wages	$10,000
Depreciation Expense (DEP)	$4,620
Total Operating Costs	$50,620
Earnings Before Interest & Taxes (EBIT)	$9,380
Interest Expense	$2,000
Earnings Before Taxes (EBT)	$7,380
Taxes	$2,509
Net Income (NI)	$4,871
Common Dividends	$1,948
Additions to Retained Earnings	$2,923

DAKOTA CORPORATION
BALANCE SHEET
FOR THE YEAR ENDED DECEMBER 31, 2000
(Thousands of Dollars, Except Per Share Data)

ASSETS		LIABILITIES	
Cash	$10,000	Accounts Payable	$12,000
Marketable Securities	$2,000	Accrued Salaries & Wages	$4,500
Accounts Receivable	$16,000	Accrued Taxes	$1,500
Inventory	$31,000	Total Current Liabilities	$18,000
Total Current Assets	$59,000	Notes Payable	$7,000
Gross Fixed Assets	$82,000	Debentures	$26,000
Accumulated Depreciation	$31,000	Total Liabilities	$51,000
Net Fixed Assets	$51,000	SHAREHOLDER'S EQUITY	
		Common Stock (par value)	$13,000
		Retained Earnings	$46,000
		Total Shareholder's Equity	$59,000
Total Assets	$110,000	Total Claims	$110,000

DAKOTA CORPORATION
INCOME STATEMENT
FOR THE YEAR ENDED DECEMBER 31, 2000
(Thousands of Dollars, Except Per Share Data)

Sales	$180,000
Cost of Goods Sold	$126,000
Salaries and Wages	$34,500
Depreciation Expense (DEP)	$2,000
Total Operating Costs	$162,500
Earnings Before Interest & Taxes (EBIT)	$17,500
Interest Expense	$4,500
Earnings Before Taxes (EBT)	$13,000
Taxes	$4,420
Net Income (NI)	$8,580
Common Dividends	$2,574
Additions to Retained Earnings	$6,006

SOLUTIONS
PRACTICE SET B: Cash Flow Statement

BALLY GEAR CORPORATION
STATEMENT OF CASH FLOWS
DECEMBER 31, 2000 (Thousands of Dollars)

CASH FLOW FROM OPERATING ACTIVITIES

Cash receipts from customers		$252,000
Cash payment for:		
Inventory	($203,000)	
Salaries and wages	($13,000)	
Interest	($3,000)	
Income taxes	($8,200)	
Total cash payments		($227,200)
Net cash provided by operating activities		$24,800

CASH FLOW FROM INVESTING ACTIVITIES

Purchase of fixed assets	($12,000)	
Purchase of marketable securities	($3,000)	
Net cash used for investing activities		($15,000)

CASH FLOW FROM FINANCING ACTIVITIES

Decrease in notes payable	($1,000)	
Repurchase of common stock	($2,000)	
Dividends paid	($4,800)	
Net cash provided by financing activities		($7,800)
Net increase in cash		$2,000
Cash at the beginning of the year		$3,000
Cash at the end of the year		$5,000

EXPLANATIONS

Sales Revenue and Accounts Receivable

Let's again begin with the first item on the income statement: namely, sales. We continue to assume that all sales were for credit. Thus, we want to compare the net income figure from the income statement with the changes in the firm's accounts receivable. In this way we can determine the amount of cash the firm collected as a result of its sales efforts. Bally Gear had total sales in 2000 of $250,000. Accounts receivable decreased by $2,000 (from $18,000 in 1999 to $16,000 in 2000). Thus, Bally collected $2,000 more in cash than the sales figure on the income statement reported.

Sales	$250,000
+Beginning accounts receivable	$18,000
Potential collections	$268,000
−Ending accounts receivable	($16,000)
Cash collections from customers	$252,000

Therefore, cash inflows from sales were $252,000 ($250,000 sales + $2,000 decrease in accounts receivable) and this is the amount we report in the cash flows from operating activities section in the cash flow statement.

Cost of Goods Sold

The income statement reports that cost of goods sold was $207,000. Remember, we have to examine inventory and accounts payable to determine cash outflows. Inventory increased by $5,000 from 1999 to 2000. This means that purchases were $5,000 more than inventory sold. The total purchases of inventory was $212,000 ($207,000 cost of goods sold + $5,000 increase in the firm's inventory account between the two periods).

Ending inventory	$31,000
+Cost of goods sold	$207,000
Inventory to account for	$238,000
–Beginning inventory	($26,000)
Purchases of inventory	$212,000

The balance sheet shows that accounts payable increased $9,000 between 1999 and 2000. This means that Bally Gear's purchases were $9,000 more than their cash payments.

Beginning accounts payable	$9,000
+Purchases	$212,000
Total amount to be paid	$221,000
–Ending accounts payable	($18,000)
Amount paid in cash	$203,000

Thus, cash outflows for inventory must have been $203,000 ($212,000 in inventory purchases – $9,000 increase in accounts payable) and we record this outflow under operating activities in the cash flow statement.

Recall that we determined that inventory purchases were $212,000. Thus cash payments for inventory must have been $203,000 ($212,000 in inventory purchased – $9,000 increase in accounts payable), and this is what we record as cash payments for inventory in the operating activities section of the statement of cash flows.

Salaries and Wages Expense and Salaries and Wages Payable

We have to ask whether $18,000 in salary and wage expense was the amount that Bally Gear actually paid (i.e., was this the actual size of the cash outflow). The accrued salary and wage account increased by $5,000 between 1999 and 2000 thereby reducing their cash outflows to employees by this accrued amount.

Beginning accrued salaries and wages	$2,000
+Salaries and wages expense	$18,000
Total amount to be paid	$20,000
–Ending accrued salaries and wages	($7,000)
Cash payments to employees	$13,000

Thus the firm would record $13,000 ($18,000 salary and wage expense – $5,000 increase in accrued salary and wage account) as cash payments to employees under operating activities.

Depreciation Expense

The next item on the income statement is depreciation of $4,000. Recall that depreciation has no effect on cash flows so we don't record it.

Interest Expense

The amount of interest expense reported on the income statement is $3,000. Again, there is no accrual of interest so we record the entire amount as a cash outflow under operating activities.

Income Tax Expense and Income Taxes Payable

The income statement reports income tax expense of $7,200. Note however, that accrued taxes declined by $1,000 from 1999 to 2000. This means that the amount of cash paid to the government in taxes was $1,000 more than the amount of the tax expense reported on the income statement.

Beginning accrued taxes	$3,000
+Income tax expense	$7,200
Total amount to be paid	$10,200
–Ending accrued taxes	($2,000)
Cash payments to IRS	$8,200

Thus the firm made payments of $8,200 ($7,200 income tax expense + $1,000 decrease in accrued taxes). This is the amount we report in cash flows from operating activities. Now it's time to move to the second section of the cash flow statement and account for any investing activities in which the firm engaged.

Determine the Cash Flows from Investing Activities

Bally Gear's balance sheet shows an increase in gross fixed assets of $12,000 between 1999 and 2000. We record this cash outflow in the investing activities section.

Besides the purchase of additional fixed assets, Bally also purchased $3,000 more in marketable securities in 2000. This represents an additional cash outflow for the firm and is also recorded in the investing activities section.

Determine the Cash Flows from Financing Activities

To determine the cash flows from financing activities we begin with the examination of the firm's long-term liability and shareholder's (equity) account. Remember, we also report any shareholder dividends paid out in this section because this is an announced (arranged) cash outflow.

Notes Payable

Bally Gear Corporation decreased their notes payable by $1,000 from $10,000 in 1999 to $9,000 in 2000. This means the firm repaid some of their bank borrowings and we record this cash outflow in the financing activities section of the statement of cash flows.

Long Term Debt

There was no change in Bally's long-term debt account.

Shareholder's Equity

Bally repurchased $2,000 of its common stock in the open market requiring a cash outflow. We record this change in cash flows in the financing activities section.

Retained Earnings

Bally Gear had an increase in retained earnings. Again, we don't record this amount because retained earnings are a netted figure (net income - dividends) and the cash flow statement should show where the cash came from and where it went. We do want to record the $4,800 in dividends Bally Gear paid to their shareholders in the financing activities section.

Summary of Findings for Bally Gear's Cash Flow Statement:

Bally Gear has net operating cash flows of $24,800. They used 60 percent of net cash provided by operating activities to purchase fixed assets and marketable securities. They repaid some of their debt as evidenced by their reduction in notes payable. They also paid out nearly 44 percent of their net income (19 percent of net operating cash flows) to shareholders as dividends and repurchased some of their own common stock in the market place. With the repurchase of common stock there are fewer shareholders to "share" in the firm's net income. This means that every shareholder now has a bigger piece of the pie because there are fewer shares of stock outstanding. A major portion of the firm's cash outflows went into inventory purchases ($203,000). This single outflow accounts for more than 80 percent of their cash flows from operating activities. Even after these moves the firm was able to increase their cash by $2,000. Based on this analysis alone, the firm is doing quite well.

2. Webster Corporation

WEBSTER CORPORATION
STATEMENT OF CASH FLOWS
DECEMBER 31, 2000 (Thousands of Dollars)

CASH FLOW FROM OPERATING ACTIVITIES		
Cash receipts from customers		$2,693,520
Cash payment for:		
Inventory	($2,156,224)	
Salaries & wages	($510,000)	
Interest	($85,000)	
Income taxes	($7,550)	
Total cash payments		($2,758,774)
Net cash provided by operating activities		($65,254)
CASH FLOW FROM INVESTING ACTIVITIES		
Purchase of fixed assets	($53,520)	
Net cash used for investing activities		($53,520)
CASH FLOW FROM FINANCING ACTIVITIES		
Increase in notes payable	$43,107	
Increase in long-term debt	$98,197	
Dividends paid	($24,150)	
Net cash provided by financing activities		$117,154
Net increase in cash		($1,620)
Cash at the beginning of the year		$40,320
Cash at the end of the year		$38,700

EXPLANATIONS

Sales Revenue and Accounts Receivable

One more time let's begin with sales and let's continue to assume that all sales were for credit. Thus, we want to compare the net income figure from the income statement with the changes in the firm's accounts receivable. In this way we can determine the amount of cash the firm collected as a result of its sales efforts. Webster had total sales in 2000 of $2,750,000. Accounts receivable account increased by $56,480 (from $245,840 in 1999 to $302,320 in 2000). Thus Webster had $56,480 more in sales than it collected in cash.

Sales	$2,750,000
+Beginning accounts receivable	$245,840
Potential collections	$2,995,840
–Ending accounts receivable	($302,320)
Cash collections from customers	$2,693,520

Therefore, cash inflows from sales were $2,693,520 ($2,750,000 sales - $56,480 increase in accounts receivable) and this is the amount we report in the cash flows from operating activities section in the statement of cash flows.

Cost of Goods Sold
The income statement reports that cost of goods sold was $2,062,500. We remember, however, that we have to examine inventory and accounts payable to determine cash outflows. Inventory increased by $150,114 from 1999 to 2000. This means that purchases were $150,114 more than inventory sold. The total purchases of inventory was $2,212,614 ($2,062,500 cost of goods sold + $150,114 increase in the firm's inventory account between the two periods). Don't forget the company made at least some of these purchases on credit.
Note from the balance sheet that accounts payable increased $56,390 between 1999 and 2000. This means that Webster's purchases were $56,390 more than their cash payments.

Ending inventory	$650,754
+Cost of goods sold	$2,062,500
Inventory to account for	$2,713,254
–Beginning inventory	($500,640)
Purchases of inventory	$2,212,614

Thus, cash outflows for inventory must have been $2,156,224 ($2,212,614 in inventory purchases - $56,390 increase in accounts payable) and we record this outflow under operating activities in the cash flow statement.

Beginning accounts payable	$101,500
+Purchases	$2,212,614
Total amount to be paid	$2,314,114
–Ending accounts payable	($157,890)
Amount paid in cash	$2,156,224

Salaries and Wages Expense and Salaries and Wages Payable
Again, we first need to know if Webster actually paid out $520,000 (i.e., was this the actual size of the cash outflow). The accrued salaries and wages account on the balance sheet increased by $10,000 between 1999 and 2000 thereby reducing their cash outflows to employees by this accrued amount.

Beginning accrued salaries and wages	$25,000
+Salaries and wages expense	$520,000
Total amount to be paid	$545,000
–Ending accrued salaries and wages	($35,000)
Cash payments to employees	$510,000

Thus the firm would record $510,000 ($520,000 in salary and wage expense - $10,000 increase in the accrued salary and wage account) as cash payments to employees in the operating activities section.

Depreciation Expense

The next item on the income statement is depreciation of $25,000. Recall that depreciation has no effect on cash flows so we don't record it.

Interest Expense

The amount of interest expense reported on the income statement is $85,000 and with no accrual account this is the amount we record as a cash outflow under operating activities.

Income Tax Expense and Income Taxes Payable

The income statement reports income tax expense of $23,000. Note however, that accrued taxes increased by $15,450 between 1999 and 2000. This means that the amount of cash paid to the government in taxes was $15,450 less than the amount of tax expense reported on the income statement.

Beginning accrued taxes	$70,200
+Income tax expense	$23,000
Total amount to be paid	$93,200
−Ending accrued taxes	($85,650)
Cash payments to IRS	$7,550

Thus the firm made payments of $7,550 ($23,000 income tax expense – $15,450 increase in accrued taxes). This is the amount we report in the cash flows from operating activities section in the statement of cash flows. Now it's time to develop the second section of the cash flow statement and account for any investing activities in which the firm engaged.

Determine the Cash Flows from Investing Activities

Webster's balance sheet shows an increase in gross fixed assets of $53,520 in 2000 and this is the amount we record in the cash flows from investing activities section in the statement of cash flows.

Webster has no investment in marketable securities. The second section was quick and easy so let's move to the third section where we account for the firm's cash inflows and outflows as the result of their financing activities.

Determine the Cash Flows from Financing Activities

Determining cash flow from financing activities generally begins with examination of the firms long-term liability and equity accounts.

Notes Payable

Webster Company increased their notes payable by $43,107 from $140,000 in 1999 to $183,107 in 2000. This means the firm obtained additional funding from their financial institution(s). We record this cash inflow in the financing activities section.

Long -Term Debt

Webster increased their long-term debt account by $98,197 in 2000. We would record this cash inflow in the financing activities section.

Shareholder's Equity

There was no change in Webster's common stock account.

Retained Earnings

Again, we don't record retained earnings but we do record the $24,150 in dividends Webster paid out to their equity investors (i.e., shareholders).

Summary of findings for Webster's Cash Flow Statement:

Webster has net operating cash flows of ($65,254). They spent $53,520 on acquiring fixed assets. Because their operations generated a negative cash flow (primarily from a significant increase in accounts receivable and inventory), they had to borrow money to pay for their fixed assets, cover the shortfalls their operations generated and pay dividends. They borrowed $43,107 from the bank in the form of notes payable and issued an additional $98,197 in long-term debt. Even with this heavy demand for funds and subsequent borrowing, the firm continued to pay a dividend in the amount of $24,150 or 70 percent of the firm's net income. Given this information it is not too surprising that their cash account declined.

In summary, from their borrowed funds of $141,304 ($43,107 + $98197) they used 38 percent to purchase additional fixed assets, they used 46 percent to cover their cash flow shortfall from operations and 17 percent to pay dividends. It's never a good sign when a firm borrows funds to pay dividends. If we saw a trend in declining cash flows this would also be cause for worry.

SOLUTIONS
PRACTICE SET C: TAXES

1. Bargain Basement Bakery (Bcubed)

Gross revenues	$20,000
+Taxable dividends[1]	$1,500
+Interest income	$2,000
−Interest expense[2]	($1,500)
Taxable income	$22,000
−Taxes at 34%	($7,480)
+Nontaxable dividends[3]	$3,500
After-tax income	$18,020
−Dividends paid	($3,000)
Addition to retained earnings	$15,020

[1]$5,000 minus the 70% exclusion = $1,500 in taxable dividends
[2]Interest expense $15,000(.10) = $1,500
[3]Have to remember to add back nontaxable dividends or we'd be understating the firm's after-tax income by $3,500.

2. Stone Products

EBIT*	$600,000
+Taxable dividends[1]	$24,000
+Interest income	$40,000
−Interest expense	($60,000)
Taxable income	$604,000
−Taxes at 34%	($205,360)
+Nontaxable dividends[2]	$56,000
After-tax income	$454,640
−Dividends paid	($20,000)
Addition to retained earnings	$434,640

*Income from operations, gross revenues and earnings before interest and taxes (EBIT) are all the same thing: sales revenues minus operating expenses such as cost of goods sold, selling and administration costs and depreciation.

[1]$80,000 minus the 70% exclusion = $24,000 in taxable dividends
[2]Have to remember to add back nontaxable dividends or we'd be understating the firm's after-tax income by $56,000.

SOLUTIONS
PRACTICE SET D: DEPRECIATION

1. Flamingo Laundry

Operating income	$300,000
−Depreciation expense[1]	($19,800)
Taxable income	$280,200
−Tax liability	($95,268)
After-tax income	$184,932
+Depreciation expense	$19,800
After-tax cash flows	$204,732

Tax savings from depreciation tax shield = $19,800(0.34)=$6,732

[1]$60,000(0.33) = $19,800

2. and 3. Flamingo Laundry

Calculating book value
$60,000(0.33) = $19,800
$60,000(0.45) = $27,000
$46,800

Book Value $60,000 − $46,800 = $13,200
or $60,000(0.22) = $13,200 to account for the depreciation not taken

Selling Price $30,000
$30,000-$13,200= $16,800
Market – Book = Gain on
Value   Value   Sale

$16,800 (0.34) = $5,712
(gain on sale × tax rate)
= Tax Liability

Cash flow from sale of machine
Market Value $30,000
– Taxes   ($5,712)
Net Cash Flow $24,288

Selling Price $5,000
$5,000-$13,200 =($8,200)
Market – Book = Loss on
Value   Value   Sale

$8,200(0.34) = $2,788
 (loss on sale × tax rate)
=Tax Saving

Cash flow from sale of machine
Market Value $5,000
+Tax Saving $2,788
Net Cash Flow $7,788

4. Crey Seafood Company

Operating income	$275,000
–Depreciation expense[1]	($14,400)
Taxable income	$260,600
–Tax liability	($88,604)
After-tax income	$171,996
+Depreciation expense	$14,400
After-tax cash flows	$186,396

Tax savings from depreciation tax shield = $14,400 (0.34)=$4,896

[1]$75,000(0.192) = $14,400

5. Challenge Problem a.$145,554, b. $282,546, c. $297,246

6. Challenge Problem a. $47,600, b.$78,400, c. $73,400, d. $111,400
e. $13,200, f. $8,800, g. $4,000

SOLUTIONS
PRACTICE SET E: CARRY-FORWARD AND CARRY-BACK

1. Silver Stone

	1998	1999	2000
Earnings Before Taxes	$50,000	$50,000	($70,000)
Carry-Back credit 1999	($50,000)		
Adjusted Profit	$0		
Taxes paid on $50,000	$17,000		
Taxes due on $0 @34%	$0		
Tax refund ($17,000–$0)			$17,000
Amount left to carry forward	$20,000		
Carry-Back credit 2000		($20,000)	
Adjusted Profit		$30,000	
Taxes paid on $50,000		$17,000	
Taxes due on $30,000 @34%		$10,200	
Tax refund ($17,000–$10,200)			$6,800

2. Waterford Tile

	1997	1998	1999[1]	2000
Earnings Before Taxes	$82,000	$82,000	($40,000)	($93,000)
Carry-Back credit 2000	($82,000)			
Adjusted Profit	$0			
Taxes paid on $82,000	$27,880			
Taxes due on $0 @34%	$0			
Tax refund ($27,880–$0)				$27,880
Amount left to carry forward	$11,000			
Carry-Back credit 2000		($11,000)		
Adjusted Profit		$71,000		
Taxes paid on $82,000		$27,880		
Taxes due on $71,000 @34%		$24,140		
Tax refund ($27,880–$24,140)				$3,740

[1]The loss in 1999 was carried back and written off in its entirety in 1996

Cartwright Oil

	1997	1998	1999	2000
Earnings Before Taxes	$50,000	$50,000	$120,000	($300,000)
Carry-Back credit 2000	($50,000)			
Adjusted Profit 1997	$0			
Taxes paid on $50,000	$17,000			
Taxes due on $0 @34%	$0			
Tax refund ($17,000–$0)				$17,000
Amount left to carry forward	$250,000			
Carry-Back credit 2000		($50,000)		
Adjusted Profit 1998		$0		
Taxes paid on $50,000		$17,000		
Taxes due on $0 @34%		$0		
Tax refund ($17,000–$0)				$17,000
Amount left to carry forward		$200,000		
Carry-Back credit 2000			($120,000)	
Adjusted Profit 1999			$0	
Taxes paid on $120,000			$40,800	
Taxes due on $0 @34%			$0	
Tax refund ($40,800–$0)				$40,800
Amount left to carry forward			$80,000	

3. Frame Galleries Corporation

	1997	1998	1999	2000
Earnings Before Taxes	$57,000	$110,000	$140,000	$175,000
Carry-Forward loss 1994	($57,000)			
Adjusted Profit	$0			
Taxes due on $0 @34%	$0			
Carry-Forward loss 1994		($93,000)		
Carry-Forward loss 1995		($17,000)		
Adjusted Profit		$0		
Taxes due on $0 @34%		$0		
Carry-Forward loss 1995			($103,000)	
Carry-Forward loss 1996			($37,000)	
Adjusted Profit			$0	
Taxes due on $0 @34%			$0	
Amount available for write-off			$0	
Carry-Forward loss 1996				($38,000)
Adjusted Profit				$137,000
Taxes due on $137,000 @34%				$46,580
Amount available for write-off				$137,000

4. **Challenge Problem** a. $0, b. ($9,490), c. $11,227, d. $34,984, e. $7,264

5. **Challenge Problem** a. $0, b. ($11,350), c. ($10,600), d. $89,450, e. $7,352

SOLUTIONS
PRACTICE SET F: Financial Analysis

1. Jurassic Industries
a. Extended DuPont equation

	profit margin	×	total asset turnover	×	equity multiplier		ROE
JURRASIC	3.15%	×	3.55	×	2.20	=	24.66%
INDUSTRY	5.00%	×	2.50	×	1.90	=	23.75%

Note how the ROE for Jurassic is very close to the ROE for the industry, yet they arrived at these similar ROEs in very different ways. Jurassic's profit margin is much lower than the industry indicating they are not very good at controlling expenses. The industry's total asset turnover is much lower than Jurassic's total asset turnover. This implies that Jurassic is either very efficient with the use of its assets or its assets may be very old relative to the rest of the industry. Jurassic uses more debt than the industry and that along with the higher total asset turnover is what gives Jurassic the superior ROE in terms of absolutes. Remember that ROE says nothing about how the firm got there. That is, Jurassic's use of debt has leveraged up their ROE, but may well be at the cost of higher risk due to the increased financial leverage employed.

b. Areas for further investigation.

The analyst should look at the income statement in more detail because Jurassic's profit margin is very low when compared to the industry. She should also investigate the firm's ability to service their debt load because we measure their usage of debt to exceed industry norms. The analyst should also examine Jurassic's asset utilization and focus on the firm's use of fixed assets to determine why the total asset turnover is so high.

c. Prepare a common size balance sheet and income statement for Jurassic.

JURASSIC INDUSTRIES
COMMON SIZE INCOME STATEMENT
FOR THE YEAR ENDED DECEMBER 31, 2000

Sales	100.00%
Cost of Goods Sold	69.23%
Salaries and Wages	22.31%
Depreciation Expense (DEP)	1.85%
Total Operating Costs	93.38%
Earnings Before Interest & Taxes (EBIT)	6.63%
Interest Expense	1.37%
Earnings Before Taxes (EBT)	5.25%
Taxes	2.10%
Net Income (NI)	3.15%

JURASSIC INDUSTRIES
COMMON SIZE BALANCE
FOR THE YEAR ENDED DECEMBER 31, 2000

ASSETS		LIABILITIES	
Cash	3.83%	Accounts Payable	2.19%
Marketable Securities	1.64%	Accrued Salaries & Wages	2.73%
Accounts Receivable	8.20%	Accrued Taxes	1.09%
Inventory	13.66%	Total Current Liabilities	6.01%
Total Current Assets	27.32%	Notes Payable	7.65%
Gross Fixed Assets	84.70%	Mortgage Bonds	21.86%
Accumulated Depreciation	12.02%	Debentures	19.13%
Net Fixed Assets	72.68%	Total Long-Term Debt	48.63%
		Total Liabilities	54.64%
		SHAREHOLDERS' EQUITY	
		Common Stock (par value)	7.10%
		Additional Paid-In Capital	13.66%
		Retained Earnings	24.59%
		Total Shareholder's Equity	45.36%
Total Assets	100.00%	Total Claims	100.00%

2. Pylon Corporation

PYLON CORPORATION – BALANCE SHEET
FOR THE YEAR ENDED DECEMBER 31, 2000

ASSETS		LIABILITIES	
Cash	$258,000	Accounts Payable	$115,000
Accounts Receivable	$125,000	Accrued Salaries & Wages	$50,000
Inventory	$175,000	Accrued Taxes	$25,000
Total Current Assets	$558,000	Total Current Liabilities	$190,000
Gross Fixed Assets	$1,100,000	Notes Payable	$50,000
Accumulated Dep.	$250,000	Mortgage Bonds	$350,000
Net Fixed Assets	$850,000	Total Long-Term Debt	$400,000
		Total Liabilities	$590,000
		SHAREHOLDERS' EQUITY	
		Common Stock (par value)	$226,000
		Additional Paid-In Capital	$392,000
		Retained Earnings	$200,000
		Total Shareholder's Equity	$818,000
Total Assets	$1,408,000	Total Claims	$1,408,000

3. Bad Dog, Inc.

We see that Bad Dog kept their ROE close to 22 percent until 2000 when it surged to 26.55 percent. They maintained this ratio even though their return on assets steadily declined.

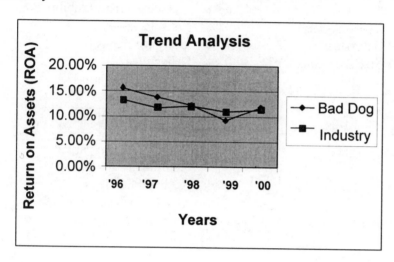

Bad Dog, Inc.	1996	1997	1998	1999	2000
ROA	15.6%	13.8%	12.1%	9.18%	11.8%
Industry, Inc.	1996	1997	1998	1999	2000
ROA	13.2%	11.7%	12.05	11.0%	11.4%

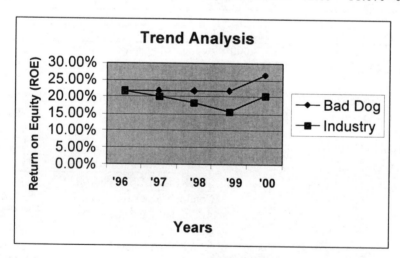

Bad Dog, Inc.	1996	1997	1998	1999	2000
ROE	21.8%	21.8%	21.8%	21.8%	26.55%
Industry, Inc.	1996	1997	1998	1999	2000
ROE	21.8%	20.0%	18.2%	15.6%	20.4%

There is only one way to do this and that is if their debt usage increased. To investigate further we should examine the profit margin, total asset turnover and equity multiplier ratios. See the graphs below.

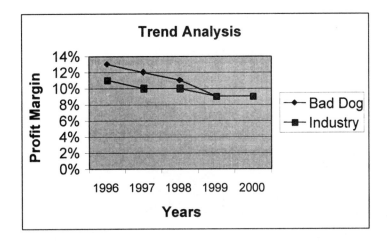

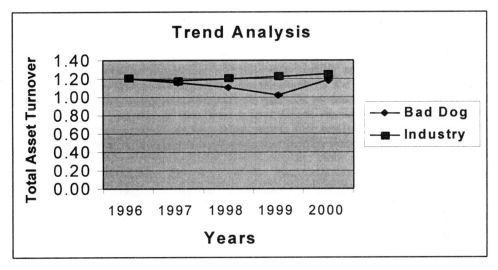

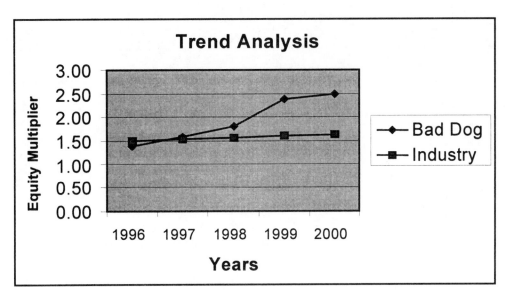

Sure enough, they made up for any shortfalls in their profit margin or total asset turnover by increasing their debt. This is a very risky strategy and one of which investors should be aware.

WATERTECH ENERGY CORPORATION

4.

a. current ratio – Increase, because the numerator is larger due to the increase in cash and inventory.

b. quick ratio – Increase because even though there is no inventory in the numerator, the cash balance increased causing the numerator to increase.

c. debt ratio – The debt ratio would decrease because more of the assets are financed with equity. From another perspective the equity portion on the right-hand side of the balance sheet is larger and the ratio of debt to equity is now smaller.

d. total asset turnover – Total asset turnover is smaller because we have a larger number of assets and there has been no commensurate increase in sales.

e. return on equity – This ratio is smaller because there has been no increase in net income as the result of this transaction, but the equity invested in the firm has increase causing the ratio to decline.

f. return on assets – This ratio will decrease because sales have not increased, but the dollar amount of assets has increased by $18 million.

5. Challenge Problem

INDIANAPOLIS INDUSTRIES BALANCE SHEET

Cash	$5,167	Accounts Payable	$13,000
Accounts Receivable	$20,833	Long-Term Debt	$19,143
Inventory	$13,000	Stockholders' Equity	$39,286
Total Current Assets	39,000		
Fixed Assets	$32,429		
Total Assets	$71,429	Total Claims	71,429

SECTION 2:
Time Value of Money

I. OVERVIEW OF THE TIME VALUE OF MONEY

The time value of money is at the very core of all finance. Whether you're investing and want to know the value of your investment at some point in the future (future value), or you expect to receive a cash inflow at a later date and want to know its value today (present value), you'll need to apply the time value of money concepts. No doubt you've had some exposure to time value in your accounting or other business courses. In these sections, however, we'll assume no prior knowledge. Instead, we'll work through each concept step by step and walk you through the mathematics.

A. Imagining Future Value

Suppose you find a bunch of dollars in your hand. You will invest those dollars at a positive interest rate for some period of time. How much money will you have at the end? That is, what is the future value of your investment? It depends: First, on how much money you started with; second, the interest rate; and third, the length of your investment period. If you invest today at a positive interest rate, then tomorrow (or at any point in the future) you will have more money than you started with. We call this financial phenomenon *compounding* or *solving for future value*.

For example, suppose you won $5 million (after taxes) in the lottery. After squandering the first couple of million, you decide to invest the remainder ($3 million) for future needs. How much will you have after one year, two years, or three years? A lot! To answer this question a bit more precisely, you would have to compound the $3 million principal forward to find out its worth at the end of your selected investment horizon. We'll hold off on the mechanics of calculating future value for now and work on clarifying the concept of present value.

B. Conceiving Present Value

The big question in finance is not who, what, or where, but when. When do we get our money? There is a price for making us wait because if we had the money today we could invest it and already have the money working for us (i.e., earning interest income). Waiting for money reduces its value. So, for instance, if we have to wait five years to get a promised sum, that means we'll have to give up five years' worth of interest income. In finance we do very little out of the goodness of our hearts, so the person who makes us wait has to pay. How much they have to pay is equal to the amount of interest income we had to give up by waiting. We call this process *discounting* or *solving for present value.*

Present value is the value today of a sum of money you expect to receive in the future. For example, you've recently learned that your rich and eccentric Aunt Lucy left you $1.2 million in a trust fund. Unfortunately, the fund doesn't pay out until you reach age 35. You're only 25 now, but not too surprisingly you want some of the cash today. You go to your local financial institution with your trust fund papers and see if, based on your promised future cash inflow, you can get any money now. They read over the papers, and say they won't give you $1.2 million because they have to wait ten years to be repaid. How much would the financial institution be willing to give you now in exchange for the promised cash inflow in the future? To answer this question, we have to discount the promised cash inflow backwards in time to find out what it's worth today. The discounted or present value of your $1.2 million depends on when the cash flow arrives (in your case that's ten years), the interest income lost on the cash inflow by having to wait for it to show up (a.k.a. an opportunity cost), and the size of the cash inflow expected in the future ($1.2 million in this example).

We need to know how time influences the value of money not only because you might win the lottery or be related to a wealthy eccentric, but because timing influences the desirability of all financial transactions. For example, the value or price of a financial security (e.g., a stock or bond) is simply the present value of all the cash flows we expect the security to generate. While the amount of cash our investment gives us is important, when we get the money is also important. As an example, suppose a firm is thinking of taking on a new project. One key element management considers is not just how big the project's cash inflows are, but when they expect to receive them. In the process of comparing projects for possible investment, the ones that give management the most money the soonest are the best.

The next two sections take a closer look at future value and present value. For convenience, we've rounded all numbers to the nearest whole dollar.

II.   MECHANICS OF TIME VALUE

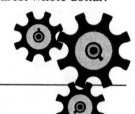

In the following sections we won't overload you with equations and notations; we'll leave that to your textbook. Unfortunately, however, the nature of the time value beast requires that we use mathematics to show you how all this works. We'll keep it simple, but you have to read carefully and think things through as you move along. If you can grasp the time value concepts and their relatively simple mechanics, your days in finance will be ever so much easier. From here on out, nearly all finance topics are, to one degree or another, based on these time value concepts.

A. The Aerodynamics of Future Value

With future value we're interested in finding out what the value of a given investment is at some future point. We already know that the future value is a function of how much we started with, how long we leave our dollars invested, and the rate of interest our investment earns. Future value is a compounding process where we earn interest not only on our initial investment (a.k.a. present value, beginning balance or principal), but we also earn interest on the interest we earned in the previous period(s). Got that?

We'll assume you've decided to invest your $3 million lottery prize for one year at an interest rate of 8 percent. You want to know how much money you'll have one year from now or the future value of your investment. We know the dollar amount you'll have one year from now will consist of your present value or the principal originally invested, plus any dollars in interest your money earned over that one-year period.

$$\text{Future Value} = \$3,000,000(1.08) = \$3,240,000 \tag{1}$$

By investing your winnings for only one year you earned $240,000 without lifting a finger. Not bad! Now, what if you wanted to leave the money invested at 8 percent for two years how much would you have at the end?

$$\text{Future Value} = \$3,000,000(1.08)(1.08)$$
$$= \$3,000,000(1.08)^2 = \$3,499,200 \tag{2}$$

You've earned $499,200 by simply investing your money and leaving it untouched for two years. Notice we calculated the future value using an exponent to indicate the length of time you invested your money. Let's think this through for a minute. If you earned $240,000 in interest in one year, as we calculated in equation [1], then shouldn't your total dollars in interest after two years be twice that amount, or $480,000? But in equation [2] we calculated the interest to be $499,200 or $19,200 more than that. What's going on here? Compounding!

In year 2 you earn interest not only on the $3 million principal as you did in year 1, but during the second year you also earn interest on the $240,000 you generated in interest during the first year. Thus you can find the future value at the end of the second year by compounding both the original $3 million in principal and the $240,000 of interest earned in the first year by 8 percent.

Interest Earned After 2 Years

$3,000,000(0.08) = $240,000	Interest on principal balance in the first year
$3,000,000(0.08) = $240,000	Interest on principal balance in the second year
$240,000(0.08) = $19,200	Interest on interest earned in the first year
$499,200	

Now what if you wanted to leave the money in at 8 percent for three years? How much would you have at the end?

Future Value = $3,000,000(1.08)(1.08)(1.08)
               = $3,000,000(1.08)^3 = $3,779,136   [3]

Without doing anything, you've earned $779,136. Again, notice we calculated the future value using an exponent to indicate the length of time you invested your money.

The best part about compounding or solving for future value is that you not only earn interest on your principal investment of $3 million, but you also earn interest on your interest and on your interest's interest (whew!). Let's do a breakdown of the interest earned for each year during your three-year investment period.

Interest Earned After 3 Years

Interest on principal balance in the first year	$3,000,000(.08)	=	$240,000
Interest on principal balance in the second year	$3,000,000(.08)	=	$240,000
Interest on the interest earned in the first year	$240,000(.08)	=	$19,200
Interest on principal balance in the third year	$3,000,000(.08)	=	$240,000
Interest on the interest earned in the first year	$240,000(.08)	=	$19,200
Interest on the interest earned in the second year	$240,000(.08)	=	$19,200
Interest on the interest's interest earned in the third year	$19,200(.08)	=	$1,536
			$779,136
Add principal balance			$3,000,000
Future value of investment			$3,779,136

Notice that in year 3, you earn interest not only on the $3 million principal, but also on the $240,000 in interest you earned in years 1 and 2 and also on the $19,200 of interest you earned on your first year's interest in the second year. What? Let's use a time line to sort this out. The time line below shows the value of each interest payment when compounded forward each year by 8 percent (e.g., $240,000(1.08) = $259,200).

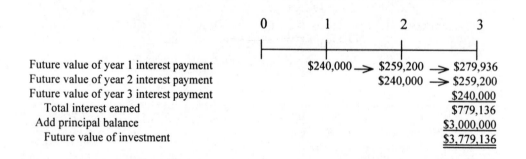

	0	1	2	3
Future value of year 1 interest payment		$240,000 →	$259,200 →	$279,936
Future value of year 2 interest payment			$240,000 →	$259,200
Future value of year 3 interest payment				$240,000
Total interest earned				$779,136
Add principal balance				$3,000,000
Future value of investment				$3,779,136

The initial interest payment received at the end of the first year is compounded forward at eight percent to the end of year 2 $240,000(1.08)=$259,000. That first interest payment earns interest again when compounded forward from the end of year 2 to the end of the third year,

$259,000(1.08)=$279,936. The $240,000 interest payment received at the end of the second year is compounded forward to the end of the third year, $240,00(1.08) = $259,000. Because you specified a three-year time horizon, the interest payment received at the end of the third year does not get compounded.

To find the future value of your investment, add the principal balance to the compounded value of the interest payments for a grand total of $3,779,136. This is the same amount we calculated in equation [3].

B. The Effect of Time and Interest Rates on Future Value

The two factors that influence future value are time and interest rates. At some given positive interest rate, the longer you leave your money invested the greater the future value. For illustrative purposes, let's hold the interest rate constant and see what happens as we vary the amount of time you invest your money. If you invest your $3 million principal at 15 percent, what would your future value be at various points in time? The table below shows the future value of your $3 million compounded at 15 percent for various investment horizons.

Number of Years Invested	Interest Earned		+	Principal	=	Future Value
1	$3,000,000(0.15)$ =	$450,000	+	$3,000,000	=	$3,450,000
5	$3,000,000(0.15)^5$ =	$3,034,072	+	$3,000,000	=	$6,034,072
10	$3,000,000(0.15)^{10}$ =	$9,136,673	+	$3,000,000	=	$12,136,673
15	$3,000,000(0.15)^{15}$ =	$21,411,185	+	$3,000,000	=	$24,411,185
20	$3,000,000(0.15)^{20}$ =	$46,099,612	+	$3,000,000	=	$49,099,612

Now if we hold time constant, you'll see that the higher the interest rate, the greater the future value. For example, if you invested your $3 million for five years, what would be your future value at various interest rates?

Interest Rate	Interest Earned		+	Principal	=	Future Value
5%	$3,000,000[(1.05)^5 - 1]$	=	$828,845 +	$3,000,000	=	$3,828,845
10%	$3,000,000[(1.10)^5 - 1]$	= $1,831,530 +		$3,000,000	=	$4,831,530
15%	$3,000,000[(1.15)^5 - 1]$	= $3,034,072 +		$3,000,000	=	$6,034,072
20%	$3,000,000[(1.20)^5 - 1]$	= $4,464,960 +		$3,000,000	=	$7,464,960
25%	$3,000,000[(1.25)^5 - 1]$	= $6,155,273 +		$3,000,000	=	$9,155,273

Theoretically, as we increase the interest rate or the time factor toward infinity, the future value approaches infinity. Now there's a theory that needs testing! Before we move on to present value explanations and calculations, let's do Practice Set A on the next page. At the end of each section (consult table of contents for exact page numbers to each practice set) we've provided detailed solutions except to the challenge problems. Good luck and keep in mind that it's only money!

PRACTICE SET A
FUTURE VALUE PROBLEMS

1. What is the future value of $200 invested for seven years at 8 percent annual interest?

2. What is the future value of $350 invested for five years at 9 percent annual interest?

3. Today Richardson Inc., an art gallery on the West Side, purchased a rare painting for $70,000. They expect the painting to increase in value at a rate of 15 percent annually for the next five years. How much will their painting be worth at the end of the fifth year if their expectations are correct? (HINT: Recognize that $70,000 is the current or present value of Richardson's investment and thus you need to solve for the future value of $70,000 to know what the value of the painting will be in five years).

4. Allegro Industries, Inc., has a defined-benefit pension plan that is under-funded. To try and catch up with their liabilities, Allegro invested $50,000 into a high-risk junk bond mutual fund that in previous years had earned as much as 17 percent annually. If their plan works and the fund continues to earn an annual rate of 17 percent over the next ten years, how much will Allegro have added to their pension fund holdings?

5. Tucker Trucking invested $4,000 in a money market mutual fund that currently pays 3.5 percent annual interest. They plan to leave their money invested for a period of eight years. What will be the value of Tucker's money at the end of their eight-year investment horizon?

6. Simpson Clothier, a men's haberdashery, invested $12,000 in a corporate bond mutual fund that offers a 7.7 percent annual return. They would like to have $20,000 at the end of nine years for an expansion project. Will Simpson Clothier reach their desired goal?

7. Howell Publishing plans to expand their operations to the West Coast in ten years. Today their CFO contributed $100,000 toward their goal of $350,000. They expect their portfolio to earn 12 percent annually. Will they reach their goal of $350,000?

8. **Challenge Problem**: The Weilers are saving up to buy a house. They have found the perfect bungalow with an eight-foot privacy fence to deter intruders. The asking price is $300,000 and their mortgage lender told them they would have to come up with at least 20 percent for a down payment in order qualify for their mortgage loan. Mrs. Weiler inherited and then invested $10,000 five years ago and Mr. Weiler sold his Ferrari and invested the $20,000 in net proceeds when they got married ten years ago. Their respective investments have been earning 10 percent annually. How much do they have available to purchase their dream house? (HINT: Use a time line to help solve this problem.)

9. **Challenge Problem**: In three years the McBeals expect to receive $20,000 from Mrs. McBeal's profit-sharing plan at work. The McBeals plan to use the entire $20,000 to finance their daughter, Ally's, education fund. Ally is 8 years old now. The McBeals estimate they will need $50,000 at the end of ten years, when Ally is 18, to pay her education expenses. They will make up any shortfalls with a home equity loan. If they invest their funds at 12 percent annual compounding, how much, if any, will they have to borrow to make up the difference? (HINT: Use a time line to help solve this problem.)

10. **Challenge Problem**: The phenomenal singer who goes simply by the name of # has made some wise and prudent investments over the years. Six years ago she invested $5 million from her record contract in an investment paying an annual rate of 8 percent. Three years ago she invested the $3 million she was paid for her first leading role in a large-scale movie production at an annual interest rate of 5 percent. What is the total value of #'s investments today? (HINT: Use a time line to help solve this problem.)

C. Thermodynamics of Present Value

Recall we said that waiting for money reduces its value because if we had the money today we could invest it and earn interest income. The interest income we have to forgo by waiting is what economists call an *opportunity cost*. To solve for present value, we must determine the cost of this lost opportunity. We do this by discounting the dollars we expect to receive in the future to account for the lost interest income opportunity.

Discounting is the opposite of compounding. Recall that to determine future value we ***multiplied*** the principal balance by one plus the interest rate raised to the appropriate exponent to account for time. To determine present value we ***divide*** the principal balance by one plus the interest rate raised to the appropriate exponent to account for time. Remember that $1.2 million trust fund from your Aunt Lucy that you had to wait ten years to get? What is the value of your trust fund today? We discount your pending cash inflow by dividing your future value ($1.2 million) by one plus the interest rate raised to the appropriate exponent to represent time. If we assume the interest rate is 8 percent, then the present value of your $1.2 million trust fund is:

$$\text{Present value} = \frac{\$1,200,000}{(1.08)^{10}} = \$555,832 \qquad [4]$$

So the financial institution you approached earlier would be willing to give you $555,832 today to have the right to your $1.2 million trust fund in ten years. They give up $644,168 ($1.2 million − $555,832) in interest income because they had to wait ten years to get your trust fund money. Remember they didn't just give up interest, but compounding of that interest as well.

Note again that discounting is the reverse of the compounding procedure. The present value of $1.2 million received in ten years <u>discounted</u> at 8 percent is $555,832. The future value in ten years of $555,832 <u>compounded</u> at 8 percent is $1.2 million [$555,832(1.08)^{10}].

Let's look at another example. What would be the value of your $3 million in lottery winnings if you had to wait one year before receiving your money? Remember that having to wait means you give up the "opportunity" to earn interest income on those dollars.

$$\text{Present value} = \frac{\$3,000,000}{(1.08)^{1}} = \$2,777,778 \qquad [5]$$

Having to wait a whole year means you give up $240,000 in interest income you would have received at the end of the first year if you'd had the money immediately available for investment. You don't, however, forego the entire $240,000. Even if you had the $3 million right now, you would have to wait until the end of the first year to receive your first interest payment. So we should discount the $240,000 to determine the *present value* of the lost interest payment.

$$\text{Present value of lost interest payment} = \frac{\$240,000}{(1.08)^{1}} = \$222,222 \qquad [6]$$

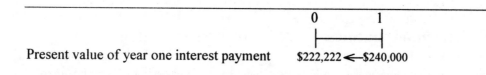

	0	1

Present value of year one interest payment $222,222 ← $240,000

The present value of that lost interest income payment is $222,222. Not coincidentally, this is also the amount of the discount calculated in equation [5] or the difference between $3,000,000 and $2,777,778.

To look at this from another angle, consider the interest you would have earned on $240,000 invested for one year at 8 percent. In the future value section we calculated this to be $240,000(0.08) = $19,200. If that is the interest you would have earned had you had the $240,000 now instead of a year from now, then what is the present value of those foregone interest dollars?

$$\text{Present value of lost interest income} = \frac{\$19,200}{(1.08)^1} = \$17,778 \qquad [7]$$

The answer is $17,778 and that is the difference between $240,000 and $222,222 or the present value of the lost interest income. Let's work through another example to get this straight.

What if you had to wait two years instead of just one year? That would mean you not only give up two years of interest, but also the compounding effects of earning interest on your interest.

$$\text{Present value} = \frac{\$3,000,000}{(1.08)^2} = \$2,572,017 \qquad [8]$$

$$\text{Amount of discount} = \$3,000,000 - \$2,572,017 = \$427,983 \qquad [9]$$

Thus having to wait two years results in a discount of $427,983. As we did in the future value section, notice we calculated the present value using an exponent to indicate time. The time line below shows the discounting of the individual cash flows whose sum equals the amount of the discount calculated in equation [9].

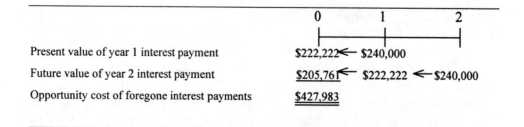

	0	1	2

Present value of year 1 interest payment $222,222 ← $240,000

Future value of year 2 interest payment $205,761 ← $222,222 ← $240,000

Opportunity cost of foregone interest payments $427,983

To tie all this together, recall the following from the future value section:

Interest Earned After 2 Years

Interest on principal balance in the first year	$3,000,000(.08) =	$240,000
Interest on principal balance in the second year	$3,000,000(.08) =	$240,000
Interest on the interest earned in the first year	$240,000(.08) =	$19,200
		$499,200

Thus, if you'd had the $3,000,000 from the get go (time 0) you would've earned $499,200 in interest income. If we calculate the present value of the $499,200 in delayed interest income (including the interest on the interest) we would again find the value of the discount:

$$\text{Present value} = \frac{\$499,200}{(1.08)^2} = \$427,983 \qquad [10]$$

And $427,983 represents the size of the discount we calculated in equation [9]. Finally, what if you were forced to wait three years for your cash inflow? What is the present value of $3 million if the discount rate is again eight percent?

$$\text{Present value} = \frac{\$3,000,000}{(1.08)^3} = \$2,381,497 \qquad [11]$$

$$\text{Amount of discount} = \$3,000,000 - \$2,381,497 = \$618,503 \qquad [12]$$

You discounted the $3 million by $618,503 for having to wait three years to receive your cash inflow. The discounting of the individual cash flows is shown on the time line below.

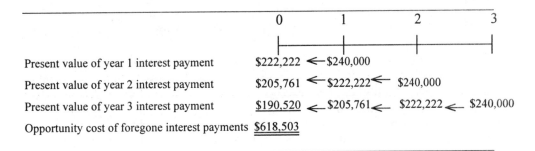

The sum of the discounted cash flows equals the amount of the discount calculated in equation [12]. Again, let's tie this together with our future value calculations.

Interest Earned After 3 Years

Interest on principal balance in the first year	$3,000,000(.08) =	$240,000
Interest on principal balance in the second year	$3,000,000(.08) =	$240,000
Interest on the interest earned in the first year	$240,000(.08) =	$19,200
Interest on principal balance in the third year	$3,000,000(.08) =	$240,000
Interest on the interest earned in the first year	$240,000(.08) =	$19,200
Interest on the interest earned in the second year	$240,000(.08) =	$19,200
Interest on the interest's interest earned in the third year	$19,200(.08) =	$1,536
Total interest earned over three years		$779,136

Thus, if we'd had the $3,000,000 from the beginning (time 0) we would have earned $779,136 in interest income. If we calculate the present value of the $779,136 in delayed interest income (that includes the interest on the interest as well as interest on the interest's interest), we again find the value of the discount:

$$\text{Present value} = \frac{\$779,136}{(1.08)^3} = \$618,503 \qquad [13]$$

And $618,503 represents the size of the discount we calculated in equation [12].

At the risk of boring you, please note again that discounting is the reverse of the compounding procedure. The present value of $3,779,136 received in three years <u>discounted</u> at 8 percent is $3 million. The future value in three years of $3 million <u>compounded</u> at 8 percent is $3,779,136.

D. The Effect of Time  and Interest Rates on Present Value

As with future value, two factors influence present value: time and interest rates. The longer you have to wait to receive your money, the greater your opportunity cost and the larger the discount you exact. Let's hold the opportunity cost for waiting constant at 15 percent. Assume you are to receive $1.2 million at some future date. What would be the present value of your sum when you vary the lengths of time you have to wait for your cash inflow?

Interest Rate	Principal	–	Present Value		=	Interest Foregone
1	$1,200,000	–	$1,200,000/(1.15)	= $1,043,478	=	$156,522
5	$1,200,000	–	$1,200,000/(1.15)^5	= $596,612	=	$603,388
10	$1,200,000	–	$1,200,000/(1.15)^{10}	= $296,622	=	$903,378
15	$1,200,000	–	$1,200,000/(1.15)^{15}	= $147,473	=	$1,052,527
20	$1,200,000	–	$1,200,000/(1.15)^{20}	= $73,320	=	$1,126,680

Now if we hold time constant, we'll see that the higher the interest rate, the smaller the present value. For example, what if you had to wait five years for your $1.2 million? What would be your present value at various interest rates? The table below shows the present value of your $1.2 million you expect to receive in five years discounted at various interest rates.

Interest Rate	Principal	–	Present Value		=	Interest Foregone
5%	$1,200,000	–	$1,200,000/(1.05)^5	= $940,231	=	$259,769
10%	$1,200,000	–	$1,200,000/(1.10)^5	= $745.106	=	$454,894
15%	$1,200,000	–	$1,200,000/(1.15)^5	= $596,612	=	$603,388
20%	$1,200,000	–	$1,200,000/(1.20)^5	= $482,253	=	$717,747
25%	$1,200,000	–	$1,200,000/(1.25)^5	= $393,216	=	$806,784

Theoretically, when we increase the interest and/or the time factor toward infinity, the present value approaches zero. Notice that while future value grew toward infinity as we increased time and/or interest rates, present value grows toward zero, not negative infinity. Why is that? Because the worst case scenario for you and your money in terms of how long you have to wait or the opportunity cost of waiting approaches zero.[1] Your money can only approach being worthless (have a value of close to zero); it cannot have a negative value. Let's do Practice Set B on the next page before we move on to multiple compounding periods.

NOTES:

_____

_____

_____

_____

_____

_____

_____

_____

_____

_____

_____

_____

_____

_____

_____

[1] Technically, your money never equals zero, but only approaches zero. In calculus terms we say that the value of your cash flows asymptotically approaches zero.

PRACTICE SET B
PRESENT VALUE PROBLEMS

1. What is the present value of $100 you expect to receive in seven years at 6 percent annual interest?

2. What is the present value of $300 you expect to receive in ten years at 8 percent annual interest?

3. Petroleum Plastics has been doing a booming business. They would like to expand in the next two years. The owners estimate they will need $37,000 to purchase and remodel the store next door. What amount of money should they set aside today assuming they can earn 4 percent on their investments? (HINT: Recognize that $37,00 is a future value and thus you need to solve for the present value of $37,000 to know what they need to invest today at an annual rate of 4 percent to have the money they will need.)

4. Coffee is out. Tea is in. Given this information, the makers of Mr. Coffee want to produce a Ms. Tea by next year. The investment required is $67,000. The firm currently has $54,000 invested in short-term Treasury securities that offer a 3 percent annual return. Will Mr. Coffee have enough funds to produce Ms. Tea? How much should they put aside to have the desired amount of funds?

5. Tyger Sweepers, Inc., needs $300,000 in eight years. If they can invest their money at 7 percent annual interest, how much should they invest today to have the $300,000 in eight years?

6. Roetronic Industries needs $400,000 in five years. They have invested $220,000 in stocks paying 15.5 percent annually. Will Roetronics have enough funds to meet their financial goal? If not, how much should they put aside to have the desired amount of funds?

7. Medical Surplus Supply will need $200,000 to build up their business. They have the option to invest in a new mutual fund that promises low risk and returns of 7 percent annually. How much should Medical Surplus Supply invest if they want to meet their financial goal?

8. **Challenge Problem**: Pacer Hotel owner Don Martin estimates he can sell his hotel in seven years for $250,000. If Don could invest that money today at an annual rate of 7 percent for the first three years and then at an annual rate of 8 percent thereafter, what is the value of his hotel today? (HINT: Use a time line to help solve this problem.)

9. **Challenge Problem**: Silver Star Productions plans to spin off two of their other interests that no longer fit their corporate mission and to help raise money for future movie projects. They plan to sell Prop Products, Inc., two years from now for $10.3 million and then sell Hollywood's Clothier Corporation five years from now for $50.7 million. If Silver Star's opportunity cost is an annual rate of 12 percent, what is the combined value of these divisions today?

10. **Challenge Problem**: Buckle Up Industries makes neon-colored seat belts for the new and improved Volkswagen Beetle. They plan to divest themselves of two nonrelated business lines. They will sell Flower Power, Inc., for $12.7 million in six years and Peace Sign Corporation for $40.8 million in eight years. The powers that be at Buckle Up Industries believe they would be able to invest the funds from the sale of Flower Power at an annual rate of 7 percent and the funds from the sale of Peace Sign at an annual rate of 9 percent. What is the combined value of these firms today?

III. TIME VALUE WITH MULTIPLE COMPOUNDING PERIODS

So far we've assumed our interest factor was compounded or discounted on an annual basis. We were either compounding our dollars forward every year to solve for future value or we were discounting our dollars backward each year to solve for present value. What happens to our calculations when compounding or discounting occurs more often, such as semiannually (twice a year), quarterly (four times a year), monthly, daily, or continuously? The more often we earn interest, the greater our future value because we earn interest on our interest more often. Oh, the joys of compounding! The opposite is true for present value. Increasing the frequency of the discounting makes the cost of waiting go up. Therefore, as the frequency of discounting increases, the discount gets bigger, making present value smaller.

To account for more frequent compounding we have to make two adjustments to our calculations. First, we multiply the number of years by the number of times compounding occurs so we get the correct number of periods. Second, we divide the interest rate by the number of times compounding occurs to determine the amount of interest earned in each period. For example, suppose we want to solve for the future value of an amount invested for five years at 6 percent compounded semiannually. We no longer earn 6 percent each year as we did with annual compounding. Instead we earn 3 percent every six months. Increasing the frequency of compounding means we get interest on our interest sooner.

We know what you're going to ask. Are we merely playing a semantics game or does this really matter? It really matters, especially if we put enough zeros in the numbers to impress you.

A. Nuclear Physics  of Future Value

Let's compare the future value of $1 million invested for five years with 12 percent annual compounding to $1 million invested for five years with semiannual compounding when the interest rate is 12 percent. With annual compounding we earn 12 percent for five periods.

Future value with annual compounding $= \$1,000,000(1+ 0.12)^5 = \$1,762,342$

With semiannual compounding we earn 6 percent for ten periods. Notice that in previous sections we used years and periods interchangeably. We are now making a notable distinction that there can be more than one period in a year. To convert our formula to handle semiannual compounding, we first have to multiply the number of years by the number of times compounding occurs to get the correct number of periods ($5 \times 2 = 10$). Next we divide the interest rate by the number of times compounding occurs to determine the interest earned during each period ($0.12 \div 2 = 0.06$).

Future value with
semiannual compounding[2] $= \$1,000,000\left(1 + \dfrac{0.12}{2}\right)^{(5)(2)} = \$1,790,848$

We have increased the future value from \$1,762,342 with annual compounding to \$1,790,848 with semiannual compounding for a difference of \$28,506 or roughly the price of a nice new car. And you thought this was all semantics. Now, what would happen if we increased the frequency of compounding from two times a year to four times a year?

Future value with
quarterly compounding $= \$1,000,000\left(1 + \dfrac{0.12}{4}\right)^{(5)(4)} = \$1,806,111$

We are now getting 3 percent every quarter ($0.12 \div 4 = 0.03$) for a total of 20 ($5 \times 4 = 20$) periods. We have increased the future value from \$1,790,848 with semiannual compounding to \$1,806,111 with quarterly compounding for a difference of \$15,263 or approximately the price of a new midsize car. What do you suppose happens to the future value of our investment when we increase the frequency of compounding from 4 times a year to 12 times a year?

Future value with
monthly compounding $= \$1,000,000\left(1 + \dfrac{0.12}{12}\right)^{(5)(12)} = \$1,816,697$

We are now getting 1 percent every month ($0.12 \div 12 = 0.01$) for a total of 60 periods ($5 \times 12 = 60$). We have increased the future value from \$1,806,111 with quarterly compounding to \$1,816,697 with monthly compounding for a difference of \$10,586 or about the price of a new compact car. Daily compounding gives us:

Future value with
daily compounding $= \$1,000,000\left(1 + \dfrac{0.12}{365}\right)^{(5)(365)} = \$1,821,939$

We are now getting interest every day for a total of 365 periods. We have increased the future value from \$1,816,697 with monthly compounding to \$1,821,939 with daily compounding for a difference of \$5,242 or just about the price of a used car. Moving to continuous compounding, we find that the calculations involve a bit more effort, but the reward for higher future value is worth the exertion.

---

[2] Your basic algebra rules require that you carry out the mathematics for what's inside the parentheses first. Remember also that division and multiplication are computed before addition and subtraction. Thus you would first divide the 12 percent by two, add one, and then take that number [1.06] to the tenth exponent. You can use the exponent button [Y^x] on most calculators as follows: With 1.06 showing on the readout, push the [Y^x] button, then enter 10 for the exponent and then press the equals button to get [1.7908].

In our previous examples we said interest was earned in each period and we kept increasing the frequency of those periods. With continuous compounding we do away with discrete intervals and recognize that the most frequent compounding of all is compounding that occurs continuously. Think of the discrete intervals as a loud windup clock that audibly ticks off each second. Continuous intervals are similar to a quartz run clock where the second hand sweeps past each second without hesitation.

Future value with
continuous compounding[3] $= \$1,000,000(e^{(0.12)(5)}) = \$1,822,119$

We now receive interest on our interest on a continuous basis. We have increased the future value from \$1,821,939 with daily compounding to \$1,822,119 with continuous compounding, a difference of \$179 or more or less the price of a pretty good bicycle.

In summary, with any positive interest rate you drive instead of walk, but the compounding frequency determines the style in which you arrive. On the next page is a figure that shows, in graphical form, the difference in interest earned for annual, semiannual, and continuous compounding.

NOTES:

_____

_____

_____

_____

_____

_____

_____

_____

_____

_____

---

[3] To move to continuous compounding, we use Euler's constant, which is approximately 2.7182. To use your calculator, multiply 12 percent by five years [(0.12)(5)=0.600], then hit the second function key [2nd] to access the [e^x] button to get [1.8221], and then multiply by our \$1 million investment to get \$1,822,119.

Annual, Semiannual and Continuous Compounding:
Future Value of $1 million invested for five years at 12 %

PANEL A: Annual Compounding

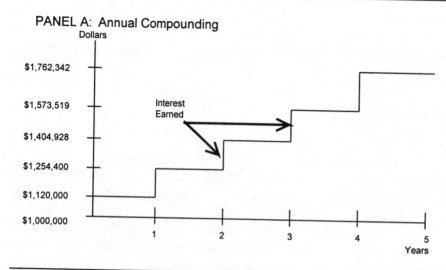

PANEL B: Semiannual Compounding

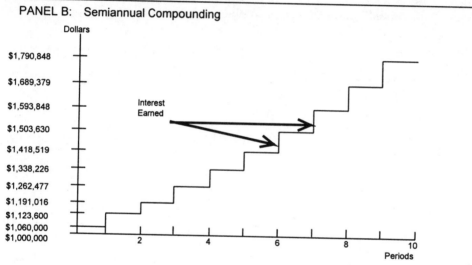

PANEL C: Continuous Compounding

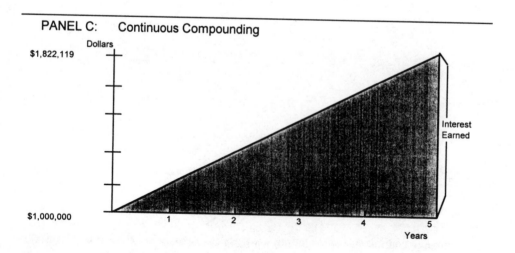

B. Astrophysics of Present Value

With present value, the greater the discounting frequency,[4] the smaller the present value (i.e., the larger the discount). We'll look at a quick example. Remember that $1.2 million cash inflow from your eccentric Aunt Lucy? You probably also remember that you had to wait ten years to get it. What is the value today of your cash inflow if you could have invested that money at an 8 percent annual return? Remember, being forced to wait means you're giving up that 8 percent annual return. You may also remember that we finance people don't give in without a price. The value of the cash flow today is:

Present value with
Annual discounting $= \dfrac{\$1,200,000}{(1.08)^{10}} = \$555,832$

Amount of discount $= \$1,200,000 - \$555,832 = \$644,168$ *cost of waiting*

Why, that's a discount of more than 50 percent! But we're just getting started. What would be your cost of waiting if you had the opportunity to invest your money over that ten-year period and earn an 8 percent *semiannual* return? You'll have to make the same two adjustments that were made in the future value section: *Divide* the interest factor by the frequency of the discounting and *multiply* the number of years by the number of times discounting occurs.

Present value with
semiannual discounting $= \$1,200,000 \left[\dfrac{1}{\left(1 + \dfrac{0.08}{2}\right)^{(2)(10)}} \right] = \$547,664$

Amount of discount $= \$1,200,000 - \$547,664 = \$652,336$ *cost of waiting*

You are now losing out on 4 percent $(0.08 \div 2 = 0.04)$ every six months for a total of 20 periods $(10 \times 2 = 20)$ causing the discount to increase to $652,336. This illustrates how the cost of waiting is higher (as measured by the size of the discount) when the frequency of discounting the cash inflow increases. In this example, the cost of waiting when you discounted the cash flows on an annual basis was $644,168, whereas the cost of waiting when you discounted the cash flows on a semiannual basis was $652,336 for a difference of $8,168. Increasing the frequency of discounting even more to, say, quarterly, monthly or continuous discounting, as shown on the next page, will further expand the size of the discount (i.e., the cost of waiting).

---

[4] Jargon Alert! When we refer to the calculation of future value we use the terms *compounding* and *number of periods* to represent the interest factor and number of times compounding occurs. When we refer to the calculation of present value we use the terms *discounting* and *frequency* to signify the interest factor and the number of times discounting occurs.

Present value with
continuous discounting $= \$1,000,000 \left[\dfrac{1}{\left(e^{(0.08)(10)}\right)} \right] = \$539,195$

As we stated earlier, time and interest rates influence present and future values. When we increase the frequency of discounting (compounding) we increase the discount causing present value (future value) to decline (increase).

Let's practice calculating present and future values when we have multiple discounting (compounding) frequencies. Practice Set C is on the next page.

NOTES:

_____

_____

_____

_____

_____

_____

_____

_____

_____

_____

_____

_____

_____

PRACTICE SET C
PRESENT AND FUTURE VALUES WITH MULTIPLE COMPOUNDING PERIODS

You've recently won a series of court battles over a severe bout of food poisoning after dining at your local Fungus Hut. The jury, impressed with your 24 hours of suffering, has awarded damages in the amount of $200 million. Rather than appeal the case, the management at Fungus Hut agrees to pay you the $200 million, but not for five years. The next six questions ask you to calculate the value of your dollars today at various discounting frequencies.

1. What is the present value of your $200 million that you expect to receive in five years when the discount rate is 6 percent annually?

2. What is the present value of your $200 million that you expect to receive in five years when the discount rate is 6 percent semiannually?

3. What is the present value of your $200 million that you expect to receive in five years when the discount rate is 6 percent quarterly?

4. What is the present value of your $200 million that you expect to receive in five years when the discount rate is 6 percent monthly?

5. What is the present value of your $200 million that you expect to receive in five years when the discount rate is 6 percent daily?

6. What is the present value of your $200 million that you expect to receive in five years when the discount rate is 6 percent continuously?

You just found out, through DNA testing, that you are a certified and verifiable relative of Benjamin Franklin. That relationship is extremely valuable because you can now successfully lay claim to your portion of his estate. A knowledgeable source close to the case, but who wishes to remain anonymous, has placed a $350 million price tag on the value of your portion of Franklin's estate. What to do with all that money? Alas, Benjamin's will stipulates that every relative must endure an excruciatingly long eight-year waiting period upon legal verification of lineage before receiving said funds. You may, however, invest your funds in the interim. The next six questions ask you to calculate the future value of your dollars at various compounding periods.

7. What is the future value of your $350 million that you have to invest for eight years when the interest rate is 6 percent annually?

8. What is the future value of your $350 million that you have to invest for eight years when the interest rate is 6 percent semiannually?

9. What is the future value of your $350 million that you have to invest for eight years when the interest rate is 6 percent quarterly?

10. What is the future value of your $350 million that you have to invest for eight years when the interest rate is 6 percent monthly?

11. What is the future value of your $350 million that you have to invest for eight years when the interest rate is 6 percent daily?

12. What is the future value of your $350 million that you have to invest for eight years when the interest rate is 6 percent continuously?

13. **Challenge Problem**: In three years the McBeals expect to receive $20,000 from Mrs. McBeal's profit-sharing plan at work. The McBeals plan to use the entire $20,000 to finance their daughter, Ally's, education fund. Ally is 8 years old now. The McBeals estimate they will need $50,000 at the end of ten years, when Ally is 18, to pay her education expenses. They will make up any shortfalls with a home equity loan. If they invest their funds at 12 percent continuous compounding, how much, if any, will they have to borrow to make up the difference? (HINT: Use a time line to help solve this problem—logic dictates that your answer should be larger than the one you calculated in Practice Set A because while the interest rate remains at 12 percent, the number of times of compounding occurs is higher.)

14. **Challenge Problem**: The phenomenal singer who goes simply by the name of # has made some wise and prudent investments over the years. Six years ago she invested $5 million from her record contract in an investment paying 8 percent with monthly compounding. Three years ago she invested the $3 million she was paid for her first leading role in a large-scale movie production at an interest rate of 5 percent with daily compounding. What is the value of #'s account today?

15. **Challenge Problem**: Pacer Hotel owner Don Martin estimates he can sell his hotel in seven years for $250,000. If Don could invest that money today at 7 percent with quarterly compounding in the first three years and then at 8 percent with semiannually compounding thereafter, what is the value of his hotel today?

16. **Challenge Problem**: Buckle Up Industries still makes neon-colored seat belts for the Volkswagen Beetle. They plan to divest themselves of two unrelated business lines. They will sell Flower Power, Inc., for $12.7 million in six years and Peace Sign Corporation for $40.8 million in eight years. The powers that be at Buckle Up Industries believe they would be able to invest the funds from the sale of Flower Power at 7 percent with quarterly compounding and the funds from the sale of Peace Sign at 9 percent with continuous compounding. What is the value of these firms today?

IV. ANNUITY

An annuity is a series of even cash flows for a specified period of time. Most of us are on the painful (or cash outflow) end of annuities. For instance, your car payment, student loan, and other installment debt are annuities where you pay a fixed amount for a specified period of time. In this section we're going to look at how to value annuities, both present and future values.

There are two types of annuities: ordinary annuities where cash flows occur at the end of the period and annuities due where cash flows occur at the beginning of the period. We'll value both kinds. As a general rule, most annuities are the ordinary kind that pay at the end of the period.

A. Future Value of an Ordinary Annuity

What if you are to receive $200 at the end of each of the next three years? You plan to reinvest each cash inflow as you receive it at an annual rate of 5 percent. You want to determine what the value of all these cash flows are at the end of the three years. In other words, you want to calculate the future value of this three-year, $200 annuity. This simply involves finding the future value of each of the cash inflows received. On a time line the cash inflows look like this:

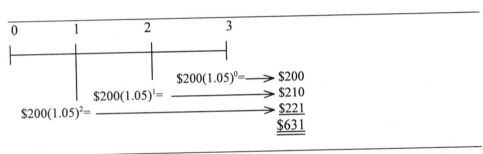

You receive the first cash inflow at the end of year 1. Keep in mind that you invest this cash inflow for two years (during years 2 and 3). You invest the second cash inflow received at the end of year 2 for one year (during year 3). Finally, we find the future value of the third cash inflow received at the end of year 3. You will not invest this cash flow for any period of time because you got it at the end of the annuity's life—at the end of the third year. The future value of this three-year, $200 annuity is the sum of the future values of the individual cash inflows.

If you pull out those cardboard annuity tables that came with your text or check the appendix of your book you can see that the future value annuity interest factor for a three-year, 5 percent annuity is 3.1525. If you multiply this number times $200 you get $631. But where did that 3.1525 come from? It's simple mathematics. Let's look at these three cash flows again with all the math worked out.

$$\$200(1.05)^2 = \$200\ (1.1025) = \$221$$
$$\$200(1.05)^1 = \$200\ (1.05) = \$210$$
$$\$200(1.05)^0 = \$200\ \underline{(1.00)} = \underline{\$200}$$
$$ 3.1525 \qquad \underline{\$631}$$

First we solved for the value of the interest rate taken to the appropriate exponent to represent time. For the first cash flow that you leave invested during years 2 and 3, the interest factor was 1.1025. Look on your future value interest factor table (for a single sum and not the annuity table) under two years, 5 percent, and you should see this number. For the second cash flow that you leave invested during year 3, the interest factor was 1.05. The final cash flow received at the end of the third year has an interest factor of 1, because you don't have the option to invest this cash flow for any amount of time. If we add up the values of the three interest factors we get 3.1525 $[(1.05)^2 + (1.05)^1 + (1.05)^0 = 3.1525]$. Not coincidentally, 3.1525 is the three-year, 5 percent, future value annuity interest factor from the *annuity* table in your text. See? There's nothing magical about these tables.

What if we want to solve for the future value of a 20-year annuity? Do we expect you to find the future value interest factor for each single sum and then add them together to find the future value interest factor for our 20-year annuity? Of course not! We can use the annuity interest factor equation as follows:

$$\text{Future Value Interest Factor of an Annuity} = \frac{(1 + \text{int. rate})^{\text{number of periods}} - 1}{\text{int. rate}}$$

Now let's put in the numbers for the annuity we're working on and calculate the future value interest factor.   Remember, we have a three-year annuity compounded at 5 percent.

$$\text{Future Value Interest Factor of a 3-year, 5\% annuity} = \frac{(1.05)^3 - 1}{0.05} = 3.1525$$

The interest factor tables can be handy reference guides as long as you're never asked to calculate a problem that involves a time period or interest rate not on the table.

As another example, suppose you expect to receive $600 at the end of each of the next five years, reinvesting each cash inflow at 8 percent as they come in. You want to determine the value of these cash flows at the end of the five years. To do this, we calculate the future value of this five-year, $600 annuity. Again, we find the future value of each of the cash inflows received.

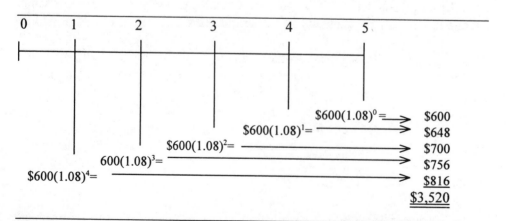

You receive the first cash inflow at the end of year 1. Keep in mind that you invest this cash inflow for four years (during years 2, 3, 4, and 5). You invest the second cash inflow received at the end of year 2 for three years (during years 3, 4, and 5). You invest the third cash flow received at the end of year 3 for two years (during years 4 and 5), and the fourth cash flow received at the end of year 4 you invest for one year (during year 5). Finally, we find the future value of the fifth cash inflow received at the end of year 5. You will not invest this cash flow for any period of time because you got it at the end of the annuity's life—at the end of the fifth year. The future value of this annuity is the sum of the future values of the individual cash inflows.

Let's revisit the future value interest factor table one more time. Below are the cash flows and their future value interest factors.

$600(1.08)^4 = $600\ (1.3605) = 816	As in the previous example, if we add
$600(1.08)^3 = $600\ (1.2597) = 756	up the values of the five interest
$600(1.08)^2 = $600\ (1.1664) = 700	factors we get 5.8666. Not surprisingly,
$600(1.08)^1 = $600\ (1.08)\ \ = 648	5.8666 is the five-year, 8 percent
$600(1.00)^0 = $600\ \underline{(1.00)}\ \ = \underline{$600}$	future value annuity interest factor
$\quad\quad\quad\quad\quad 5.8666\quad \underline{$3,520}$	from the annuity tables.

All right, using our general formula:

$$\text{Future Value Interest Factor of an Annuity} = \frac{(1+\text{int. rate})^{\text{number of periods}} - 1}{\text{int. rate}}$$

We get the same result as adding the future value interest factors together:

$$\text{Future Value Interest Factor of a 5-year, 8\% annuity} = \frac{(1.08)^5 - 1}{0.08} = 5.8666$$

B. Future Value of an Annuity Due

In this case, we receive our cash inflows at the beginning of each period. If we use the same example as before with a three-year, $200 annuity earning 5 percent annual compounding, we get the following solution. Notice how all the cash inflows are one period closer.

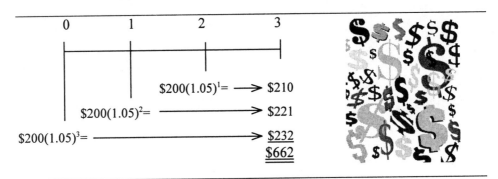

You receive the first cash inflow at the beginning of year 1. We must keep in mind that we will invest this cash inflow for three years now instead of two (during years 1, 2, and 3). Next you invest the second cash inflow for two years (during years 2 and 3). Finally, you invest the last cash flow for one year (during year 3). Thus, each cash flow in the annuity due example received one more year of compounding then the ordinary annuity cash flow. This is all based on the implicit assumption that the investor's time horizon of three years hasn't changed. That is, the investor is still interested in the value of the annuity at the end of three years, regardless of whether it's an ordinary annuity or an annuity due.

We could also solve for this value by taking the value of an ordinary annuity and multiplying it by one plus the interest rate to recognize that each cash flow earns one more period of interest.

$$\$631(1.05) = \$662$$

If we look at each cash flow and multiply it by its new interest factor we get the same result. Notice that the cumulative interest factor is now 3.3101.

$$\$200(1.05)^3 = \$200 \ (1.1576) \quad = \$232$$
$$\$200(1.05)^2 = \$200 \ (1.1025) \quad = \$221$$
$$\$200(1.05)^1 = \$200 \ \underline{(1.05)} \quad = \underline{\$210}$$
$$\qquad\qquad\qquad\quad 3.3101 \qquad \$663$$

Please note that 3.3101 is not on your future value interest factor table. The tables do not make allowances for an annuity due.[5]

We could also multiply our ordinary annuity interest factor by one plus the interest rate and that would give us the correct annuity due interest factor as shown below:

$$3.1525(1.05) = 3.3101$$

Multiplying our annual cash flow by this annuity interest factor gives us the value of our annuity due.

$$\$200(3.3101) = \$662$$

If we use the second example again of a five-year, $600 annuity due earning 8 percent annual compounding, we get the following solution. Again, notice all the cash inflows are one period closer.

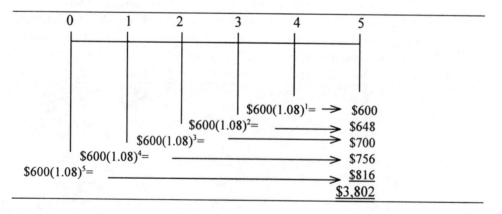

---

[5] The reason our calculator gives us an answer of $663 instead of $662 is due to rounding. The numbers we're using to calculate these problems by hand are rounded to the nearest fourth decimal place, whereas the calculator rounds to the nearest twelfth decimal place.

You receive the first cash inflow at the beginning of year 1. You must keep in mind that you will invest this cash inflow for five years now instead of four (during years 1, 2, 3, 4, and 5). Next you invest the second cash inflow for four years (during years 2, 3, 4, and 5). Next you invest the third cash flow for three years (during years 3, 4, and 5) and the fourth cash flow for two years (during years 4 and 5). Finally, you invest the last cash flow for one year (during year 5). Thus, each cash flow in the annuity due example received one more year of compounding than the ordinary annuity cash flow.

We could also solve for this value by taking the value of an ordinary annuity and multiplying it by one plus the interest rate to recognize that each cash flow earns one more period of interest.

$$\$3,520(1.08) = \$3,802$$

Let's look at the individual cash flows. If we multiplied the values of each cash flow we found in our ordinary annuity by one plus the interest rate we could account for the extra period of compounding on an individual basis. This is what we've calculated below.

Ordinary Annuity	(1+interest rate) =	Annuity Due
$816	(1.08) =	$882
$756	(1.08) =	$816
$700	(1.08) =	$756
$648	(1.08) =	$700
$600	(1.08) =	$648
$3,520		$3,802

No, we are not having fun yet, but hopefully this gives you an idea of exactly how an annuity due differs from ordinary annuities.

C. Present Value of an Ordinary Annuity

Your great Uncle Jorge died (you hardly knew him) and left you an annuity contract that stated you were to receive $250 at the end of each of the next four years. Your annual opportunity cost of funds is 6 percent. In other words, if you had the money now you could invest it at an annual rate of 6 percent. Someone has offered to pay you $800 to purchase the right to your inherited cash flows. Should you keep the annuity or sell to the prospective buyer and get $800 today?

If we ignore your desperate desire for cash, the only way to answer this question is to figure the value of all these cash flows today. To do this, calculate the present value of this four-year, $250 annuity. This simply involves finding the present value of the individual cash flows.

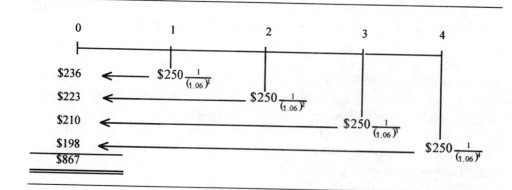

You have to wait one year to get the first cash inflow of $250 so you forgo interest during that year. The present value of the first cash inflow received at the end of year 1 is $236. You have to wait two years to get the second cash inflow of $250 so you forgo earning interest for two years on this payment as well as any interest on interest you would have gotten. Discounting this payment for two years gives a present value of the second cash flow of $223. Three years go by before you receive the third cash inflow of $250. This means you give up three years of interest. Present value of the third cash inflow received at the end of year three is $210. Finally, the last cash flow arrives at the end of the fourth year. Present value of the fourth cash inflow received at the end of year 4 is $198. Thus, the present value of this annuity is the sum of the present value of the individual cash inflows. Let's digress for a moment. . . .

If you look again at those cardboard annuity tables you will find the present value interest factor for a four-year, 6 percent annuity is 3.4651. If you multiply this number times $250 you get $867. But, where did that 3.4651 come from? Let's look at these four cash flows more closely.

$$\$250\frac{1}{(1.06)^4} = \$250(0.7921) = \$198$$

$$\$250\frac{1}{(1.06)^3} = \$250(0.8396) = \$210$$

$$\$250\frac{1}{(1.06)^2} = \$250(0.8900) = \$223$$

$$\$250\frac{1}{(1.06)^1} = \$250\underset{3.4651}{(\underline{0.9434})} = \underset{\$867}{\underline{\$236}}$$

First we solve for the value of the interest rate taken to the appropriate exponent to represent time. For the first cash flow—that you have to wait one year to receive—the interest factor is 0.9434. Look on your present value interest factor table for a single sum under one year, 6 percent, and you should see this number. For the second cash flow for which you have to wait two years, the interest factor is 0.8900. You have to wait three years for the third cash inflow so the interest factor is 0.8396. The final cash flow received at the end of the fourth year has an interest factor of 0.7921. If we add up the values of the four interest factors we get 3.4651. Not coincidentally, 3.4651 is the four-year, 6 percent present value annuity interest factor from the *annuity* table in your text.

What if we want to solve for the present value of a 15-year annuity? Do we expect you to find the present value interest factor for each single sum and then add them together to find the present value interest factor for our 15-year annuity? No way! We can write the general annuity interest factor equation as follows:

$$\text{Present Value Interest Factor of an Annuity} = \frac{1}{\text{int. rate}} - \frac{1}{\text{int. rate}(1+\text{int. rate})^{\text{number of periods}}}$$

Now let's insert the numbers for the annuity we're working on and calculate the present value interest factor for an annuity. In this instance we have a four-year annuity discounted at 6 percent.

$$\text{Present Value Interest Factor of a 4 year, 6\% annuity} = \frac{1}{0.06} - \frac{1}{0.06(1.06)^4} = 3.465$$

This is the same number we got before by adding up the present value interest factors for each individual cash inflow.

What if you are to receive $400 at the end of each of the next two years? Your annual opportunity cost of funds is 7 percent. You want to determine the value of all these cash flows today. To do this, calculate the present value of this two-year, $400 annuity. Again, we find the present value of each of the cash inflows received.

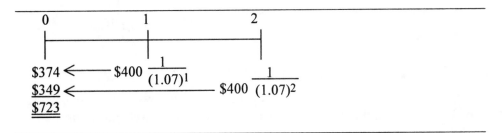

Present value of the first cash inflow received at the end of year one is $374. The present value of the second cash inflow received at the end of year two is $349. Thus, the present value of this annuity is the sum of the present value of the individual cash inflows. Looking at the individual cash flows more closely we see the following:

$$\$400\frac{1}{(1.07)^2} = \$400(0.8734) = \$349$$

$$\$400\frac{1}{(1.07)^1} = \$400\underset{1.8080}{\underline{(0.9346)}} = \underset{\$723}{\underline{\$374}}$$

What if we want to solve for the present value of a long-term annuity? We can't be expected to find the present value interest factor for each single sum and then add them together. We can, however, use the general present value interest factor of an annuity equation as follows:

Present Value Interest Factor of an Annuity $= \dfrac{1}{\text{int. rate}} - \dfrac{1}{\text{int. rate}(1+\text{int. rate})^{\text{number of periods}}}$

Now let's insert the numbers for the annuity we're working on and calculate the present value interest factor of an annuity. Recall that we have a two-year annuity discounted at an annual rate of 7 percent.

Present Value Interest Factor of a 2-year, 7% annuity $= \dfrac{1}{0.07} - \dfrac{1}{0.07(1.07)^2} = 1.8080$

This is the same number we got before when adding up the single sum present value interest factors.

D. Present Value of an Annuity Due

In this case you receive your cash inflows at the *beginning* of each period. Let's use our four-year, $250 annuity example from before and discount it at 6 percent annually:

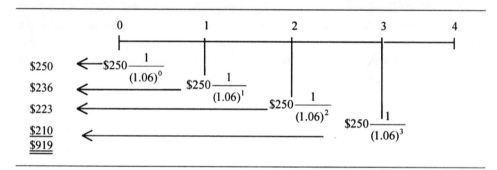

You receive the first cash inflow of $250 right away so you don't forgo any interest during this first year. Therefore, we do not discount the first year's cash flows. [6]   Present value of the second cash inflow received at the beginning of year 2 is $236. Present value of the third cash inflow received at the beginning of year 3 is $223. Present value of the fourth cash inflow received at the beginning of year 3 is $210. Thus, the present value of this annuity due is the sum of the present value of the individual cash inflows.

We could also solve for this value by taking the value of an ordinary annuity and multiplying it by one plus the interest rate to recognize that each cash flow foregoes losing one period of interest:

$867(1.06) = $919

---

[6] We hear you wondering when would you ever get a cash flow immediately as in this example? What kind of annuity is it where you get the first inflow without having to wait? Ever rent an apartment? The landlord will almost always require the first month's rent up front (besides the security deposit). From that point on you pay your rent at the beginning of each period, so this series of cash inflows represents an annuity due for the landlord. Another example would be financing a car. The financial institution that lends you the money typically requires the first payment at the time of signing. Thereafter your monthly payments are due at the beginning of each month, creating an annuity due for the lender.

We could also multiply our present value interest factor of an annuity by one plus the interest rate and that would give us the correct annuity due interest factor as shown below:

$$3.4651(1.06) = 3.673$$

Multiplying our annual cash flow by this annuity interest factor gives us the value of our annuity:

$$\$250(3.673) = \$919$$

Notice the annuity due is more valuable ($919) than an ordinary annuity ($866) because we get each of our cash flows one period sooner with an annuity due.

Let's calculate the value of our two-year $400 annuity due discounted at 7 percent annually:

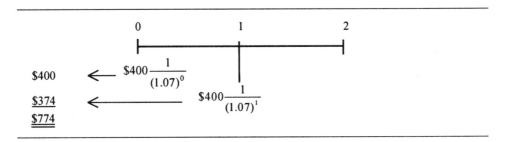

Remember, we could also solve for this value by taking the value of an ordinary annuity and multiplying it by one plus the interest rate to recognize that each cash flow foregoes losing one period of interest.

$$\$723(1.07) = \$774$$

Let's look at the individual cash flows. If we multiply the values of each cash flow we found in our ordinary annuity by one plus the interest rate we could account for the lost period of discounting on an individual basis.

Ordinary Annuity	(1+interest rate)	=	Annuity Due
$374	(1.07) =		$400
$349	(1.07) =		$374
$723			$774

E. Lost in Space

You can't believe so many decisions have to be made. You've got present values, future values, annuities, and annuities due floating in your brain and have trouble making the distinction from one to the other. First and foremost, draw a time line. Yes, it takes a moment or two longer, but you're less likely to make a mistake and eventually once you get all this down you'll be able to visualize time lines in your head.

The first question the time line will answer is whether you are solving for a single sum or an annuity. If the problem says you pay or receive the stated cash flow each year or every year then you've got an annuity. If the problem indicates that this is a one-time occurrence then you're dealing with a single sum. The second question the time line will answer is whether the problem is looking for future value or present value. This is a hard one to wave our arms about and explain, but the time line can answer each of these questions. For the more visually minded, let's use the flowchart.

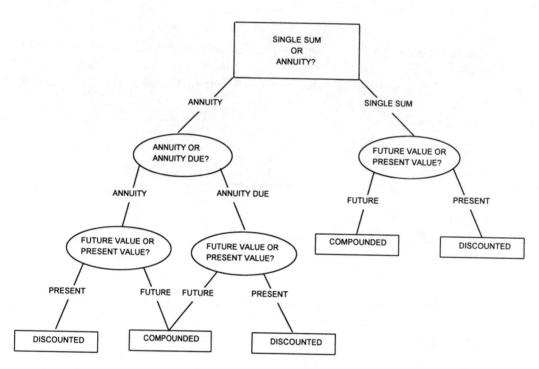

Practice Set D will give you some hands-on experience carrying out these annuity calculations. Before you whip out your calculators and start punching buttons, respond to the first question about what value is being sought before you compute the answer. Make sure you can answer this question! You must first decide whether the problem is asking for present value or future value, whether it is the present or future value of a single sum or an annuity, AND if the problem is seeking the value of an annuity, you must determine if it is an ordinary annuity or an annuity due.

NOTES:

_____

_____

_____

_____

PRACTICE SET D
ANNUITIES

1. Renaissance Paper, Inc. needs to invest $8,000 at the end of each of the next five years to keep their current project going. If they can earn 7.5 percent annual compounding on their invested dollars, how much will they have to set aside today to ensure they will have the level of cash inflows they will need? (Be sure to recognize that the $8,000 annual investment needed is the <u>annuity</u> payment, then draw a time line to determine if you are solving for future value or present value.)

a. What value is being sought in this problem?

b. Compute the value.

2. The owners of Beagle Brothers Automotive Store want to have $500,000 at the end of 15 years to supplement their pension income. They are currently investing $30,000 at the end of each year earning 8.2 percent compounded annually. Are the Beagle Brothers investing enough to finance their supplementary retirement fund?

a. What value is being sought in this problem?

b. Compute the value.

3. A competitor has approached the owners of the Linger Longer Lounge with an offer to purchase their establishment. The potential purchasers offered the owners of Linger Longer $25,000 to be paid at the beginning of each year for the next 10 years. When news of the offer became public knowledge, another competitor offered to pay the owners of the Linger Longer Lounge $200,000 today. If the opportunity cost of investing for the owners of Linger Longer is 6 percent annual discounting, which offer should they accept?

a. What value is being sought in this problem?

b. Compute the value.

4. Indiana "Hoosier" Insurance Agency offered to sell Dr. Natasha Phelps an annuity contract at a price of $40,000. In return, the contract stipulates that Indiana will pay Dr. Phelps $5,000 at the end of each of the next 10 years. Dr. Phelps's opportunity cost of investment is 8 percent annually. Should she purchase the annuity contract?

a. What value is being sought in this problem?

b. Compute the value.

5. Avenue Florist wants to purchase a new delivery truck. The truck has a purchase price of $65,000. The owners of the Avenue Florist have been setting aside $5,000 at the beginning of each year for the past 10 years in an account paying 7.7 percent annually. Do they have enough to make their purchase?

a. What value is being sought in this problem?

b. Compute the value.

6. Mr. Fox and his partner have created a database of security prices. This database is the most comprehensive of its kind. To manufacture the CD discs once all the data have been entered, the partners will need $8,000 at the end of each of the next five years. If they can earn 7.5 percent annual compounding on their invested dollars, how much will they have to set aside today to ensure they will have the level of cash inflows they will need?

a. What value is being sought in this problem?

b. Compute the value.

7. **Challenge Problem**: The Bicycle Shop has been in business for a number of years. They want to purchase a $46,000 tire machine. For the past eight years the owners invested $2,000 every six months in an investment paying 6.9 percent semiannual compounding. Do the owners have enough to purchase their tire machine?

a. What value is being sought in this problem?

b. Compute the value.

8. **Challenge Problem**: Carol Kessler won the Reader's Digest Sweepstakes and has an option to receive $100,000 today or receive equal periodic payments at the end of each of the next five years. Her opportunity cost on investments is 14 percent compounded annually. What annual payment should Ms. Kessler receive to equal the $100,000 lump-sum payment today?

a. What value is being sought in this problem?

b. Compute the value.

V. ADDITIONAL TOPICS

A. Uneven Cash Flows

Besides calculating the present and future values of single sums and annuities, there are other important time value calculations. The most important to businesses are uneven cash flows.

Cash flows do not always come in a single sum or as an annuity. Cash flows are frequently uneven. In this section we will learn how to solve for the present value of uneven cash flow series. For example, suppose you expect the following cash flow series. $100 at the end of year 1; $200 at the end of years 2 through 5; $1,000 at the end of year 7. The discount rate is an annual 6 percent. You want to know the value of these cash flows today. The first order of business is to put this on a time line so we can visualize the cash flows.

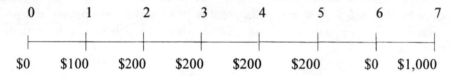

0	1	2	3	4	5	6	7
$0	$100	$200	$200	$200	$200	$0	$1,000

There are a few things to notice. The first cash flow at time 0 is $0. Also notice that during years 2 through 5 we have a four-year $200 annuity imbedded in this uneven series of cash flows. When we solve for the present value of this series we can take advantage of the embedded annuity. Let's begin with the first year's cash inflow.

$\underline{\text{Year 1}}$ $100 $\dfrac{1}{(1.06)^1}$ = $94.34

When solving for an embedded annuity we have to take two steps. First, we find the value of the annuity like we did in the previous section. Second, we have to discount the annuity back to time 0.

Step One: Find the present value of the four-year $200 annuity:

$\underline{\text{Years 2-5}}$ $\dfrac{1}{\text{int. rate}} - \dfrac{1}{\text{int. rate}(1+\text{int. rate})^{\text{number of periods}}} = \dfrac{1}{.06} - \dfrac{1}{.06(1.06)^4} = 3.4651$

3.4651($200) = $693.02

Step Two: Discount the annuity back to time 0:

We found the present value of the embedded annuity, but the annuity doesn't know that we didn't start at time 0. The annuity thinks that year 1 is time 0. Thus, our calculation shows us the value of the annuity at the end of year 1, not at time 0 so we have to discount the annuity back one more time period.

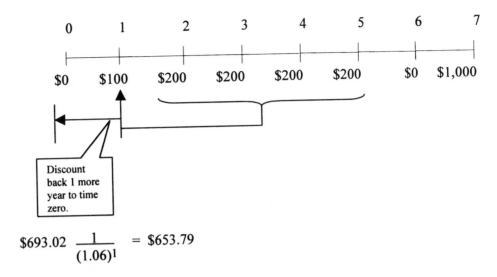

$$\$693.02 \ \frac{1}{(1.06)^1} \ = \$653.79$$

<u>Year 6</u> we can ignore because the cash flow was zero.

<u>Year 7</u> had a $1,000 cash flow that occurs at the end of the cash flow series.

$$\$1,000 \ \frac{1}{(1.06)^7} = \$665.06$$

As our last order of business, we sum the discounted cash flows to determine the present value of this uneven series of cash flows.

Year 1	$94.34
Years 2-5	$653.79
Year 6	$0
Year 7	$665.06
Total Value	$1,413.19

As another example, suppose we have the following cash flow series. $100 in year 1; $200 in year 2; $300 in year 3; $400 in years 4 through 10. The annual discount rate is 4 percent. First things first, let's put this on a time line so we can see exactly what we have.

Notice that during years 4 through 10 we have a seven-year $400 annuity imbedded in this uneven series of cash flows. Let's start with the first three years of uneven cash flows.

<u>Year 1</u> $100 $\frac{1}{(1.04)^1}$ = $94.15

<u>Year 2</u> $200 $\frac{1}{(1.04)^2}$ = $184.91

Year 3 $300 $\dfrac{1}{(1.04)^3} = \$266.70$

Again, when solving for an embedded annuity we have to take two steps. First, we find the value of the annuity as we did in the previous section. Second, we have to discount the annuity back to time 0.

Step One: Find the present value of the seven-year $400 annuity:

Years 4-10 $\dfrac{1}{\text{int. rate}} - \dfrac{1}{\text{int. rate}(1 + \text{int. rate})^{\text{number of periods}}} = \dfrac{1}{.04} - \dfrac{1}{.04(1.04)^7} = 6.0021$

$6.0021\,(\$400) = \$2,400.82$

Step Two: Discount the annuity back to time 0:

We found the present value of the embedded annuity, but the annuity doesn't know that we didn't start at time 0. The annuity thinks that year 3 is time 0. Thus, our calculation shows us the value of the annuity at the end of year 3, not at time 0 so we have to discount the annuity back three more time periods.

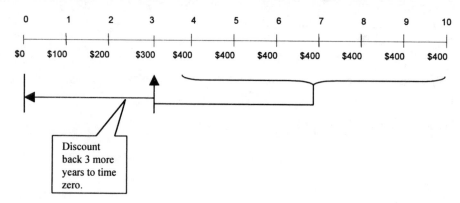

$\$2,400.82\ \dfrac{1}{(1.04)^3} = \$2,134.32$

When we add up the present value of this uneven cash flow series, we find that its value today is $2,680.08.

Year 1	$94.15
Year 2	$184.91
Year 3	$266.70
Years 4-10	$2,134.32
Total Value	$2,680.08

As another example, suppose we have the following cash flow series: $300 in year 1; $100 in year 2; $600 in years 3 through 6; an outflow of $700 in year 7; $400 in years 8 through 10. The annual discount rate is 9 percent. On the time line this cash flow series looks like:

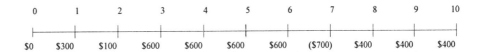

Notice we have two annuities imbedded in this uneven series of cash flows. We have a four-year $600 annuity during years 3 through 6. This is followed by a negative cash flow (an outflow) of $700 in year 7. Then we have a three-year, $400 annuity during years 8 through 10. We begin the process by solving for the present value of the cash flows in years 1 and 2.

<u>Year 1</u> $300 $\dfrac{1}{(1.09)^1} = \$275.23$

<u>Year 2</u> $100 $\dfrac{1}{(1.09)^2} = \$84.17$

When solving for either embedded annuity we have to take two steps. First, we find the value of the annuity like we did in the previous section. Second, we have to discount the annuity back to time 0.

Step One: Find the present value of the four-year $600 annuity:

<u>Years 3-6</u> $\dfrac{1}{\text{int. rate}} - \dfrac{1}{\text{int. rate}(1+\text{int. rate})^{\text{number of periods}}} = \dfrac{1}{.09} - \dfrac{1}{.09(1.09)^4} = 3.2397$

3.2397 ($600) = $1,943.83

Step Two: Discount this first annuity back to time 0:

We found the present value of the embedded annuity, but the annuity doesn't know that we didn't start at time 0. The annuity thinks that year 2 is time 0. Thus, our calculation shows us the value of the annuity at the end of year 2, not at time 0, so we have to discount the annuity back two more time periods.

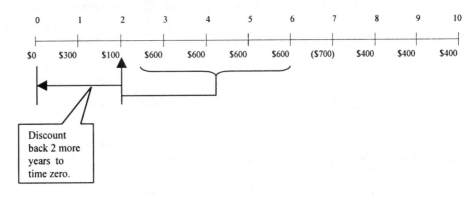

$1,943.83 $\dfrac{1}{(1.09)^2} = \$1,636.08$

<u>Year 7</u> ($700) $\dfrac{1}{(1.09)^7} = (\$382.92)$

Step One: Find the present value of the three-year $400 annuity:

$$\text{Years 8-10} \quad \frac{1}{\text{int. rate}} - \frac{1}{\text{int. rate}(1+\text{int. rate})^{\text{number of periods}}} = \frac{1}{.09} - \frac{1}{.09(1.09)^3} = 2.5313$$

2.5313 ($400) = $1,012.52

Step Two: Discount the second annuity back to time 0:

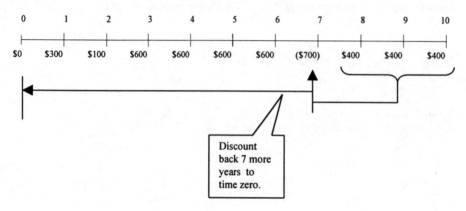

Discount back 7 more years to time zero.

$$\$1,012.52 \ \frac{1}{(1.09)^7} = \$553.88$$

When we add the present values for all the cash flows in this uneven series, the total equals $2,166.44.

Year 1	$275.23
Year 2	$84.17
Years 3-6	$1,636.08
Year 7	($382.92)
Years 8-10	$553.88
Total Value	$2,166.44

As our final example, suppose we have the following cash flow series. An investment (cash outflow) of $1,000 at time zero; $200 in years 1 through 3; no cash inflows in years 4 through 6; $700 in years 7 through 10. The annual discount rate is 7 percent. On the time line this cash flow series looks like:

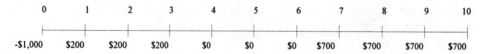

When solving for this first embedded annuity we take only one step because the annuity starts in the first year and is therefore already discounted back to time 0.

Step One: Find the present value of the three-year $200 annuity:

$$\text{Years 1-3} \quad \frac{1}{\text{int. rate}} - \frac{1}{\text{int. rate}(1+\text{int. rate})^{\text{number of periods}}} = \frac{1}{.07} - \frac{1}{.07(1.07)^3} = 2.6243$$

2.6243 ($200) = $524.86

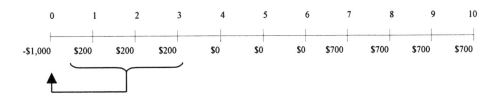

Years 4- 6 $0

Step One: Find the present value of the four-year $700 annuity:

Years 7-10 $$\frac{1}{\text{int. rate}} - \frac{1}{\text{int. rate}(1+\text{int. rate})^{\text{number of periods}}} = \frac{1}{.07} - \frac{1}{.07(1.07)^4} = 3.3872$$

3.3872 ($700) = $2,371.05

Step Two: Discount the second annuity back to time 0:

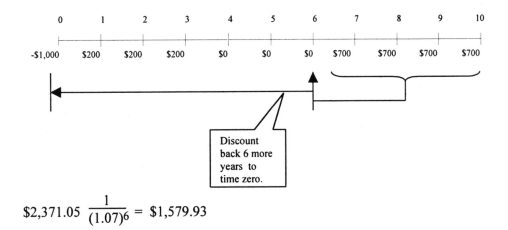

$$\$2,371.05 \; \frac{1}{(1.07)^6} = \$1,579.93$$

Add the discounted cash flows to get the total value of this uneven cash flow series of $1,104.79.

Year 0	−$1,000.00
Years 1-3	$524.86
Years 4-6	$0
Years 7-10	$1,579.93
Total Value	$1,104.79

These examples should now have you ready to go out on your own. On the next page is Practice Set E. By the time you finish working these problems you should be an expert at handling embedded annuities and finding the value of uneven cash flows.

PRACTICE SET E
UNEVEN CASH FLOWS

Assume all cash inflows occur at the end of the period. The free advice department advocates that you draw a time line for each of these problems to assist you in the proper setup of the cash flows.

1. You had a rich Aunt Ernestine who recently passed on. In her will, she stipulated you would receive $1,000 a year through age 25, then you will receive $2,500 a year through age 30, then you are to get $5,000 a year through age 40, at which time your payments will cease. You just had your twentieth birthday today (HINT: Your first cash flow occurs one year from now on your twenty-first birthday). At your twentieth birthday party, a woman offered you $30,000 for the right to your inherited cash flow. Should you take the offer given that your opportunity cost for investment is an annual rate of 8 percent?

2. Canine Corporation is planning on investing in a line of brand of stationery. Sales are expected to be $50,000 for the first two years, then drop to $30,000 for the next three years, and then decline to $15,000 for the remaining five years of the product's life cycle. Management has determined the firm would have to invest $180,000 at the beginning of the project's life for a new printing press and miscellaneous equipment. The firm's opportunity cost for investment is an annual rate of 12 percent. Should the firm invest in this project?

3. Dr. Frazier Crane is interested in syndicating his radio talk show. With the help of his brother Niles, Dr. Crane has estimated the following cash flows: $2,000 year 1; $3,000 years 2 through 6; $5,000 years 7 through 10; $2,000 years 11 and 12, and $1,000 in year 13. The startup cost is $25,000 and the Crane Brothers' investment portfolio is currently earning an annual rate of 5 percent. Should Dr. Crane sign the syndication contract?

4. **Challenge Problem:** Load Off Your Mind moving company is considering investing in a new moving van in order to expand their business operations. The cost of the new van is $75,000. The firm is currently earning an annual rate of 8 percent on their investment portfolio. The company expects to have the following cash flows from the expansion project. $33,000 in year 1; $35,000 in years 2 through 7; and $27,000 in years 9 through 12. The motor for the van will have to be rebuilt in year 8, costing the company an additional cash outflow of $41,000. Should the firm make the investment?

5. **Challenge Problem:** You own two IBM bonds and expect to receive $2,000 in five years when these bonds mature. In the interim you will receive $240 annual interest payments at the end of each year until the bonds mature. What is the present value of your investment? Assume your investment opportunity cost is an annual rate of 11 percent.

B. Determining Interest Rates

So far when we've solved for future and present values, we have always supplied the interest rate. What if we know the present value, future value and the time factor, but we don't know the interest rate? For example, your bank tells you that if you invest $1,000 in a certificate of deposit (CD), you will receive $1,200 in three years. What rate of interest is the bank offering?

Future value = Present value (1 + interest rate)TIME

Let's plug in the numbers we know:

$1,200 = $1,000(1 + interest rate)^3

Put what we do know on one side of the equation:

$\dfrac{\$1,200}{\$1,000}$ = (1 + interest rate)^3

Solve: 1.200 = (1 + interest rate)^3

Take the cubed root of the left-hand side to remove the exponent[7]:

1.0627 = (1 + interest rate)

Subtract one from both sides of the equation:

1.0627 − 1 = 1 + interest rate − 1

6.27% = interest rate

As another example, suppose a friend asks to borrow $12,000 to start her own pet grooming service. She says she will repay you $17,500 in five years. What rate of return is your friend offering you for the use of your money?

Future value = Present value (1 + interest rate)TIME

Plug in the numbers we know:

$17,500 = $12,000(1 + interest rate)^5

---

[7] 1.200 = (1 + interest rate)^3
$(1.200)^{1/3}$ = [(1 + interest rate)^3]$^{1/3}$ = 1.0627 = (1 + interest rate)

Put what we do know on one side of the equation:

$$\frac{\$17,500}{\$12,000} = (1 + \text{interest rate})^5$$

Solve: $1.4583 = (1 + \text{interest rate})^5$

Take the fifth root of the left-hand side to remove the exponent [8]:

$1.0784 = (1 + \text{interest rate})$

Subtract one from both sides of the equation:

$1.0784 - 1 = 1 + \text{interest rate} - 1$

$7.84\% = \text{interest rate}$

See this isn't so hard if you just keep in mind that you need to input the three variables you do know – present value, future value and time – to solve for what you don't know – the interest rate.

What about solving for the interest rate when the cash flows aren't a single sum, but an annuity? To solve for the interest rate we must have the present OR future value of the annuity, the size of the payment and the number of years over which the payments stretch. For example, suppose a mortgage lender offers to loan you $73,000 to buy a home. You sign a mortgage agreement calling for payments of $6,484 at the end of each year for the next 30 years. What interest rate is the mortgage lender charging you?

Present Value = pmt(Present Value Interest Factor of an Annuity)

$73,000 = $6,484(Present Value Interest Factor of an Annuity)

$$\frac{\$73,000}{\$6,484} = (\text{Present Value Interest Factor of an Annuity})$$

$$\frac{\$73,000}{\$6,484} = 11.25$$

Without a calculator to solve for this variable we use the tables in your text. Look on the Present Value Interest Factor of an Annuity table across 30 years and search for the number 11.25. The number is under the 8 percent column.

You borrow money from mom and dad to purchase your first home. You decide to treat the transaction as a formal loan so that there is no misunderstanding about the agreement. You put into writing that you will

---

[8] $1.4583 = (1 + \text{interest rate})^5$
$(1.4583)^{1/5} = [\,(1 + \text{interest rate})^3\,]^{1/5} = 1.0784 = (1 + \text{interest rate})$

borrow $20,000 and repay $2,717 each year over a ten-year period. What rate of interest are you paying?

Present Value = pmt(Present Value Interest Factor of an Annuity)

$20,000 = $2,717(Present Value Interest Factor of an Annuity)

$\frac{\$20,000}{\$2,717}$ = (Present Value Interest Factor of an Annuity)

$\frac{\$20,000}{\$2,717}$ = 7.36

Again, look on the Present Value Interest Factor of an Annuity table across ten years and search for the number 7.36. The number is under the 6 percent column.

　　　As our final example, suppose you determine that you will need $1,500,000 in 30 years to retire comfortably. You can put aside $9,119 each year for the next 30 years. What rate of interest will you have to earn in order to accumulate the amount you'll need when you retire?

Future Value = pmt(Future Value Interest Factor of an Annuity)

$1,500,000 = $9,119 (Future Value Interest Factor of an Annuity)

$\frac{\$1,500,000}{\$9,119}$ = (Future Value Interest Factor of an Annuity)

$\frac{\$1,5000,000}{\$9,119}$ = 164.49

Again, without a calculator to solve for this variable we use the tables in your text. Look in the Future Value Interest Factor of an Annuity table across 30 years and search for the number 164.49. The number is under the ten percent column.

　　　What if the interest rate is compounded more frequently than on an annual basis? Uh oh! You purchase an old Corvette from your brother-in-law for $17,000. You plan to fix it up and, after expenses, sell it for twice the amount you paid for it. The two of you work out the following deal: You will pay him $2,073 every six months until the loan is paid off in five years. What rate of interest are you paying your brother-in-law?

Present Value = pmt(Present Value Interest Factor of an Annuity)

$17,000 = $2,073 (Present Value Interest Factor of an Annuity)

$\frac{\$17,000}{\$2,073}$ = (Present Value Interest Factor of an Annuity)

$\dfrac{\$17,000}{\$2,073}$ = 8.20/2 (for semiannual) = 4.10

Once more, use the tables in your text. Look in the Present Value Interest Factor of an Annuity table across five years and search for the number 4.10. The number is under the 7 percent column.

Let's look at one more example of multiple compounding periods. Suppose an insurance salesperson offers to sell you an annuity contract for $55,000. Your contract will start paying you $446 at the end of each month for the next 30 years. What interest rate are you earning on your initial investment?

Present Value = pmt(Present Value Interest Factor of an Annuity)

$55,000 = $446(Present Value Interest Factor of an Annuity)

$\dfrac{\$55,000}{\$446}$ = (Present Value Interest Factor of an Annuity)

$\dfrac{\$55,000}{\$446}$ = 123.24/12 (for monthly) = 10.27

Using the tables in your text, look at the Present Value Interest Factor of an Annuity table across 30 years and search for the number 10.27. The number is under the 9 percent column.

Again, take note that we had to divide the number of years by 12 to account for monthly payments.

Well, what if the cash flows are at one interval say semiannual, but compounding of the interest is quarterly? We'll take a look at that scenario in the next section where we convert all these different compounding periods to an effective annual rate. For now, let's take a few minutes to work Practice Set F on the following page.

NOTES:

_____

_____

_____

_____

_____

_____

_____

PRACTICE SET F
DETERMINING INTEREST RATES

1. You need $3,000 in six years. You now have $1,200. What rate of return will you have to earn to obtain your desired amount of money?

2. Cybercollege is offering the following tuition arrangement. They told Mr. Saylor that if he gave them $10,000 now, when his son reaches college age, all of his first-year expenses would be paid. They estimate his son's first-year college expenses will be $15,000. Mr. Saylor's son is 8 years old and will begin college at age 18 (in ten years). What is the implied rate of return? What is your recommendation to Mr. Saylor?

3. Mr. Ulee invested the vast majority of his wealth ($500,000) in a honey bee farm. Today (20 years later) his wealth is estimated to be $1 million. Please advise Mr. Ulee on his investment portfolio.

4. Your broker offers to sell you a partnership in an oil and gas syndicate. The investment required is $10,000. There is a 10 percent commission on all sales executed. The commission comes out of your initial $10,000 investment. At the end of five years the syndicate will pay you $12,000. What course of action would you take and why?

5. You expect to receive $5,000 at the end of every month from a well-to-do relative. You plan to reinvest each of these cash flows into an investment that pays monthly compounding. You believe these cash flows will continue for at least five years and you expect to have $331,536 at the end of five years. What rate of return did you earn to reach this ending amount?

6. **Challenge Problem**: You need to have $17,000 in one year to pay off a gambling debt or large men with big fists will be after you. You now have $200. What annual rate of return will your $200 have to earn to so you obtain the cash you need?

7. **Challenge Problem**: You need to have $1,000,000 for retirement. You can put aside $15,000 each year towards your goal. Your investments have, on average, paid an annual rate of 12 percent. How many years will you have to wait until you can retire?

C. Stated, Nominal, or Quoted Rates

What do these terms have in common? They represent the rate that lenders quote to their borrowers. We can compare nominal rates of various investments as long as the number of compounding periods is the same. But when the compounding rates differ (e.g., one lender quotes a semiannual rate while another quotes a quarterly rate) we find ourselves comparing apples with oranges. Therefore, we need to convert each rate to an annualized rate so we are comparing apples with apples.

D. Annual Percentage Rate (APR)

The annual percentage rate that the government *requires* lenders to prominently display on all loan documents is not always the actual rate you will pay for the loan. Amazing, but true! The regulation requires lenders to report the rate charge per period (e.g., monthly) times the number of periods in a year (12). So if your credit card has a monthly charge of 1.5% your APR is 18% (1.5% × 12). If your credit card has a 21% APR that means you are paying 1.75% (21% ÷ 12) per month on your outstanding balance. Is that what the lender is actually charging you to carry a balance on your credit cards? No. To figure out what you are really paying, you have to convert the 18 or 21 percent to an effective annual rate. Using effective annual rate conversions allows us to compare different investment returns and borrowing costs.

E. Effective Annual Rate (EAR)

If we have different frequencies in compounding across investment choices it's difficult to make meaningful comparison. Therefore, we convert all stated, nominal, quoted, or APR rates of interest to an effective annual rate (affectionately known as the EAR equation). The EAR equation allows investors to choose which investments offer the greatest return and which loans are the least costly.

For example, suppose one investment alternative offered a stated rate of 6 percent semiannual return while another offered a stated rate of 5.8 percent quarterly return and yet another quoted you a rate of 5.6 percent monthly return. We know that the more frequent the compounding, the more valuable the ending balance. But in this case, while the frequency of compounding increases, the stated interest rate decreases. So what's a woman to do? Should she opt for the larger stated rate of interest or should she choose the more frequent compounding? What she needs to do first is determine the effective annual rate of each investment choice and choose whichever has the largest return. Stating all the rates of interest in annual terms levels the proverbial playing field. Easier done then said! We use the following to transform various rates into effective annual rates.

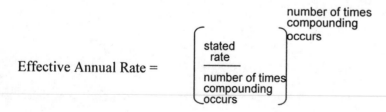

Effective Annual Rate = $\left(\dfrac{\text{stated rate}}{\text{number of times compounding occurs}} \right)^{\text{number of times compounding occurs}}$

What is the effective annual rate of 6 percent compounded semiannually?

$$\text{Effective Annual Rate} = \left(1 + \frac{0.06}{2}\right)^2 - 1 = 6.09\%$$

What is the effective annual rate of 5.8 percent compounded quarterly?

$$\text{Effective Annual Rate} = \left(1 + \frac{0.058}{4}\right)^4 - 1 = 5.927\%$$

What is the effective annual rate of 5.6 percent compounded monthly?

$$\text{Effective Annual Rate} = \left(1 + \frac{0.056}{12}\right)^{12} - 1 = 5.746\%$$

She can see from the calculations above that the 6 percent semiannual rate offers the greatest return. Converting each interest rate to an annual percentage allowed her to make that comparison without having to weigh which was better, the higher percentage or the more frequent compounding. Thus, if she had a number of investment opportunities where each offered a different interest rate and compounding period, she would be able to make sense of all the numbers and make an informed decision about which investment offers the greatest rate of return.

Now, about those credit cards. The one that had an 18% APR is really costing you 19.56%.

$$\text{Effective Annual Rate} = \left(1 + \frac{0.18}{12}\right)^{12} - 1 = 19.56\%$$

The 21% credit card is really charging you 23.14% on any outstanding balances you may be carrying.

$$\text{Effective Annual Rate} = \left(1 + \frac{0.21}{12}\right)^{12} - 1 = 23.14\%$$

Nothing is as it seems. We can't blame the credit card companies or bank loan departments for these discrepancies. After all, they are only doing what the law mandates – reporting APR. Next time you want to know what you're really paying, put your ear to the ground and figure it out for yourself.

F. Amortization Schedules

A loan that is paid off in equal installments over its life is an *amortized loan*. Your mortgage and car payments are amortized loans. An amortization schedule breaks down the loan payments into two parts to show how much of each payment is applied to pay off the principal balance and how much goes toward the interest portion. An amortization schedule also allows us to calculate the total interest expense of taking out a loan – a real show stopper when you consider that the typical homeowner pays three times the actual purchase price simply because of the interest expense involved in a mortgage loan. Another feature of amortized loans is that the interest portion decreases over time while the portion of each payment that goes toward the principal increases.

To set up an amortization schedule, we first need to solve for the payment and then we can figure how much of each payment goes toward principal and how much toward interest. Let's start with a three-year $1,000 loan for which the lender is charging an annual rate of 6 percent. We are to repay the loan in equal annual installments.

Step One: Determine the payment.

Present Value = pmt(Present Value Interest Factor of an Annuity)

$1,000 = pmt(6%, 3 years)

We look up the present value interest factor for three years at 6%. The corresponding number on the table is 2.6730

$1,000 = pmt(2.6730)

$$\frac{\$1,000}{2.6730} = pmt$$

$$\frac{\$1,000}{2.6730} = \$374.11$$

Thus, our annual installment payment is $374.11. Our next step is to create an amortization table that shows how much of each payment goes toward interest and how much toward principal.

Step Two: Create an amortization schedule

Year	Payment	Interest	Principal	Remaining Balance
0				$1,000.00
1	$374.11	$60.00	$314.11	$685.89
2	$374.11	$41.15	$332.96	$352.93
3	$374.11	$21.18	$352.93	$0
	$1,122.33	$122.33	$1,000.00	

INTEREST	PRINCIPAL	BALANCE
Balance × 6%	Payment − Interest	Balance − Principal
($1,000)(0.06) = $60.00	$374.11 − $60.00 = $314.11	$1,000 − $314.11 = $685.89
($685.89)(0.06) = $41.15	$374.11 − $41.15 = $332.96	$685.89 − $332.96 = $352.93
($352.93)(0.06) = $21.18	$374.11 − $21.18 = $352.93	$352.93 − $352.93 = $0

These calculations show that the total payments amounted to $1,122.33, of which $122.33 went to pay the interest on the loan and the remainder repaid the principal. Using this format you can easily calculate the total cost of the loan (finance charges + repayment of principal).

Let's look at one more example. Suppose you borrowed $5,000 from your local credit union and that you agreed to repay the loan in five years. The annual rate of interest is 8 percent. Again, we want to create an amortization table that shows how much of your annual payment goes toward interest and how much goes toward principal.

Step One: Determine the payment.

Present Value = pmt(Present Value Interest Factor of an Annuity)

$5,000 = pmt(8%, 5 years)

We look up the present value interest factor for five years at 8%. The corresponding number on your table is 3.9927

$5,000 = pmt(3.9927)

$$\frac{\$5,000}{3.9927} = pmt$$

$$\frac{\$5,000}{3.9927} = \$1,252.29$$

Step Two: Create an amortization schedule

Year	Payment	Interest	Principal	Remaining Balance
0				$5,000.00
1	$1,252.29	$400.00	$314.11	$4,147.71
2	$1,252.29	$331.82	$332.96	$3,227.24
3	$1,252.29	$258.18	$332.96	$2,233.13
4	$1,252.29	$178.65	$332.96	$1,159.46
5	$1,252.29	$92.76	$352.93	$0
	$6,261.45	$1,261.41	$5,000.00	

INTEREST	**PRINCIPAL**	**BALANCE**
Balance × 8%	Payment – Interest	Balance – Principal
($5,000)(0.08) = $400.00	$1,252.29 – $400.00 = $852.29	$5,000 – $852.29 = $4,147.71
($4,147.71)(0.08) = $331.82	$1,252.29 – $331.82 = $920.47	$4,147.71 – $920.47 = $3,227.24
($3,227.24)(0.08) = $258.18	$1,252.29 – $258.18= $994.11	$3,227.24 – $994.11 = $2,233.13
($2,233.13)(0.08) = $178.65	$1,252.29 – $178.65 = $1,073.67	$2,233.13 – $1,073.67 = $1,159.46
($1,159.46)(0.08) = $92.76	$1,252.29 – $92.76 = $1,159.53	$1,159.46 $1,159.53 = $0.07 [9]

Practice Set G for effective annual rates and amortization schedules is on the next page.

NOTES:

_____

_____

_____

_____

_____

_____

_____

_____

_____

_____

[9] Difference is due to rounding and is considered negligible.

PRACTICE SET G
Effective Annual Rates and Amortization

1. What is the effective annual rate for a deposit account that pays 3.2 percent interest compounded monthly?

2. What is the effective annual rate for an investment that pays 8 percent interest compounded annually?

3. What is the effective annual rate for the loan shark that charges 25 percent compounded monthly?

4. Your Wal-Mart charge card has an APR of 1.25%. What is the effective annual rate on your outstanding balance?

5. Set up an amortization schedule for a $20,000 loan to be repaid in equal installments over the next five years at an annual interest rate of 7 percent.

6. **Challenge Problem:** What is the payment on a $125,000 mortgage to be repaid monthly over 30 years when the rate is 11.5 percent monthly?

SOLUTIONS
PRACTICE SET A: Future Value Problems

1. What is the future value of $200 invested for seven years at 8 percent annual interest?

Future value = $200(1.08)^7$
$= $200(1.7138) = 343

2. What is the future value of $350 invested for five years at 9 percent annual interest?

Future value $= $350(1.09)^5$
$= $350(1.5139) = 539

3. Today Richardson Inc., an art gallery on the West Side, purchased a rare painting for $70,000. They expect the painting to increase in value at a rate of 15 percent annually for the next five years. How much will their painting be worth at the end of the fifth year if their expectations are correct? (HINT: Recognize that $70,000 is the current or present value of Richardson's investment and thus you need to solve for the future value of $70,000 to know what the value of the painting will be in five years.)

Future value $= $70,000(1.15)^5$
$= $70,000(2.0114) = $140,795$

4. Allegro Industries, Inc., has a defined-benefit pension plan that is under-funded. To try and catch up with their liabilities, Allegro invested $50,000 into a high-risk junk bond mutual fund that in previous years had earned as much as 17 percent annually. If their plan works and the fund continues to earn an annual rate of 17 percent over the next ten years, how much will Allegro have added to their pension fund holdings?

Future value $= $50,000(1.17)^{10}$
$= $50,000(4.8068) = $240,341$

5. Tucker Trucking invested $4,000 in a money market mutual fund that currently pays 3.5 percent annual interest. They plan to leave their money invested for a period of eight years. What will be the value of Tucker's money at the end of their eight-year investment horizon?

Future value $= $4,000(1.035)^8$
$= $4,000(1.3168) = $5,267$

6. Simpson Clothier, a men's haberdashery, invested $12,000 in a corporate bond mutual fund that offers a 7.7 percent annual return. They would like to have $20,000 at the end of nine years for an expansion project. Will Simpson Clothier reach their desired goal?

Future value $\quad = \$12,000(1.077)^9$
$\qquad\qquad\quad\; = \$12,000(1.9496) = \$23,395$

7. Howell Publishing plans to expand their operations to the West Coast in ten years. Today their CFO contributed $100,000 toward their goal of $350,000. They expect their portfolio to earn 12 percent annually. Will they reach their goal of $350,000?

Future value $\quad = \$100,000(1.12)^{10}$
$\qquad\qquad\quad\; = \$100,000(3.1058) = \$310,585$

8. **Challenge Problem**: $67,980

9. **Challenge Problem**: $5,786

10. **Challenge Problem**: $11,407,247

SOLUTIONS
PRACTICE SET B: Present Value Problems

1. What is the present value of $100 you expect to receive in seven years at 6 percent annual interest?

Present value $= \$100(1/(1.06))^7$
$= \$100(0.6651) = \$66.51$

2. What is the present value of $300 you expect to receive in ten years at 8 percent annual interest?

Present value $= \$300(1/(1.08))^{10}$
$= \$300(0.4632) = \$138.96$

3. Petroleum Plastics has been doing a booming business. They would like to expand in the next two years. The owners estimate they will need $37,000 to purchase and remodel the store next door. What amount of money should they set aside today assuming they can earn 4 percent on their investments? (HINT: Recognize that $37,000 is a future value and that you need to solve for the present value of $37,000 to know what the company needs to invest today at an annual rate of 4 percent to have the money they will need.)

Present value $= \$37,000(1/(1.04))^2$
$= \$37,000(0.9246) = \$34,208.58$

4. Coffee is out. Tea is in. Given this information, the makers of Mr. Coffee want to produce a Ms. Tea by next year. The investment required is $67,000. The firm currently has $54,000 invested in short-term Treasury securities that offer a 3 percent annual return. Will Mr. Coffee have enough funds to produce Ms. Tea? How much should they put aside to have the desired amount of funds?

Future value $= \$54,000(1.03)^1 = \$55,620$

Present value $= \$67,000(1/(1.03))^1$
$= \$67,000(0.9709) = \$65,048.54$

5. Tyger Sweepers, Inc., needs $300,000 in eight years. If they can invest their money at 7 percent annual interest, how much should they invest today to have the $300,000 in eight years?

Present value $= \$300,000(1/(1.07))^8$
$= \$300,000(0.5820) = \$174,602.73$

6. Roetronic Industries needs $400,000 in five years. They have invested $220,000 in stocks paying 15.5 percent annually. Will Roetronics have enough funds to meet their financial goal? How much should they put aside to have the desired amount of funds?

Future value $= \$220,000(1.155)^5 = \$452,202.13$

Present value $= \$400,000(1/(1.155))^5$
$= \$400,000(0.4865) = \$194,603.24$

7. Medical Surplus Supply will need $200,000 to build up their business. They have the option to invest in a new mutual fund that promises low risk and returns of 7 percent annually. How much should Medical Surplus Supply invest if they want to meet their financial goal?

Present value $= \$200,000(1/(1.07))^2$
$= \$200,000(0.8734) = \$174,687.75$

8. **Challenge Problem**: $150,000

9. **Challenge Problem**: $36,979,639

10. **Challenge Problem**: $28,938,690

SOLUTIONS
PRACTICE SET C: Present and Future Values With Multiple Compounding Periods

1. What is the present value of your $200 million that you expect to receive in five years when the discount rate is 6 percent annually?

Present value $= \$200(1/(1 + 0.06))^{(5)}$

$= \$200(0.7473) = \$149,451,635$

2. What is the present value of your $200 million that you expect to receive in five years when the discount rate is 6 percent semiannually?

Present value $= \$200(1/(1 + 0.06/2))^{(5)(2)}$

$= \$200(1/(1 + 0.03))^{(10)}$

$= \$200(0.7441) = \$148,818,783$

3. What is the present value of your $200 million that you expect to receive in five years when the discount rate is 6 percent quarterly?

Present value $= \$200(1/(1 + 0.06/4))^{(5)(4)}$

$= \$200(1/(1 + 0.015))^{(20)}$

$= \$200(0.7425) = \$148,494,084$

4. What is the present value of your $200 million that you expect to receive in five years when the discount rate is 6 percent monthly?

Present value $= \$200(1/(1 + 0.06/12))^{(5)(12)}$

$= \$200(1/(1 + 0.005))^{(60)}$

$= \$200(0.7414) = \$148,274,439$

5. What is the present value of your $200 million that you expect to receive in five years when the discount rate is 6 percent daily?

Present value $= \$200(1/(1 + 0.06/365))^{(5)(365)}$

$= \$200(1/(1 + 0.00016))^{(1825)}$

$= \$200(0.7408) = \$148,167,298$

6. What is the present value of your $200 million that you expect to receive in five years when the discount rate is 6 percent continuously?

Present value $= \$200(1/(e^{(.06)(5)})) = \$148,163,644$

7. What is the future value of your $350 million that you have to invest for eight years when the interest rate is 6 percent annually?

Future value $= \$350(1 + .06)^{(8)}$

$= \$300(1.5938) = \$557,846,826$

8. What is the future value of your $350 million that you have to invest for eight years when the interest rate is 6 percent semiannually?

Future value $= \$350(1 + .06/2)^{(8)(2)}$

$= \$350(1 + .03)^{(16)}$

$= \$350(1.6047) = \$561,647,254$

9. What is the future value of your $350 million that you have to invest for eight years when the interest rate is 6 percent quarterly?

Future value $= \$350(1 + .06/4)^{(8)(4)}$

$= \$350(1 + .015)^{(32)}$

$= \$350(1.6103) = \$563,613,512$

10. What is the future value of your $350 million that you have to invest for eight years when the interest rate is 6 percent monthly?

Future value $= \$350(1 + .06/12)^{(8)(12)}$

$= \$350(1 + .005)^{(96)}$

$= \$350(1.6141) = \$564,949,948$

11. What is the future value of your $350 million that you have to invest for eight years when the interest rate is 6 percent daily?

Future value $= \$350(1 + .06/365)^{(8)(365)}$

$= \$350(1 + .000164)^{(2920)}$

$= \$350(1.6160) = \$565,603,726$

12. What is the future value of your $350 million that you have to invest for eight years when the interest rate is 6 percent continuously?

Future value $= \$350(e^{(.06)(8)}) = \$565,626,041$

13. **Challenge Problem**: $3,673

14. **Challenge Problem**: $11,552,978

15. **Challenge Problem**: $148,341

16. **Challenge Problem**: $28,234,355

SOLUTIONS
PRACTICE SET D: Annuities

1. Renaissance Paper, Inc., needs to invest $8,000 at the end of each of the next five years to keep their current project going. If they can earn 7.5 percent annual compounding on their invested dollars, how much will they have to set aside today to ensure they will have the level of cash inflows they will need? (Be sure to recognize that the $8,000 annual investment needed is the <u>annuity</u> payment, then draw a time line to determine if you are solving for future value or present value.)

a. Present value of an ordinary annuity.

b. Present Value Interest Factor of a 5 year 7.5% annuity

$$= \frac{1}{0.075} - \frac{1}{0.075(1.075)^5} = 4.0459$$

$8,000(4.0459) = $32,367

2. The owners of Beagle Brothers Automotive Store want to have $500,000 at the end of 15 years to supplement their pension income. They are currently investing $30,000 at the end of each year earning 8.2 percent compounded annually. Are the Beagle Brothers investing enough to finance their supplementary retirement fund?

a. Future value of an ordinary annuity.

b. Future Value Interest Factor of a 15-year 8.2% annuity

$$= \frac{(1.082)^{15} - 1}{0.082} = 27.5785$$

$15,000(27.5785) = $827,355

3. A competitor has approached the owners of the Linger Longer Lounge with an offer to purchase their establishment. The potential purchasers offered the owners of Linger Longer $25,000 to be paid at the beginning of each year for the next 10 years. When news of the offer became public knowledge, another competitor offered to pay the owners of the Linger Longer Lounge $200,000 today. If the opportunity cost of investing for the owners of Linger Longer is 6 percent annual discounting, which offer should they accept?

a. Present value of an annuity due.

b. Present Value Interest Factor of a 10-year 6% annuity

$$= \frac{1}{0.06} - \frac{1}{0.06(1.06)^{10}} = 7.3601$$

to convert to a present value interest factor for an annuity due multiply by (1 + interest rate)

7.3601(1.06)= 7.8017

$25,000(7.8017) = $195,043

They would be better off taking the $200,000 now rather than receive $25,000 at the beginning of each year for 10 years.

4. Indiana "Hoosier" Insurance Agency offered to sell Dr. Natasha Phelps an annuity contract at a price of $40,000. In return, the contract stipulates that Indiana will pay Dr. Phelps $5,000 at the end of each of the next 10 years. Dr. Phelps's opportunity cost of investment is 8 percent annually. Should she purchase the annuity contract?

a. Present value of an ordinary annuity.

b. Present Value Interest Factor of a 10-year 8% annuity

$$= \frac{1}{0.08} - \frac{1}{0.08(1.08)^{10}} = 6.7101$$

$5,000(6.7101)= $33,550

Dr. Phelps should not purchase the contract because its value is only $33,500 and they are asking her to pay $40,000. This contract is overpriced and if she makes the investment she will earn less than her required 8 percent.

5. Avenue Florist wants to purchase a new delivery truck. The truck has a purchase price of $65,000. The owners of the Avenue Florist have been setting aside $5,000 at the beginning of each year for the past 10 years in an account paying 7.7 percent annually. Do they have enough to make their purchase?

a. Future value of an annuity due.

b. Future Value Interest Factor of a 10-year 7.7% annuity

$$= \frac{(1.077)^{10} - 1}{0.077} = 14.2818$$

to convert to a future value interest factor for an annuity due multiply by (1 + interest rate)

14.2818 (1.077)= 15.3815

$5,000(15.3815)= $76,908

6. Mr. Fox and his partner have created a database of security prices. This database is the most comprehensive of its kind. To manufacture the CD discs once all the data have been entered, the partners will need $8,000 at the end of each of the next five years. If they can earn 7.5 percent annual compounding on their invested dollars, how much will they have to set aside today to ensure they will have the level of cash inflows they will need?

a. Present value of an ordinary annuity

b. Present Value Interest Factor of a 5-year 7.5% annuity

$$= \frac{1}{0.075} - \frac{1}{0.075(1.075)^5} = 4.0459$$

$8,000(4.0459)= $32,367

7. **Challenge Problem**: Solving for the future value of an annuity with multiple compounding periods. $41,776

8. **Challenge Problem**: Solving for the size of the payment. $29,128

SOLUTIONS
PRACTICE SET E: Uneven Cash Flows

1. You had a rich Aunt Ernestine who recently passed on. In her will, she stipulated you would receive $1,000 a year through age 25, then you will receive $2,500 a year through age 30, then you are to get $5,000 a year through 40 years of age at which time your payments will cease. You just had your twentieth birthday today (HINT: Your first cash flow occurs one year from now on your twenty-first birthday.) At your twentieth birthday party, a woman offered you $30,000 for the right to your inherited cash flow. Should you take the offer given that your opportunity cost for investment is an annual rate of 8 percent?

Notice that during years 1 through 5 we have a five-year $1,000 annuity imbedded in this uneven series of cash flows.

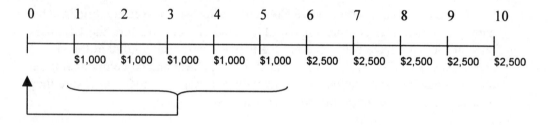

Step One: Find the present value of the 5-year $1,000 annuity:

$$\text{Years 4-10} \quad \frac{1}{\text{int. rate}} - \frac{1}{\text{int. rate}(1+\text{int. rate})^{\text{number of periods}}} = \frac{1}{.08} - \frac{1}{.08(1.08)^5} = 3.9927$$

3.9927 ($1,000) = $3,993

Notice that during years 6 through 10 we have a 5-year $2,500 annuity imbedded in this uneven series of cash flows.

Step One: Find the present value of the 5-year $2,500 annuity:

$$\text{Years 4-10} \quad \frac{1}{\text{int. rate}} - \frac{1}{\text{int. rate}(1+\text{int. rate})^{\text{number of periods}}} = \frac{1}{.08} - \frac{1}{.08(1.08)^5} = 3.9927$$

3.9927 ($2,500) = $9,982

Step Two: Discount the annuity back to time 0:

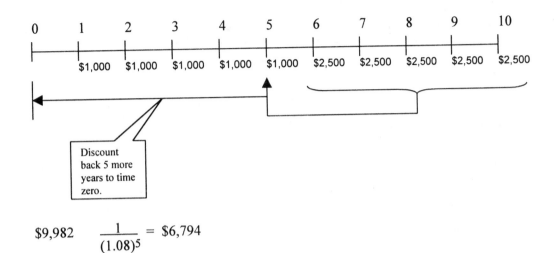

$$\$9,982 \quad \frac{1}{(1.08)^5} = \$6,794$$

Notice that during years 6 through 10 we have a 5-year $2,500 annuity imbedded in this uneven series of cash flows.

Step One: Find the present value of the ten-year, $5,000 annuity:

$$\text{Years 11-20} \quad \frac{1}{\text{int. rate}} - \frac{1}{\text{int. rate}(1+\text{int. rate})^{\text{number of periods}}} = \frac{1}{.08} - \frac{1}{.08(1.08)^{10}} = 6.7101$$

$$6.7101 \, (\$5,000) = \$33,550$$

Step Two: Discount the annuity back to time 0:

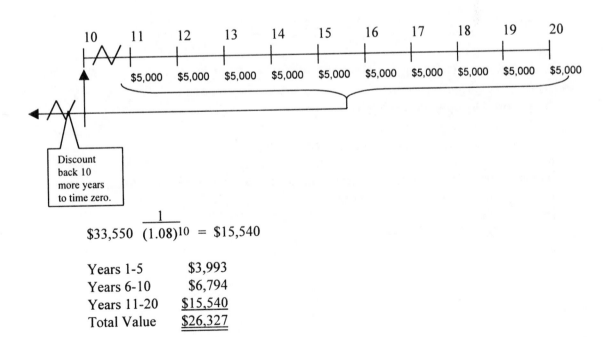

$$\$33,550 \, \frac{1}{(1.08)^{10}} = \$15,540$$

Years 1-5	$3,993
Years 6-10	$6,794
Years 11-20	$15,540
Total Value	$26,327

2. Canine Corporation is planning on investing in a line of brand of stationery. Sales are expected to be $50,000 for the first two years, then drop to $30,000 for the next three years, and then decline to $15,000 for the remaining five years of the product's life cycle. Management has determined the firm would have to invest $180,000 at the beginning of the project's life for a new printing press and miscellaneous equipment. The firm's opportunity cost for investment is an annual rate of 12 percent. Should the firm invest in this project?

Notice that during years 1 and 2 we have a 2-year $50,000 annuity imbedded in this uneven series of cash flows.

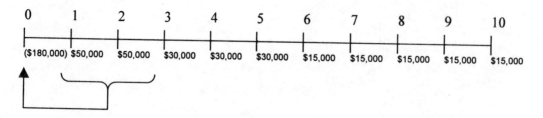

Step One: Find the present value of the 2-year $50,000 annuity:

$$\text{Years } 4\text{-}10 \quad \frac{1}{\text{int. rate}} - \frac{1}{\text{int. rate}(1+\text{int. rate})^{\text{number of periods}}} = \frac{1}{.12} - \frac{1}{.12(1.12)^2} = 1.6901$$

1.6901 ($50,000) = $84,503

Notice that during years 3 through 5 we have a 3-year $30,000 annuity imbedded in this uneven series of cash flows.

Step One: Find the present value of the 3-year $30,000 annuity:

$$\text{Years } 3\text{-}5 \quad \frac{1}{\text{int. rate}} - \frac{1}{\text{int. rate}(1+\text{int. rate})^{\text{number of periods}}} = \frac{1}{.12} - \frac{1}{.12(1.12)^3} = 2.4018$$

2.4018 ($30,000) = $72,055

Step Two: Discount the annuity back to time 0:

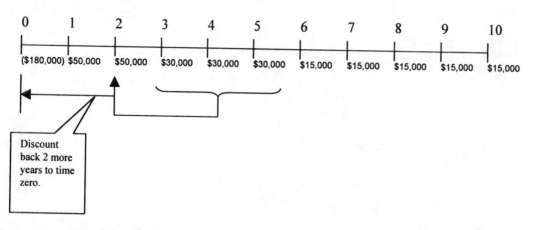

Discount back 2 more years to time zero.

$72,055 $\dfrac{1}{(1.12)^2}$ = $57,442

Notice that during years 6 through 10 we have a 5-year $15,000 annuity imbedded in this uneven series of cash flows.

Step One: Find the present value of the 5-year $30,000 annuity:

Years 6-10 $\dfrac{1}{\text{int. rate}} - \dfrac{1}{\text{int. rate}(1+\text{int. rate})^{\text{number of periods}}} = \dfrac{1}{.12} - \dfrac{1}{.12(1.12)^5} = 3.6048$

3.6048 ($15,000) = $54,072

Step Two: Discount the annuity back to time 0:

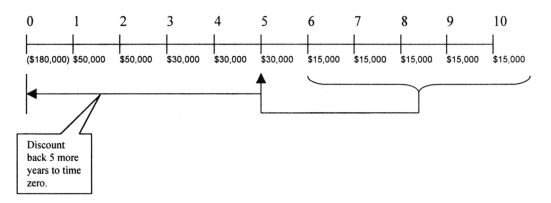

$54,072 $\dfrac{1}{(1.12)^5}$ = $30,682

Year 0	−$180,000
Years 1-2	$84,503
Years 3-5	$57,442
Years 6-10	$30,682
Total Value	−$7,373

3. Dr. Frazier Crane is interested in syndicating his radio talk show. With the help of his brother Niles, Dr. Crane has estimated the following cash flows. $2,000 year 1; $3,000 years 2 through 6; $5,000 years 7 through 10; $2,000 years 11 and 12, and $1,000 in year 13. The startup cost is $25,000 and the Crane Brothers' investment portfolio is currently earning an annual rate of 5 percent. Should Dr. Crane sign the syndication contract?

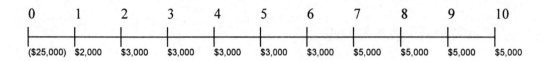

Year 1 $2,000 $\dfrac{1}{(1.05)^1}$ = $1,905

Notice that during years 2 and 6 we have a 5-year $3,000 annuity imbedded in this uneven series of cash flows.

Step One: Find the present value of the 5-year $3,000 annuity:

Years 2-6 $\dfrac{1}{\text{int. rate}} - \dfrac{1}{\text{int. rate}(1+\text{int. rate})^{\text{number of periods}}} = \dfrac{1}{.05} - \dfrac{1}{.05\,(1.05)^5} = 4.3295$

4.3295 ($3,000) = $12,988

Step Two: Discount the annuity back to time 0:

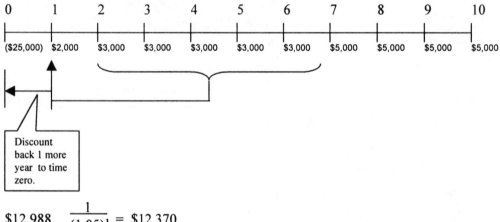

Discount back 1 more year to time zero.

$12,988 $\dfrac{1}{(1.05)^1}$ = $12,370

Notice that during years 7 through 10 we have a 4-year $5,000 annuity imbedded in this uneven series of cash flows.

Step One: Find the present value of the 4-year $5,000 annuity:

Years 7-10 $\dfrac{1}{\text{int. rate}} - \dfrac{1}{\text{int. rate}(1+\text{int. rate})^{\text{number of periods}}} = \dfrac{1}{.05} - \dfrac{1}{.05\,(1.05)^4} = 3.5460$

3.5460 ($5,000) = $17,730

Step Two: Discount the annuity back to time 0:

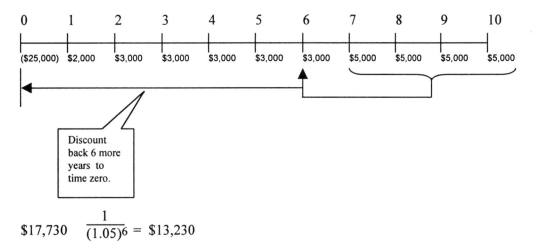

$$\$17,730 \quad \frac{1}{(1.05)^6} = \$13,230$$

Notice that during years 11 and 12 we have a 5-year $2,000 annuity imbedded in this uneven series of cash flows.

Step One: Find the present value of the 2-year $2,000 annuity:

$$\text{Years 11-12} \quad \frac{1}{\text{int. rate}} - \frac{1}{\text{int. rate}(1 + \text{int. rate})^{\text{number of periods}}} = \frac{1}{.05} - \frac{1}{.05\,(1.05)^2} = 1.8594$$

1.8594 ($2,000) = $3,719

Step Two: Discount the annuity back to time 0:

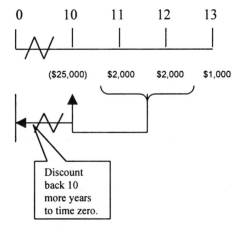

$$\$3,719 \quad \frac{1}{(1.05)^{10}} = \$2,283$$

Discount the cash flow in year 13 back to time zero:

$$\$1,000 \ \frac{1}{(1.05)^{13}} \ = \$530$$

Year 0	−$25,000
Year 1	$1,905
Years 2-5	$12,370
Years 6-10	$13,230
Years 11-12	$2,283
Year 13	$530
Total Value	$5,318

4. **Challenge Problem**: $131,535

5. **Challenge Problem**: $2,074

SOLUTIONS
PRACTICE SET F: Determining Interest Rates

1. You need $3,000 in six years. You now have $1,200. What rate of return will you have to earn to obtain your desired amount of money?

Future value = Present value $(1 + \text{interest rate})^{\text{TIME}}$

$3,000 = $1,200$(1 + \text{interest rate})^6$

Put what we do know on one side of the equation:

$\dfrac{\$3,000}{\$1,200} = (1 + \text{interest rate})^6$

Solve: $2.500 = (1 + \text{interest rate})^6$

Take the sixth root of the left-hand side to remove the exponent:

$1.1650 = (1 + \text{interest rate})$

Subtract one from both sides of the equation:

$1.1650 - 1 = 1 + \text{interest rate} - 1$

$16.5\% = \text{interest rate}$

2. Cybercollege is offering the following tuition arrangement. They told Mr. Saylor that if he gave them $10,000 now, when his son reaches college age, all his first-year expenses would be paid. They estimate his son's first-year college expenses will be $15,000. Mr. Saylor's son is 8 years old and will begin college at age 18 (in ten years). What is the implied rate of return? What is your recommendation to Mr. Saylor?

Future value = Present value $(1 + \text{interest rate})^{\text{TIME}}$

$15,000 = $10,00$(1 + \text{interest rate})^{10}$

Put what we do know on one side of the equation:

$\dfrac{\$15,000}{\$10,000} = (1 + \text{interest rate})^{10}$

Solve: $1.500 = (1 + \text{interest rate})^{10}$

Take the ten root of the left-hand side to remove the exponent:

1.0414 = (1 + interest rate)

Subtract one from both sides of the equation:

1.0414 – 1 = 1 + interest rate – 1

4.14 % = interest rate

<u>Recommendation</u>: Given that Mr. Saylor has ten years to meet his son's college expenses, Mr. Saylor could get a much better rate of return on his investment dollars by investing directly in the securities market where his money should grow by a greater annual return than 4.14%.

2. Mr. Ulee invested the vast majority of his wealth ($500,000) in a honey bee farm. Today (20 years later) his wealth is estimated to be $1 million. Please advise Mr. Ulee on his investment portfolio.

Future value = Present value $(1 + \text{interest rate})^{\text{TIME}}$

$1,000,000 = $500,00$(1 + \text{interest rate})^{20}$

Put what we do know on one side of the equation:

$\dfrac{\$1,000,000}{\$500,000} = (1 + \text{interest rate})^{20}$

Solve: 2.000 = $(1 + \text{interest rate})^{20}$

Take the twentieth root of the left-hand side to remove the exponent:

1.0353 = (1 + interest rate)

Subtract one from both sides of the equation:

1.0353 – 1 = 1 + interest rate – 1

3.53% = interest rate

<u>Recommendation:</u> Mr. Ulee has made only 3.53% on his investment portfolio. Given his original time horizon of 20 years, he could have gotten a much better rate of return on his investment dollars by investing directly in the securities market where his money should grow by a greater annual return than 3.53%. Because it is too late to counsel Mr. Ulee, a sensitive advisor would not convey this information to Mr. Ulee because it would only create angst and not serve any constructive purpose.

4. Your broker offers to sell you a partnership in an oil and gas syndicate. The investment required is $10,000. There is a 10 percent commission on all sales

executed. The commission comes out of your initial $10,000 investment. At the end of five years the syndicate will pay you $12,000. What course of action would you take and why?

Future value = Present value $(1 + \text{interest rate})^{\text{TIME}}$

$12,000 = $9,000$(1 + \text{interest rate})^5$

Put what we do know on one side of the equation:

$$\frac{\$12,000}{\$9,000} = (1 + \text{interest rate})^5$$

Solve: $1.333 = (1 + \text{interest rate})^5$

Take the fifth root of the left-hand side to remove the exponent:

$1.0592 = (1 + \text{interest rate})$

Subtract one from both sides of the equation:

$1.0592 - 1 = 1 + \text{interest rate} - 1$

$5.92\% = \text{interest rate}$

Recommendation: Given the inherent risk of such an investment, the investor would be right in demanding a rate of return that reflects the level of risk exposure. You should chide your broker for charging such an outrageous commission, complain loudly about his lackluster promised return, and get a new financial advisor immediately.

5. You expect to receive $5,000 at the end of every month from a well-to-do relative. You plan to reinvest each of these cash flows into an investment that pays monthly compounding. You believe these cash flows will continue for at least five years and you expect to have $331,536 at the end of five years. What rate of return did you earn to reach this ending amount?

Future Value = pmt(Future Value Interest Factor of an Annuity)

$331,536 = $5,000(Future Value Interest Factor of an Annuity)

$$\frac{\$331,536}{\$5,000} = (\text{Future Value Interest Factor of an Annuity})$$

$$\frac{\$331,536}{\$5,000} = 66.3072/12 \text{ (for monthly)} = 5.5256$$

Look in the Future Value Interest Factor of an Annuity table across five years and search for the number 5.5256. This number is under the 5% column.

6. **Challenge Problem**: 8,400%

7. **Challenge Problem**: 19.39 years

SOLUTIONS
PRACTICE SET G: Effective Annual Rates & Amortization

1. What is the effective annual rate for a deposit account that pays 3.2 percent interest compounded monthly?

Effective Annual Rate = $\left(1 + \dfrac{0.032}{12}\right)^{12} - 1 =$ 3.25%

2. What is the effective annual rate for an investment that pays 8 percent interest compounded annually?

Effective Annual Rate = $\left(1 + \dfrac{0.08}{1}\right)^{1} - 1 =$ 8.00%

3. What is the effective annual rate for the loan shark that charges 25 percent compounded monthly?

Effective Annual Rate = $\left(1 + \dfrac{0.25}{12}\right)^{12} - 1 =$ 28.07%

4. Your Wal-Mart charge card has an APR of 1.25%. What is the effective annual rate on your outstanding balance?

Effective Annual Rate = $\left(1 + \dfrac{0.15}{12}\right)^{12} - 1 =$ 16.08%

5. Set up an amortization schedule for a $20,000 loan to be repaid in equal installments over the next five years at an annual interest rate of 7 percent.

Step One: Determine the payment.

$20,000 = pmt(7%, 5 years)

We look up the present value interest factor for five years at 8 percent. That corresponding number on your tables is 4.1002

$20,000 = pmt(4.1002)

$\dfrac{\$20,000}{4.1002} = \$4,877.81$

Step Two: Create an amortization schedule

Year	Payment	Interest	Principal	Remaining Balance
0				$20,000.00
1	$4,877.81	$1,400.00	$3,477.81	$16,522.19
2	$4,877.81	$1,156.55	$3,721.26	$12,800.93
3	$4,877.81	$896.07	$3,981.74	$8,819.19
4	$4,877.81	$617.34	$4,260.47	$4,558.72
5	$4,877.81	$319.11	$4,558.70	$0
	$24,389.05	$4,389.07	$20,000.00	

INTEREST	PRINCIPAL	BALANCE
Balance x 7%	Payment – Interest	Balance – Principal
($20,000)(0.07) = $1,400.00	$4,877.81 – $1,400.00= $3,477.81	$20,000 – $3,477.81= $16,522.19
($16,522.19)(0.07) = $1,156.55	$4,877.81 – $331.82 = $3,721.26	$16,522.19 – $3,721.26 = $12,800.93
($12,800.93)(0.07) = $896.07	$4,877.81 – $896.07= $3,981.74	$12,800.93 – $3,981.74 = $8,819.19
($8,819.19)(0.07) = $617.34	$4,877.81 – $617.34 = $4,260.47	$8,819.19 – $4,588.70 = $4,558.72
($4,558.72)(0.07) = $319.11	$4,877.81 – $319.11 = $4,558.70	$4,558.72 – $4,558.70 = $0.02

6. **Challenge Problem:** $1,238

SECTION **3**:
Risk and Return

I. RISK AND RETURN

Your textbook will provide a more rigorous explanation of risk and return and the wonders of diversification, but we'll do an overview to give you the basics. We begin with the assumption that investors are rational. That doesn't mean we are going to delve into their psyche, only that they will demand additional compensation before they will accept more risk. Thus, for the rational investor, risk and return have a direct relationship; the greater the risk the more return the investor requires (i.e., the greater the required rate of return).

By investing in only one firm you take on all the risks associated with that firm and your fortunes rise and fall with the fortunes of that particular company. What would happen if you invested in the stock of another firm so that you now have two firms? We call this collection of securities a *portfolio*. Now when one firm isn't performing up to your expectations because of a poorly executed marketing program, perhaps your other firm is doing quite well. Thus, the higher-than-expected returns from one firm serves to offset the lower-than-expected returns from the other. Behold the marvel of diversification.

The degree to which diversification will work depends on how correlated the returns are as measured by the correlation coefficient. That is, how much the returns of the two firms tend to move up and down together. If their tendency is to move in opposite directions with equal emphasis we eliminate all the risk. Thus, when one stock return falls 20 percent below its average, its mate rises 20 percent above its average. This exactly offsets the loss so you are, in effect, guaranteed your return. This only occurs when two stocks are *perfectly negatively correlated* (correlation coefficient = −1.0).

A brief look at the other side of the coin shows us that it's possible to combine two stocks that are *perfectly positively correlated* (correlation coefficient = +1.0) and achieve no benefit from diversification because these two stocks move in perfect tandem. Thus, when one goes down 20 percent the other goes down 20 percent. With this combination we have not reduced the risk of our portfolio one iota.

Neither of these extremes fits reality. The tendency is for stocks to be positively correlated, but not perfectly so. Therefore, when we combine securities, we get a reduction in the risk, but we can't eliminate it all. Up to a point, the more securities we add to our portfolio the more risk we can eliminate because the returns are not perfectly positively correlated. With enough securities we can diversify away (a.k.a. get rid of) *company-specific risks* such as bad marketing programs, contract disputes, liability losses from litigious consumers, etc. What we cannot eliminate or diversify away is *market risk*. Market risks such as recessions and interest rate fluctuations impact all firms to one degree or another. Through diversification (combining securities whose correlation coefficients are less than +1.0) we can eliminate the risks associated with a specific company and only be left with market risk. Thus, for the sophisticated (i.e., not stupid) investor, market risk is the only relevant risk.

By now you are asking yourself "If the only relevant risk after diversification is market risk, how do I measure market risk?" While the details of these calculations are best left to your text, we will show you how we measure a stock's risk relative to movements in the market place with the stock's beta coefficient. The beta coefficient is simply the slope of the regression line that best describes the movement of a particular stock with movements in the market place. We generally use a proxy variable such as the Standard and Poor's 500 Index as our measurement of movement in the market place. By definition, the market has a beta coefficient equal to 1.0.

A. Capital Asset Pricing Model

If we know the risk (as measured by beta) of a particular stock we can use the capital asset pricing model to determine that security's required rate of return. The capital asset pricing model, affectionately known as CAPM, is a model developed to help determine a stock's required rate of return for a given level of risk. If an individual chooses to invest her money, then she must postpone consumption. In other words, our investor can't shop and invest with the same dollar (Too bad!). What rate of return would our investor demand just to postpone her consumption? We implicitly assume the investor takes on no risk whatsoever, but merely postpones consumption. She'll want compensation for the wait plus an additional return for any inflationary pressures (an inflation premium). So, if our investor demands a 3 percent return to postpone consumption, and another 2 percent to cover the expected rate of inflation, she would require a 5 percent rate of return. That is, the *risk-free rate of return* is 5 percent. For now let's put her funds into a riskless security that pays a 5 percent rate of return.

Remember that there is no compensation for risk because we currently have her invested in a riskless asset. The riskless asset, by definition, has a beta coefficient of 0.0. So our investor's required rate of return would be equal to risk-free rate of return. We tend to think of Treasury securities as a good proxy for a riskless asset because there is no default risk.

Required rate = Risk-free = 5%
of return   rate

Now, what would it take to get our investor to move from a risk-free asset to a risky asset? That would depend on the quantity of risk the asset had and what price our investor charges for risk.

Additional
compensation = $\left[\begin{array}{c} \text{Price per} \\ \text{unit of risk} \end{array}\right]$ $\begin{array}{c} \text{Quantity} \\ \text{of risk} \end{array}$
required for
investment in
a risky asset

We measure the price of risk as the difference between the rate of return on the market as measured by the rate of return on the S&P 500 Index and the risk-free rate of return.

Price per   = $\left[\begin{array}{ccc} \text{Return on} & - & \text{Risk-free} \\ \text{the market} & & \text{rate} \end{array}\right]$
unit of risk

We can measure the quantity of risk with a stock's beta coefficient. Recall that by definition our riskless asset has a beta of 0.0, and the market has a beta coefficient equal to 1.0. The market, therefore, has one unit of risk. If we multiply the price of risk times the quantity of risk, we can determine what our investor is charging per unit of risk.

$$\begin{array}{l}
\text{Additional} \\
\text{compensation} \\
\text{required for} \\
\text{investment in} \\
\text{a risky asset}
\end{array} = \left[\begin{array}{l}\text{Price per} \\ \text{unit of risk}\end{array}\right]\begin{array}{l}\text{Quantity} \\ \text{of risk}\end{array}$$

If we add this to the risk-free rate, we get the required rate of return on that security.

$$\begin{array}{l}\text{Required rate} \\ \text{of return}\end{array} = \begin{array}{l}\text{Risk-free} \\ \text{rate}\end{array} + \left[\begin{array}{l}\text{Price per} \\ \text{unit of risk}\end{array}\right]\begin{array}{l}\text{Quantity} \\ \text{of risk}\end{array}$$

Let's put all the parts back in to get the following:

$$\begin{array}{l}\text{Required rate} \\ \text{of return}\end{array} = \begin{array}{l}\text{Risk-free} \\ \text{rate}\end{array} + \left[\begin{array}{l}\text{Return on} \\ \text{the market}\end{array} - \begin{array}{l}\text{Risk-free} \\ \text{rate}\end{array}\right]\begin{array}{l}\text{Quantity} \\ \text{of risk}\end{array}$$

This is our capital asset pricing model. To see how it works suppose we have a risk-free rate of 5 percent, a rate of return on the market of 12 percent, and a quantity of risk (a.k.a. beta) of 1.5. Then our required rate of return would be:

$$\begin{array}{l}\text{Required rate} \\ \text{of return}\end{array} = 5\% + (12\% - 5\%)1.5 = 15.5\%$$

Thus, the required rate of return is equal to the risk-free rate of return plus price of risk times the quantity of risk. The <u>additional</u> return needed to induce our investor to move from a risk-free investment that has zero units of risk (beta = 0.0) to an investment that has one and a half units of risk (beta = 1.5) is 10.5 percent $(12\% - 5\%)1.5$.

What is the required rate of return for a security that has two units of risk (beta = 2.0)? We know intuitively that our investor will demand a greater rate of return for this larger quantity of risk.

$$\begin{array}{l}\text{Required rate} \\ \text{of return}\end{array} = 5\% + (12\% - 5\%)2.0 = 19\%$$

Notice the price of risk is still the same $[(12\% - 5\%)=7\%]$ and the return on the risk-free asset is still 5 percent. It is only the quantity of risk that has changed. At the risk of belaboring the point, let's reiterate. The <u>additional</u> return needed to induce an investor to move from a risk-free investment that has zero units of risk (beta = 0.0) to an investment that has two units of risk (beta = 2.0) is 14% $[(12\% - 5\%)2.0 = 14\%]$.

Before we move ahead, let's work a practice set to make sure you're comfortable with calculating the required rate of return for an individual security. Practice Set A is on the next page.

NOTES: _____

_____

_____

_____

_____

PRACTICE SET A
DETERMINING THE PRICE AND QUANTITY OF RISK

1. Sterling Corporation has a beta coefficient of 1.6. The current rate of return on Treasury securities is 9 percent. Analysts estimate the return on the market portfolio to be 13 percent.

a. What rate of return will an investor require to invest in a risk-free asset?

b. What components make up the risk-free rate of return?

c. What is the price per unit of risk?

d. What is the quantity of risk?

e. What rate of return will an investor require to invest in Sterling Corporation?

f. What <u>additional</u> return did an investor require to move from a risk-free asset with zero units of risk to an asset that has 1.6 units of risk?

g. Without doing any calculations, what do you think would happen to our investor's required rate of return if the quantity of risk went from 1.6 units to 2.4 units? Explain your logic making sure to answer in words only.

h. Now do the calculation for part g. What rate of return would an investor require if the amount of risk increased from 1.6 units to 2.4 units?

B. Security Market Line

We can look at the risk and return relationship expressed by the capital asset pricing model in a graphical format called the *security market line*.

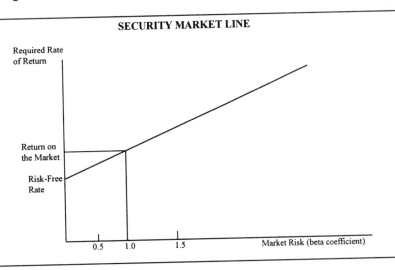

SECURITY MARKET LINE

Notice the horizontal axis shows market risk as measured by the beta coefficient and the vertical axis shows required rates of return. The slope of the security market line represents the amount of risk aversion in the economy; the more risk the steeper the slope. If investors didn't care about risk (unthinkable!), the security market line would be flat. This would mean that investors require no compensation to take on additional risk. If investors loved risk, the line would slope downward. How do you interpret a security market line that slopes downward? Literally, it would mean that as investors take on more risk they require less return (unbelievable!). The security market line always has an upward slope. This indicates that investors always require a positive return, but the price of risk will change in response to changes in investors' aversion to risk.

Analysts consider a security to be in equilibrium (i.e., fairly priced) when the expected rate of return is equal to the required rate of return and therefore plots on the security market line (SML). What happens if a security doesn't plot on the security market line? What if a security plots at point U?

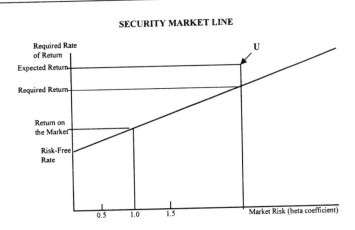

SECURITY MARKET LINE

At point U the expected rate of return is greater than the required rate. That means you expect to get a greater rate of return than you currently demand for the given quantity and current price of risk. Is this a good deal? You bet! Any time you expect to get more return than you asked for, buy it.

How does a stock get to point U? This stock is underpriced. When the marketplace realizes this stock is underpriced, like you just did, everyone will want to buy it. A bidding war will ensue that will push the price of the stock up and its expected rate of return down. The stock price will continue to increase and its return to decrease until the stock plots on the security market line and is in equilibrium (expected rate of return equals required rate of return).

What if a security plots at point O?

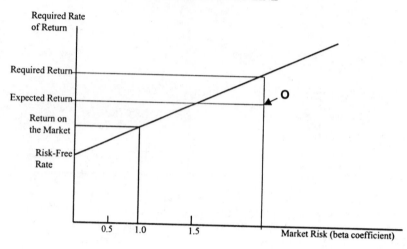

SECURITY MARKET LINE

At point O the expected rate of return is less than the required rate. That means you expect to get a lower rate of return than you currently demand for the given quantity and current price of risk. Is this a good deal? No way! Any time you expect to get less than you require, don't buy it. How does a stock get to point O? This stock is overpriced. When the marketplace comes to the same realization as you, they will all want to sell. The stock price will decrease as investors try to unload their holdings of this overpriced security. The stock price will continue to decrease and its return to increase until the stock plots on the security market line and is in equilibrium (expected rate of return equals required rate of return).

C. Changes in Risk Aversion

What happens to the security market line if the level of risk aversion increases (decreases)? This will cause the slope of the security market line to increase (decrease) and the price of risk will rise (fall). When there is an increase in risk aversion, the securities with the greatest quantity of risk, as measured by beta, are the hardest hit in terms of having to offer a greater required rate of return. Let's look at an example (on the next page).

Suppose the level of risk aversion increased. What could cause such an event? Suppose there is an economic collapse of several countries in South America that triggers investors' fears of a worldwide recession. This may cause all investors, as a group, to demand a greater level of return for any given level of risk causing the security market line to rotate up.

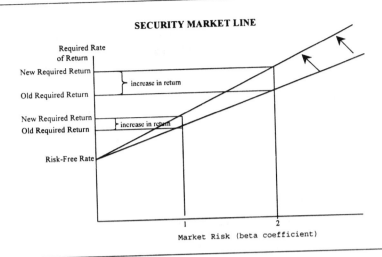

SECURITY MARKET LINE

Notice how the security that has two units of risk (beta=2) has a much greater increase in required return than the security that has only one unit of risk (beta=1). The quantity of risk has not changed, the aforementioned securities still have one and two units of risk respectively, but the price of risk has changed. Using our capital asset pricing model we will look at the old required return and the new required return when investors' aversion to risk has increased.

$$\text{Required rate of return} = \text{Risk-free rate} + \left[\text{Return on the market} - \text{Risk-free rate}\right]\text{Quantity of risk}$$

If we continue to assume that the risk-free rate is 5 percent and that the return on the market is 12 percent, we have the following:

Old required rate of return $= 5\% + (12\% - 5\%)2.0 = 19\%$

The price per unit of risk is 7 percent $(12\% - 5\%)$. With the increase in risk aversion, however, the market now requires a 14 percent return.

New required rate of return $= 5\% + (14\% - 5\%)2.0 = 23\%$

The new price of risk is now 9 percent $(14\% - 5\%)$. The new price of risk of 9 percent causes our required rate of return to increase from 19 to 23 percent. Notice the risk-free rate remained at 5 percent. This is true because even though the level of risk aversion has increased, the risk-free asset still has a beta of 0. We can increase risk aversion all day long and the risk-free asset will still have a beta of 0.

Note the change in required return for an asset that has one unit of risk (beta=1).

Old required rate of return $= 5\% + (12\% - 5\%)1.0 = 12\%$

With the increase in risk aversion, the required rate of return increases to 14 percent.

New required rate of return $= 5\% + (14\% - 5\%)1.0 = 14\%$

Notice that the asset with two units of risk increased its required rate of return from 19 percent to 23 percent for an increase of four percentage points. The asset with only one unit of risk increased its required rate of return from 12 percent to 14 percent for an increase of only two percentage points. This demonstrates the direct relationship of risk aversion to the level of risk of each asset. The more risk, the greater the change in the required return. The less risky asset increased its required return by only two percentage points compared to the more risky asset's increase of four percentage points.

D. Changes in Inflation Rates

What happens to security returns if inflation goes up (down)? This affects all securities to the same degree and causes a parallel <u>shift</u> up (down) in the security market line. Thus, if the risk-free rate, which includes an inflation premium, goes up (down), then the required rate of return on all securities increases (decreases).

What if inflation went up by one percentage point? On the graph below we see that all security returns including the risk-free rate of return are impacted to the same degree.

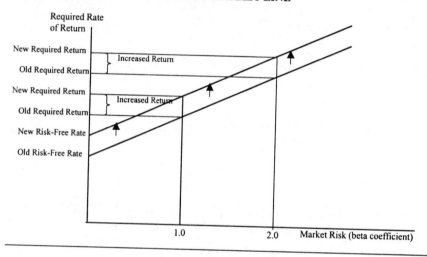

SECURITY MARKET LINE

Let's look at this using our required rate of return equation.

Old required $= 5\% + (12\% - 5\%)1.0 = 12\%$
rate of return

Suppose we have a 1 percent increase in inflation. Because an increase in inflation affects all securities equally, the risk-free rate would go up by one percentage point as would the market rate of return. Thus, from our previous example, the risk-free rate would increase from 5 to 6 percent, the return on the market would increase from 12 to 13 percent and the quantity of risk would remain the same (beta=1).

New required $= 6\% + (13\% - 6\%)1.0 = 13\%$
rate of return

Remember that the price of risk did not change, but now every security holder demands one percentage point more because of the one percentage point increase in inflation. The one percentage point increase impacts all securities equally regardless or risk. To show you what we mean, let's look at the change in required return for our security that had two units of risk (beta=2).

Old required rate of return $= 5\% + (12\% - 5\%)2.0 = 19\%$

As with our previous example, the risk-free rate would increase from 5 to 6 percent, the return on the market would increase from 12 to 13 percent and the quantity of risk would remain the same (beta=2).

New required rate of return $= 6\% + (13\% - 6\%)2.0 = 20\%$

We really don't need these calculations to refigure the required rate of return. Because inflation affects all securities equally, we can merely add the percentage increase in inflation onto the old required return to determine the new required rate of return. We would use the same procedure if the rate of inflation decreased, subtracting the percentage decrease from the old required return to determine the new required rate of return. Let's work another practice set examining the changes to required rates of return when there are changes in risk aversion and inflation rates. Practice Set B is on the next page.

NOTES:

_____

_____

_____

_____

_____

_____

_____

_____

_____

_____

_____

_____

_____

_____

PRACTICE SET B
SECURITY MARKET LINE

1. The security market line (SML) is a graphical representation of the capital asset pricing model (CAPM). What relationship does this graph depict?

2. What does the slope of the security market line represent?

3. How would the security market line show changes in aversion to risk?

4. How would the security market line show changes in the rate of inflation?

5. Recall from Practice Set A that Sterling Corporation has a beta of 1.6. The current rate of return on 30-year Treasury securities was 9 percent. Analysts estimate the return on the market portfolio to be 13 percent. What is the required rate of return for Sterling Corporation? What is the price per unit of risk?

6. If investors became more risk averse and the rate of return on an average risk stock (beta=1) went from 13 to 15 percent, what would be the required rate of return for Sterling Corporation? What happens to the security market line? What is the price per unit of risk?

7. If investors became less risk averse and the rate of return on the market portfolio went from 13 to 11 percent, what would be the required rate of return for Sterling Corporation? What happens to the security market line? What is the price per unit of risk?

8. If the Consumer Price Index (CPI) went from the 3 to 4 percent what would be the required rate of return for Sterling Corporation? What happens to the security market line? What is the price of risk?

9. If the rate of inflation went from 3 to 2 percent, what would be the required rate of return for Sterling Corporation? What happens to the security market line? What is the price per unit of risk?

E. Portfolios

We can use the same modeling technique to find the required rate of return on a portfolio of securities. Remember, a portfolio is a collection of securities instead of only one security. The risk of the portfolio is the weighted average of the betas of the individual securities included in the portfolio. Let's work through an example.

Indiana Investment Management Group has the following securities in their $1.5 million portfolio. Using the information given below, what is the beta coefficient for the portfolio?

Security	Amount Invested	Beta Coefficient
A	$600,000	1.7
B	$500,000	0.8
C	$400,000	2.0

The first step is to determine what percentage of the portfolio each stock represents (i.e., determine the weight of each security in the portfolio). To get the weights we take the amount invested in each security divided by the total value of the portfolio.

Security	Amount Invested	Beta Coefficient
A	$600,000/$1,500,000 = 0.40	1.7
B	$500,000/$1,500,000 = 0.33	0.8
C	$400,000/$1,500,000 = 0.27	2.0

To get a weighted average we multiply the weight times the beta for each security and sum to get the beta for the portfolio.

Security	Amount Invested		Beta Coefficient
A	$600,000/1,500,000 = 0.40	×	1.7 = 0.68
B	$500,000/1,500,000 = 0.33	×	0.8 = 0.26
C	$400,000/1,500,000 = 0.27	×	2.0 = 0.54
			Portfolio Beta = 1.48

Now that we know the portfolio's quantity of risk, as measured by the beta coefficient, we can use the capital asset pricing model to determine the portfolio's required rate of return. If we assume the risk-free rate is again 5 percent and the return on the market is 12 percent, the required return for the portfolio is:

Required rate $= 6\% + (12\% - 6\%)1.48 = 15.36\%$
of return

Thus, using the capital asset pricing model, well-diversified investors can find the required rate of return for an individual security as well as for a portfolio of securities. Let's work Practice Set C on the next page.

PRACTICE SET C
PORTFOLIO REQUIRED RETURNS

1. Reynolds Mutual Fund has a total of $800 million dollars invested in the following stocks.

COMPANY	AMOUNT	BETA
Delphi's Pizzeria	$120	1.2
Foundry Machine Corporation	$184	0.5
Nordic Winery	$64	2.0
All Tell Cellular Phones	$96	0.75
Franklin Utilities	$80	1.6
Version II Computers	$40	3.0
Web Based Commerce, Inc.	$216	1.0

a. What is the beta for this portfolio?

b. The current yield on Treasury securities is 9 percent. Analysts estimate the return on market portfolio to be 13 percent. What is the required rate of return for this portfolio?

c. Reynolds has the opportunity to purchase a new stock. The new stock has an expected rate of return of 12 percent with an estimated beta coefficient of 3.0. Should they purchase the stock? Explain why or why not.

d. In terms of risk, what does beta measure?

2. Martin Capital Management has a total of $650 million dollars invested in the following stocks.

COMPANY	AMOUNT	BETA
Ruskin Shoes, Inc.	$65	1.00
Satellite Towers	$130	1.75
ATP Security Corp.	$150	2.25
Bellford Insurance Company	$85	3.00
KLI Ambulance Conversions	$220	0.75

a. What is the beta for this portfolio?

b. The current yield on Treasury securities is 7.5 percent. The return on the market portfolio is currently 10 percent. What is the required rate of return for this portfolio?

3. Bowers Mutual Fund has a total of $900 million dollars invested in the following stocks.

COMPANY	AMOUNT	BETA
Just Shoot Me Publishing, Inc.	$200	1.9
Celldone, Ltd.	$110	0.8
Silvert Computers, Inc.	$220	2.0
Website Bottom Line, Inc.	$90	3.5
A-Market Discount Stores	$100	2.6
Package Wrap Products	$180	0.52

a. What is the beta for this portfolio?

b. The current yield on Treasury securities is 6.5 percent. The return on the market portfolio is currently 12 percent. What is the required rate of return for this portfolio?

4. **Challenge Problem:** Referring to Problem 2, suppose Martin Capital Management is thinking about investing $70 million in Kohl's Medical Supplies, Inc. The expected return on Kohl's is 12 percent and its beta coefficient is 1.0.

a. Should Martin Capital Management purchase this stock? Explain why or why not.

b. If the beta were 2.0, what would be your recommendation and why?

5. **Challenge Problem:** Referring to Problem 3, suppose Bowers Mutual Fund has the opportunity to purchase a new stock called Waste Recycle Corporation (WRC). WRC has an expected return of 15.75 percent; and its estimated beta coefficient is 2.0.

a. Should Bower Mutual Fund purchase WRC stock?

b. What would make the management of Bowers Mutual Fund indifferent to buying the stock?

SOLUTIONS
PRACTICE SET A: Determining the Price and Quantity of Risk

1.a. What rate of return will an investor require to invest in a risk-free asset?

9%

b. What components make up the risk-free rate of return?

Real rate of interest that is the rate of return it takes to get investors to postpone consumption plus an inflation premium to protect the investor against rising price levels.

c. What is the price per unit of risk?

$(13\% - 9\%) = 4\%$

d. What is the quantity of risk?

1.6 units

e. What rate of return will an investor require to invest in Sterling Corporation?

Required rate of return = 9%+ $(13\% - 9\%)1.6 = 15.4\%$

f. What additional return did an investor require to move from a risk-free asset with zero units of risk to an asset that has 1.6 units of risk?

$(13\% - 9\%)1.6$
$(4\%)1.6$
6.4% additional return needed to induce an investor to move from the risk-free asset to an asset that has 1.6 units of risk.

g. Without doing any calculations, what do you think would happen to our investor's required rate of return if the quantity of risk went from 1.6 units to 2.4 units. Explain your logic making sure to answer in words only.

Our investor would require a greater rate of return to compensate for the additional risk. Recall we assume that all rational investors are risk averse. This means that investors don't like risk and if we want an investor to take on more risk we have to offer inducements (higher returns).

h. Now do the calculation for part g. What rate of return would an investor require if the amount of risk increased from 1.6 units to 2.4 units?

Required rate of return = 9%+ $(13\% - 9\%)2.4 = 18.6\%$

SOLUTIONS
PRACTICE SET B: Security Market Line

1. The security market line (SML) is a graphical representation of the capital asset pricing model (CAPM). What relationship does this graph depict?

> Depicts the relationship between market risk and required rate of return.

2. What does the slope of the security market line represent?

> The slope illustrates the level of risk aversion in the economy.

3. How would the security market line show changes in aversion to risk?

> The greater the level of risk aversion, the steeper the slope of the security market line.

4. How would the security market line show changes in the rate of inflation?

> The security market line makes a parallel shift when there are changes in the rate of inflation. When inflation increases the security market line shifts up by the amount of the increase and when inflation decreases the security market line shifts down by the amount of the decrease.

5. Recall from Practice Set A that Sterling Corporation has a beta of 1.6. The current rate of return on 30-year Treasury securities is 9 percent. Analysts estimate the return on the market portfolio to be 13 percent. What is the required rate of return for Sterling Corporation? What is the price per unit of risk?

> Required rate of return = 9%+ (13% − 9%)1.6 = 15.4%
> Price per unit of risk is (13% − 9%)= 4.0%

6. If investors became more risk averse and the rate of return on an average risk stock (beta=1) went from 13 to 15 percent, what would be the required rate of return for Sterling Corporation? What happens to the security market line? What is the price per unit of risk?

> Required rate of return = 9% + (15% − 9%)1.6 = 18.6%
> SML rotates up (price per unit of risk 6%)

7. If investors became less risk averse and the rate of return on the market portfolio went from 13 to 11 percent, what would be the required rate of return for Sterling Corporation? What happens to the security market line? What is the price per unit of risk?

> Required rate of return = 9% + (11% − 9%)1.6 = 12.2%
> SML rotates down (price per unit of risk 2%)

8. If the Consumer Price Index (CPI) went from 3 to 4 percent what would be the required rate of return for Sterling Corporation? What happens to the security market line? What is the price per unit of risk?

> Required rate of return = 10% + (14% − 10%)1.6 = 16.4%
> SML shifts up parallel (price per unit of risk is 4%)

9. If the rate of inflation went from the three percent to two percent, what would be the required rate of return for Sterling Corporation? What happens to the security market line? What is the price per unit of risk?

> Required rate of return = 8% + (12% − 8%)1.6 = 14.4%
> SML shifts down parallel (price per unit of risk is 4%)

SOLUTIONS
PRACTICE SET C: Portfolio Required Returns

1. Reynolds Mutual Fund has a total of $800 million dollars invested in the following stocks.

COMPANY	AMOUNT		BETA
Delphi's Pizzeria	$120/$800 =	.15 × 1.2 =	0.18
Foundry Machine Corporation	$184/$800 =	.23 × 0.5 =	0.115
Nordic Winery	$64/$800 =	.08 × 2.0 =	0.16
All Tell Cellular Phones	$96/$800 =	.12 × 0.75 =	0.09
Franklin Utilities	$80/$800 =	.10 × 1.6 =	0.16
Version II Computers	$40/$800 =	.05 × 3.0 =	0.15
Web Based Commerce, Inc.	$216/$800 =	.27 × 1.0 =	0.27
		Portfolio beta =	1.125

a. Portfolio beta = 1.125

b. 9% + (13% − 9%)1.125 = 13.5% is the required rate of return on this portfolio.

c. 9% + (13% − 9%)3.0 = 21% Do not purchase this stock. The required rate of return is greater than the expected rate of return.

d. Beta measures the volatility of a security (or portfolio of securities) with movements in the marketplace and, as such, beta measures market risk.

2. Martin Capital Management has a total of $650 million dollars invested in the following stocks.

COMPANY	AMOUNT		BETA
Ruskin Shoes, Inc.	$65/$650 =	0.10 × 1.00 =	0.10
Satellite Towers	$130/$650 =	0.20 × 1.75 =	0.35
ATP Security Corp.	$150/$650 =	0.23 × 2.25 =	0.52
Bellford Insurance Company	$85/$650 =	0.13 × 3.00 =	0.39
KLI Ambulance Conversions	$220/$650 =	0.34 × 0.75 =	0.26
		Portfolio beta =	1.62

a. Portfolio beta = 1.62

b. The current yield on Treasury securities is 7.5 percent. The return on the market portfolio is currently 10 percent. What is the required rate of return for this portfolio?

$$= 7.5\% + (10\% − 7.5\%)1.6125 = 11.53\%$$

3. Bowers Mutual Fund has a total of $900 million dollars invested in the following stocks.

COMPANY	AMOUNT		BETA
Just Shoot Me Publishing, Inc.	$200/$900 =	$0.2222 \times 1.9 =$	0.42
Celldone, Ltd	$110/$900 =	$0.1222 \times 0.8 =$	0.10
Silvert Computers, Inc.	$220/$900 =	$0.2444 \times 2.0 =$	0.49
Website Bottom Line, Inc.	$90/$900 =	$0.1000 \times 3.5 =$	0.35
A-Market Discount Stores	$100/$900 =	$0.1111 \times 2.6 =$	0.29
Package Wrap Products	$180/$900 =	$0.2000 \times .52 =$	0.10
		Portfolio beta =	1.75

a. Portfolio beta=1.75

b. The current yield on Treasury securities is 6.5 percent. The return on the market portfolio is currently 12 percent. What is the required rate of return for this portfolio?

$$= 6.5\% + (12\% - 6.5\%)1.7518 = 16.13\%$$

4. **Challenge Problem**: **a.** Purchase.   Expected > Required
                                            Return   Return

  b. Don't purchase. Expected < Required
                           Return   Return

5. **Challenge Problem:** **a.** Don't purchase. Expected < Required
                                              Return   Return

  b. When Expected Return = Required Return

SECTION 4: Security Valuation

I. OVERVIEW OF SECURITY VALUATION

Now that you have learned the basics of compounding and discounting, we will put your knowledge to good use. This section looks at how investors use discounted cash flows to determine the value of a security such as a stock or bond. The perspective of this course is to look at security valuation from the corporate manager's point of view. Management has an interest in how investors value securities because they want to know which variables investors consider important. Knowing how investors value securities helps managers maximize shareholder wealth.

In the next section we will use these valuation methods to determine a firm's cost of financing. Why do we care about that? Because managers want to make sure they don't invest in projects that have a rate of return lower than their cost of funds. No one stays in business very long doing that. For a lot of corporations, the biggest expense is the cost of raising funds. If managers can find ways to minimize financing costs they will further maximize shareholder wealth.

We will first examine how to value corporate bonds and then move through the valuation of preferred stock. Last, we will examine the techniques used to value common stock.

II. BOND VALUATION

Bonds are long-term promissory notes issued by corporations, governments and others to raise money. Firms issue bonds in standard increments of $1,000 (a.k.a. par value). The money the firm gets from the bond sale represents a loan and the corporation records the transaction as a liability on their balance sheet. In return for the loan, the firm will pay interest (rent) on each bond issued and, when the bond matures, repay the principle. The bond's maturity date is set before the sale so investors know when the company will repay the liability.

How do we know what the correct price is for a particular bond? As we mentioned in the time value of money section, the value of a financial security is the present value of all the cash inflows an investor expects that security to generate. Thus, to find the value of a bond we find the present value of all the cash flows it produces. Bonds generate two cash inflows. First, as we already said, the investor receives interest payments every year from the issuing firm as a form of rent paid on the money borrowed. Second, when the bond matures, the firm repays the investor the $1,000 principal balance.

The coupon payment[1] is the annual rent paid on the loan. Bonds are fixed income securities. That is, the firm sets the coupon payment when the firm issues the bond and it stays fixed for the entire duration of the loan. That sounds suspiciously like the definition of an annuity—a fixed payment for a specified period of time! Over the life of the bond the coupon payment remains constant, but the price of the bond may not. As with our other present value calculations, there is an inverse relationship between interest rates and bond prices. As we'll see in the following sections, if market interest rates rise our bond will sell at a discount (< $1,000). If rates fall our bond will sell at a premium (>$1,000), and if market rates remain constant, our bond will sell at its par value (=$1,000).

The coupon rate is the fixed interest payment guaranteed to the bondholder over the life of the bond stated as a percentage of the par value. Thus, a 15 percent coupon rate would give the bondholder $150 ($1,000 × 0.15) in annual coupon payments. After issuance, the coupon rate remains fixed while the market interest rate moves in response to economic conditions. Let's first look at par value bonds.

A.  Par Value Bond

As we'll see in a minute, a bond will always be worth its par value ($1,000) as long as the coupon interest rate is the same as the market interest rate. Before we leap to the calculator, let's look at the mechanics for valuing a bond. For example, suppose StillWave International Corporation issues 2,500 bonds today that mature in 20 years. Each bond in this issue has a coupon rate of 12 percent so every year the bond pays $120 ($1,000 × 0.12). To determine the value of one of these bonds we need to find the present value of all the cash inflows this bond is going to generate over its lifetime. The bond is going to produce cash inflows of $120 per year for 20 years and then repay $1,000 when the bond matures. We discount each of these cash inflows by the market interest rate to determine their present value and then add them to solve for the value or price of the bond.

$$\text{Bond Value} = \frac{\$120}{(1.12)^1} + \frac{\$120}{(1.12)^2} + \frac{\$120}{(1.12)^3} + \ldots + \frac{\$120}{(1.12)^{20}} + \frac{\$1,000}{(1.12)^{20}} = \$1,000$$

Notice that again we are using exponents to show time. Thus an exponent of 20 means that this cash flow is 20 years away. We next solve for the present value of each cash flow and sum them to solve for the value of the bond.

$$\text{Bond Value} = \$107 + \$96 + \$85 + \ldots + \$12 + \$104 = \$1,000$$

Sure enough, we find that the summed value of all the discounted cash flows is equal to $1,000, which is the price of the bond.

But, as you can see, this equation gets unruly pretty fast. We can consolidate if we recognize that we have two components to bond valuation. The interest payments are an annuity (a fixed stream of cash inflows for a specified

---

[1] This term originated when firms issued bonds with coupons attached. The investor clipped a coupon and mailed it in to receive the coupon payment. Firms no longer issue coupon bonds. Instead, firms issue registered bonds where the interest payments due are automatically sent to the registered owner of the bond.

period of time) and the repayment of principal is a single sum. Thus, we can write our valuation as follows:

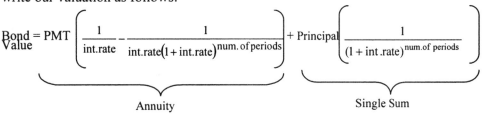

$$\text{Bond Value} = \text{PMT} \left[\frac{1}{\text{int.rate}} - \frac{1}{\text{int.rate}(1 + \text{int.rate})^{\text{num. of periods}}} \right] + \text{Principal} \left[\frac{1}{(1 + \text{int .rate})^{\text{num.of periods}}} \right]$$

Annuity   Single Sum

Now our equation says just what we said before, that if we sum the present value of all the coupon payments and add to that the present value of the principal portion of the bond, we have the bond's value or price.

Again, at the risk of belaboring the point, note we have two components to our equation. The interest payments are an annuity (a fixed stream of cash inflows for a specified period of time) and the repayment of principal is a single sum. There remains one further complication in valuing bonds—semiannual interest payments.

Bonds typically pay interest every six months instead of annually so we have to make the appropriate changes to find the correct value. We cut the annual interest payment in two to get the semiannual interest payment $60 ($120 ÷ 2). Then we make the same adjustments we did in the time value of money section when we were faced with multiple periods. First, we divide the interest rate by two to show semiannual discounting (0.12 ÷ 2 = 0.06). Second, we multiply the number of years by two to indicate the correct number of periods (20 × 2 = 40 periods). Notice that your prior knowledge about how to handle semiannual interest makes bond valuation easier to learn (just thought we'd throw that in). Now our bond valuation equation looks like this:

$$\text{Bond Value} = \$60 \left(\frac{1}{0.06} - \frac{1}{0.06(1.06)^{40}} \right) + \$1,000 \left(\frac{1}{(1.06)^{40}} \right) = \$1,000$$

Annuity   Single Sum

$902.78 $97.22

A bond's coupon rate remains fixed over the life of the bond. That means the investor who buys a StillWave International bond will get $60 every six months no matter what happens to market interest rates. Again, this is why financial experts refer to bonds as fixed income securities—because the income they produce never varies. The market interest rate, however, moves as conditions in the economy change. When a firm makes a bond offering, it sets the coupon rate equal to the market interest rate so the bonds will sell for their par value.

Assuming the market interest rate stays equal to the coupon rate, what is the value of this bond one year after StillWave International issued the security? Remember this bond has made two interest payments of $60 each. Your instincts will no doubt tell you that the value of the bond declined because the bond's cash flows now include only 38 interest payments instead of 40. Let's again use our bond value equation to determine the value of the bond one year later.

$$\text{Bond Value} = \$60 \left(\frac{1}{0.06} - \frac{1}{0.06(1.06)^{38}} \right) + \$1,000 \left(\frac{1}{(1.06)^{38}} \right) = \$1,000$$

Annuity   Single Sum

$890.76 $109.24

The value of the bond did not decline! How can it still be worth $1,000? Because the cash inflow from the remaining interest payments and the principal are all two periods closer. Remember from the time value section, the closer the cash inflows, the more value (in present value terms). The increase in value from the principal portion offsets the relatively small decrease in the annuity portion of the bond.

To really appreciate what happened let's separate the two cash inflows; the annuity and the single sum. The present value of the annuity portion with 40 periods remaining when market interest rates are 12 percent is $902.78 and the present value of the principal is worth $97.22 for a combined total of $1,000. When the number of periods drops to 38 (assuming that market rates remain unchanged) the present value of the annuity portion drops by $12.02 to $890.76. The present value of the principal increased by $12.02 to $109.24 that when added together still equals $1,000.

		Present Value of Interest Pmts		Present Value of Principal		
Bond Value @	40 periods	$902.78	+	$97.22	=	$1,000
Bond Value @	38 periods	$890.76	+	$109.24	=	$1,000
Difference in value		($12.02)		$12.02		

In fact, and we are not making this up, as long as the coupon rate and the market interest rate are equal, the bond will sell for its par value ($1,000). We even call this a par value bond! After this message we'll be right back!

B. Outstanding in Their Field

When we discuss interest rate movements and their resultant impact on bonds keep firmly in mind that the discussion relates only to bonds that firms have already issued. Interest rate movements impact bonds that trade in the secondary market, not the primary market. This may be obvious, but if overlooked can be a stumbling block to understanding bond price movements. When interest rates go up, bond prices go down, but only those bonds that are already trading among investors.

It is the static nature of the coupon payment that creates this relationship between interest rates and bond prices. When a firm establishes the coupon rate they set it to equal the current market rate so investors will purchase the bonds for their par value ($1,000). After issuance, the market rate freely moves in response to economic conditions, but the coupon payment remains fixed.

Let's look at an example. Suppose the current market rate on 20-year corporate bonds that have the highest credit rating is 10 percent. Suppose further that IBM wants to issue 20-year triple-A rated bonds to raise capital for acquisition of another company. If IBM wants to sell their bonds for $1,000 (par value) they will set the coupon rate equal to 10 percent. Now let's say a year later that market interest rates have increased to 11 percent. The value of the IBM bonds will decline, because they trade in the secondary market. New bonds issued in the primary market will set their coupon rate to 11 percent and sell at their par value. In this scenario it was only the bonds in the secondary market that "felt" the impact of market interest rate movements, whereas the bond prices in the primary market were unaffected.

Now for the fun part. What happens when the market interest rate is no longer equal to the coupon rate?

C. Discount Bond

Bond prices move inversely with movements in interest rates. When interest rates go down, bond prices in the secondary market go up and when interest rates go up, bond prices in the secondary market go down. Got it?

Let's look at an example. What happens to the value of our StillWave International bond if two years after the firm issued the securities, market interest rates increased from 12 to 14 percent? Any firm planning to issue new bonds will now have to offer coupon payments of $140 (or $70 semiannually) to attract investors. Why did the market interest rate go up? An increase in the market interest rate could be the result of the Federal Reserve's worries about inflation. If the Federal Reserve believes inflation is on the rise, they may force market interest rates up in an effort to reduce economic growth and thus put the brakes on inflation.

If new bonds are offering a 14 percent return, then no one will pay $1,000 for a bond that offers only a 12 percent return. To sell our StillWave International bond, we would have to lower our selling price until it offered the same rate of return (14 percent) as the new bonds. That is, because the coupon interest rate on our bond is fixed at 12 percent, the only way to increase the return to 14 percent is to lower the price an investor would have to pay for the bond. How low will the price have to go? The price on our 12 percent coupon bond will have to drop until it is offering the same rate of return (14 percent in this case) as the new bonds. Let us demonstrate.

We begin our demonstration by finding the value of our StillWave International bond when market interest rates have increased to 14 percent. Keep in mind this is still a "fixed income" security, and regardless of movements in market interest rates the coupon rate stays at 12 percent so the cash inflow remains at $60 every six months. We now have 36 periods remaining in the life of this bond.

$$\text{Bond Value} = \$60\left(\frac{1}{0.07} - \frac{1}{0.07(1.07)^{36}}\right) + \$1,000\left(\frac{1}{(1.07)^{36}}\right) = \$869.65$$

This is a discount bond because it sells below its par value. At the new price, investors would be indifferent between paying $1,000 for a 14 percent ($140) coupon bond or paying $869.65 for our 12 percent ($120) StillWave International bond. At a price of $869.65, the StillWave bond offers a 14 percent rate of return. Is that really true? Lets find out!

We can calculate an annual rate of return (ROR) by dividing the security's annual cash inflows by the price of the security. For example, before market interest rates increased to 14 percent our bond sold for $1,000 and the annual cash inflow was $120 producing an annual rate of return of:

$$\text{Annual cash inflow} \div \text{Investment} = \text{ROR}$$
$$\$120 \div \$1,000 = 12\%$$

When market interest rates increased to 14 percent our bond's value dropped to $869.65. Interest income is the annual cash inflow ($120) and the investment is the price of the bond ($869.65) so our rate of return (ROR) is equal to $120 ÷ $869.65 = 13.80 percent. Wait a minute! We said the StillWave International bond would have to offer a 14 percent return to make investors indifferent. Where is the other 0.20 percent? The answer is, capital gains.

The investor makes up the 0.20 percent difference as the bond's value increases over time. Remember, the bond's value on the day it matures is $1,000. Regardless of what market interest rates have done over the bond's life, the firm returns the principal ($1,000) to the owner when the bond matures. This increase in value toward the $1,000 maturity value doesn't happen overnight, but instead occurs slowly over the remainder of the bond's life. Thus, if a bond sells at a discount, the bond's price will have to increase in value as it approaches maturity where it will, by definition, be worth $1,000.

Let's prove it. We'll assume there are no additional movements in the market interest rates. We'll also assume our investor purchases the bond for $869.65, holds the bond for one year, and then sells it to another investor. But for how much?

$$\text{Bond Value} = \$60\left(\frac{1}{0.07} - \frac{1}{0.07(1.07)^{34}}\right) + \$1,000\left(\frac{1}{(1.07)^{34}}\right) = \$871.46$$

Notice we set the number of periods at 34 because our investor sold the bond one year, or two periods, later. She sold the bond for $1.81 more than she paid for the bond originally ($871.46 – $869.65). This produced a capital gain. We know our investor gets $120 ÷ $869.65 = 13.80 percent from the interest portion of the bond and we call this the bond's <u>current yield</u>.

Now if we combine the current yield with the capital yield, she gets the full 14 percent return.

Current yield = $120 ÷ $869.65 = 0.138
Capital yield = $1.81 ÷ $869.65 = 0.002
                                   ≈ 14%

If we combine the interest payment cash inflow ($120) and the capital gain cash inflow ($1.81) we can use our original equation to solve for the total annual rate of return:

Annual cash inflow ÷ Investment = ROR
$121.81 ÷ $869.65 = 14%

Thus, investors are indifferent between paying $1,000 for a 14 percent ($140) coupon bond or paying $869.65 for our 12 percent ($120) coupon bond. At a price of $869.65, the StillWave International bond does offer a 14 percent rate of return.

Why did our investor's bond drop by exactly $130.35, from $1,000 to $869.65? Because this is the present value of the lost annuity. What? Remember, our investor's bond pays $60 and new bonds pay $70—a difference of $10. How long does that $10 difference persist? Over the remaining life of the bond, 36 more periods. So what is the present value of a –$10 annuity discounted at the market interest rate of 7 percent (14% ÷ 2) for 36 periods? The answer is the amount of the discount, or –$130.35. Could we use this to find the value of the bond? You bet!

Par value – Present value of foregone cash flows = Price
$1,000 – $130.35 = $869.65

A cautionary note: During our analysis we made a few pretty big assumptions. For starters, we assumed that market interest rates had a one-time swing to 14 percent and then didn't move again. The truth is that market interest rates are rarely stable over the life of a bond. We also assumed that our investor purchased her bond after the movement in interest rates so we could ignore the capital loss of the original owner – the poor investor who purchased the bond for $1,000 and then had to sell it for $869.65.

D. Premium Bond

Now what do you think will happen to our investor's bond price if interest rates decrease? You've probably caught on by now that the inverse relationship with bonds in the secondary and interest rates would dictate a price increase. Let's see how much our investor's bond price increases if two years after StillWave International issued the securities, market interest rates decreased; falling from 12 percent to 9 percent. New bonds now pay $90. Everyone wants a bond like our investor's because it's paying $120. As a result, investors will bid up the price of the StillWave International bond in their quest to have the larger cash inflow ($120 versus $90). They will bid up the price to where our investor's bond is offering a 9 percent return—the same as newly issued bonds.

$$\text{Bond Value} = \$60\left(\frac{1}{0.045} - \frac{1}{0.045(1.045)^{36}}\right) + \$1,000\left(\frac{1}{(1.045)^{36}}\right) = \$1,265.00$$

This is a premium bond because it sells for a premium above the par value. At this new price of $1,265, investors don't care if they pay $1,000 for a 9 percent ($90) coupon bond or pay $1,265 for our investor's 12 percent ($120) StillWave International bond. At a price of $1,265, the two bonds offer the same 9 percent rate of return.

$$\text{Annual cash inflow} \div \text{Investment} = \text{ROR}$$
$$\$120 \div \$1,265 = 9.5\%$$

Didn't we say the StillWave International bond would have to offer a 9 percent return to make investors indifferent? But the yield calculation above shows a return that is greater than 9 percent. So what happened? Capital loss. Remember, the bond's value on the day it matures is $1,000 regardless of what interest rates have done over the bond's life. Thus, if a bond sells at a premium, the bond will have to decrease in value as it approaches maturity where it will, by definition, be worth $1,000.

To figure the capital loss we calculate the value of the bond one year or two periods later. Notice we now have the number of periods set at 34 because our investor sold the bond one year, or two periods, later.

$$\text{Bond Value} = \$60\left(\frac{1}{0.045} - \frac{1}{0.045(1.045)^{34}}\right) + \$1,000\left(\frac{1}{(1.045)^{34}}\right) = \$1,258.70$$

She sold the bond for $6.30 less than she paid for the bond originally ($1,265.00 − $1,258.70). This produced a capital loss. Now if we separate the total rate of return into the two components, current yield and capital yield, we get the following:

Current yield = $120 ÷ $1,265.00 = 9.50%
Capital yield = −$6.30 ÷ $1,265.00 = −0.5%
                                         ≈ 9%

If we combine the interest payment cash inflows ($120) with the capital cash flow (−$6.30) we can solve for the total rate of return (ROR):

$$\text{Annual cash inflow} \div \text{Investment} = \text{ROR}$$
$$\$113.70 \div \$1,265 = 9\%$$

Again we assumed our investor purchased the bond after the movement in interest rates so we could ignore the capital gain of the previous owner.

Now we ask, why did our investor's bond value go up by exactly $265, from $1,000 to $1,265? Because this is the present value of the extra annuity. Okay, remember our investor's bond produces semiannual cash flows of $60 and new bonds offer a semiannual cash flow of $45 for a difference of $15. How long does that $15 difference persist? Over the remaining life of the bond, 36 more periods. So what is the present value of a $15 annuity discounted at the market interest rate of 4.5 percent (9% ÷ 2) for 36 periods? The answer is the amount of the premium or $265. Could we use this to find the value of the bond? Absolutely!

Par value + Present value of extra cash flows = Price
    $1,000 + $265 = $1,265

This merely proves that there is more than one way to value a bond!

E. Tracking Bond Values

The figure below tracks the various paths our StillWave International bond value followed when market interest rates went from 12 percent to 14 percent and from 12 percent to 9 percent.

TRACKING BOND VALUES

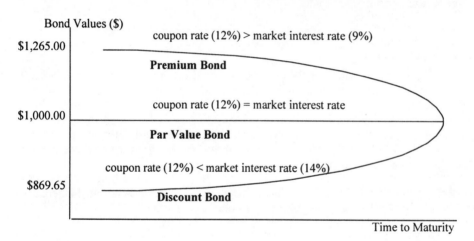

Maintaining our assumption that there are no subsequent movements in interest rates, this figure shows how the bond approaches its par value as it nears maturity.

F. Yield to Maturity (YTM)

What if our investor wanted to know the rate of return she would earn if she bought a bond and then held it until it matured? For example, what rate of return would our investor earn if she bought a seven-year, 8 percent coupon rate bond for $1,242.12 and held the bond until it matured? In other words, what is the bond's yield to maturity (YTM)? This is the obvious question any investor might ask. "If I buy a bond for $1,242.12 and hold it until it matures, what rate of return will my invested dollars earn?"

Why is the bond selling for $1,242.12 instead of $1,000? Because market interest rates have decreased. Recall that a decrease in market interest rates causes an increase in bond prices. Finding the yield to maturity takes a bit of trial and error. Keep in mind that our bond has an 8 percent coupon rate so it pays $40 semiannually and there are 14 periods (seven years) until the bond matures. Because this bond has a $1,000 payoff at the end it is not a pure annuity. We begin our effort to solve for YTM using the following formula.

$$\text{Bond Value} = \text{PMT}\left(\frac{1}{\text{int.rate}} - \frac{1}{\text{int.rate}(1+\text{int.rate})^{\text{num. of periods}}}\right) + \text{Principal}\left(\frac{1}{(1+\text{int. rate})^{\text{num. of periods}}}\right)$$

$$\underbrace{\hphantom{\text{Bond Value} = \text{PMT}\left(\frac{1}{\text{int.rate}} - \frac{1}{\text{int.rate}(1+\text{int.rate})^{\text{num. of periods}}}\right)}}_{\text{Annuity}} \qquad \underbrace{\hphantom{\text{Principal}\left(\frac{1}{(1+\text{int. rate})^{\text{num. of periods}}}\right)}}_{\text{Single Sum}}$$

She needs to find the interest rate that forces the value of the bond to be $1,242.12. To begin with, we know that the interest rate must be below the 8 percent coupon rate because the bond is selling at a premium. Let's begin with 6 percent.

$$\text{Bond Value} = \$60\left(\frac{1}{0.03} - \frac{1}{0.03(1.03)^{14}}\right) + \$1,000\left(\frac{1}{(1.03)^{14}}\right) = \$1,112.96$$

Using 3 percent as the semiannual discount rate gives us too low a price. From a present value standpoint this means that in order to increase this value we need to lower the discount rate. In other words, we are discounting the cash flows by too large a discount rate. To increase the present value we need to decrease the discount rate. Let's try 4 percent.

$$\text{Bond Value} = \$60\left(\frac{1}{0.02} - \frac{1}{0.02(1.02)^{14}}\right) + \$1,000\left(\frac{1}{(1.02)^{14}}\right) = \$1,242.12$$

Here we have the exact number we want so we know the correct YTM is 4 percent. Thus, If our investor buys this bond for $1,242.12, gets fourteen $40 semiannual coupon payments, and then receives the $1,000 maturity at the end of the fourteen periods, she will have earned a 4 percent return on her investment. Remember, we have to multiply our semiannual discount rate by two to move from a semiannual return (2%) to an annual return (4%).

Don't confuse the yield to maturity with the current (or interest) yield. Current yield is the coupon payment divided by the bond's price. The yield to maturity is the return the investor would earn if she bought this bond for the current price ($1,242.12 in this case) and held it until it matures. Thus, this calculation takes into account the interest payments received as well as any capital gains or losses. This is the same as solving for the annual rate of return where we took into account both the current and capital yields, except we're solving for the entire time span of investment between purchase and maturity. Again, as before, we assumed there was a one-time movement in interest rates. That is, we assumed that after market interest rates decreased to 4 percent, they did not change again throughout the life of the bond. If rates move again, this would change the value of the bond and thus change the investor's yield to maturity.

Why does the yield to maturity change if interest rates move? Because the bond valuation model implicitly assumes that the coupon payments are reinvested at the going market rate. If the market rate increases, then our investor's cash inflows are discounted at a greater rate causing their value to drop. This happens because when interest rates increase the cost of waiting goes up. A decline in rates would have the opposite impact. When an investor buys a bond, if she holds it to maturity she will earn the yield to maturity that existed on the date she purchased the bond.

G. Interest Rate Risk

Investors call the change in bond prices in response to movements in market interest rates the interest rate risk. The longer the term to maturity, the greater the change in bond prices when market interest rates move. Thus, a longer term bond is more sensitive to changes in interest rates (i.e., has bigger price swings) than a shorter term bond.

Let's examine two bonds that are identical in every way except one bond has 5 years until maturity and the other has 20 years to maturity. What happens to the value of these bonds if market interest rates move? We'll assume, for the sake of argument, that both bonds are 10 percent coupon bonds. Below we've listed the value of both bonds at various market interest rates.

Market Interest Rate	10% Coupon 5-Year Bond	10% Coupon 20-Year Bond
5%	$1,219	$1,628
10%	$1,000	$1,000
15%	$828	$685
20%	$693	$511

Notice that when market interest rates decreased to 5 percent the 5-year bond increased in value by $219, or 23 percent, while the 20-year bond increased in value by $628, or 63 percent. Alternatively, when market interest rates increased to 20 percent the value of the 5-year bond declined by $307, or 31 percent, while the 20-year bond declined in value by $489, or 49 percent. We can see this in the graphical representation below.

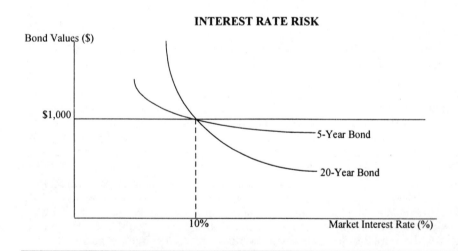

INTEREST RATE RISK

Thus, longer term bonds are more sensitive to changes in market interest rates and therefore have greater interest rate risk. From a present value standpoint this makes sense because the larger cash flow (return of the principal balance, $1,000) is further away with the 20-year bond. Remember the two things that impact present value are time and interest rates. When interest rates go up, present value declines and the effect is magnified when the largest cash flow is further away (20 years versus 5 years).

H. Zero-Coupon Bonds

Some bonds make no coupon payments at all; hence the name zero-coupon bonds. If they're not receiving any "rental" on their principal investment, what's in it for the investor? That is, why would an investor want to purchase a bond that pays zero income? Because they can buy the bond at a deep discount. Say you had the chance to purchase an 8 percent coupon bond that has 20 years left until maturity or you could buy a zero-coupon bond that also matures in 20 years. If the market interest rate is 8 percent what would you pay for each bond? The coupon bond would sell for its par value (because the coupon rate and market interest rate are equal). The zero-coupon bond's value is the present value of the $1,000, the only cash inflow this bond will produce. So the present value of $1,000 discounted at 4 percent for 40 periods is $208. So if you plunk down $208 today, you'll get $1,000 in 20 years.

Why would corporations want to issue zero-coupon bonds? Because they don't have to worry about making all those pesky interest payments. Remember interest payments made to bondholders are a contractual obligation. If the firm should fail to make an interest payment, the bondholders would force the firm into bankruptcy and sell the firm's assets to recoup their investment. With a zero-coupon bond the firm does not have that threat hanging over their head.

The caveat for our investor is the mistaken notion that she won't have to pay any taxes because there are no interim cash flows. She assumes she only has to pay taxes on capital gains and then only when those gains are realized either at the end of the bond's life or at such time that she should sell the bond. The IRS has a few choice words about this assumption—"It's a felony!" The IRS says she has to recognize the gain each year and pay taxes on the gains as the bond approaches its maturity date. So even though she received no cash inflows, she still owes taxes on the <u>unrealized</u> capital gains. Because of this quirk in the tax laws, most owners of zero-coupon bonds are tax-exempt organizations such as pension funds.

There are many other types of corporate bonds such as mortgage bonds, debentures, subordinated debentures, callable, and convertible bonds. Your textbook will explain the important differences among these types of bonds. In the next section we examine a special type of bond not issued by corporations.

I. Municipal Bonds

States, cities and towns issue municipal bonds to pay for schools, roads, waterworks projects, and the like. To encourage these municipalities to raise their own funds, the federal government doesn't tax the revenues investors receive from these bonds. This allows municipalities to issue bonds that have coupon payments lower than corporate bonds of equal risk, because the revenue isn't taxed. Investors only care about after-tax returns. This means that an investor would be indifferent between an 8 percent municipal bond that is tax free and an 11.4 percent corporate bond in which she is taxed at a rate of 30 percent. Here's the proof:

	Municipal Bond	*Corporate Bond*
Annual interest payment	$80	$114
Less: taxes on income	($0)	($34)
After-tax cash flows	$80	$80

The investor doesn't care whether she receives $80 and pays no taxes or receives $114 and pays $34 in taxes. The after-tax cash flow to her is the same in either case. What coupon rate does a corporate bond have to offer the investor to make her indifferent? We can use the following equation to find out.

Corporate bond coupon rate = $\dfrac{\text{Municipal bond coupon rate}}{(1 - \text{marginal tax rate})}$

So in our example we would have the following: $\dfrac{8\%}{(1-30\%)}$ = 11.4%

Practice Set A on the next page will give you a chance to value some bonds and calculate interest and capital yields. There are also a couple of challenge problems for those who feel ready for, well, a challenge.

NOTES:

_____

_____

_____

_____

_____

_____

_____

_____

_____

_____

_____

_____

_____

_____

_____

_____

_____

_____

_____

PRACTICE SET A
BOND VALUATION

All bonds pay interest semiannually unless otherwise noted.

1. DragonFly Robotics, Inc., issued 15 percent coupon bonds that have five years left until maturity. Market interest rates have fallen to 12 percent. What is the current value or price of a DragonFly Robotics bond?

2. Bullseye Game Corporation issued 11 percent coupon bonds that have 15 years until they mature. Market interest rates have increased to 13 percent. What is the current value or price of a Bullseye bond?

3. Cynthia doesn't want to pay $1,000 for Carry's 15-year bond that had an original maturity of 20 years. Although both the bond's coupon rate and market interest rate are 10 percent, she says she will receive 5 years fewer in interest payments. Therefore, she claims, she shouldn't have to pay the same price she did when she bought the bond. Explain to Cynthia why the bond still sells for its par value of $1,000.

4. Contrarian Investments Corporation issued 18 percent junk bonds 3 years ago. The bonds have 17 years remaining until they mature. The current market rate of interest for this type of speculative debt remains at 18 percent. What is the current value or price of a Contrarian bond?

5. NightOwl Corporation issued twenty thousand $1,000 par value, 13 percent, coupon bonds. The market rate of interest on similar debt instruments is 11 percent. The bonds have ten years until maturity. At what price will an investor be indifferent between the NightOwl bond and any new (equivalent) bond being issued? Please prove your argument numerically by showing interest and capital yields. Now assume that the market rate of interest on similar debt instruments is 15 percent instead of 11 percent. At what price will an investor be indifferent between the NightOwl bond and any new (equivalent) bond being issued? Please prove your argument numerically by showing interest and capital yields.

6. Genetic Engineering, Inc., issued two hundred $1,000 par value bonds on September 30, 1998. The bonds mature in 20 years and have an 8 percent coupon.

a. What is the value of the bond on September 30, 1999, if the market interest rate on comparable debt is 8 percent?

b. What is the value of the bond on September 30, 1999, if the market interest on comparable debt is 12 percent?

c . What is the value of the bond on September 30, 1999, if the market interest on comparable debt is 5 percent?

d. Track the path of value of an 8 percent coupon, $1,000 par value bond when market interest rates are 5, 8, and 12 percent.

7. You purchased an 18-year, 12 percent coupon bond for $1,165.47. What is your current yield? What is your yield to maturity?

8. Your marginal tax rate is 28 percent and you want to purchase a municipal bond that has a coupon rate of 7 percent. What would a corporate bond have to offer you as a coupon rate to make you indifferent between the two bonds?

9. Graphics Art Products, Inc., issued two-thousand 20-year, zero-coupon bonds. The market interest rate is 12 percent. What is the value or price of a Graphic Art's bond?

10. **Challenge Problem:** As a portfolio manager you purchased the following bonds. Two 10 percent coupon rate bonds from Zephyr Co. that had an original maturity of 10 years when they were purchased 2 years ago. Three 12 percent bonds from Kiosk Corp. that have 6 years until maturity. You also purchased seven 8 percent coupon bonds from Telnet Inc. that have 5 years until maturity. Finally, you purchased six zero-coupon Disney bonds that have 20 years until they mature. If current market interest rates are 9 percent, what is the value of your portfolio? Round to the nearest whole dollar.

11. **Challenge Problem** You expect interest rates to increase in the very near future. You want to take full advantage of the resultant price swing in the bond market. Market interest rates are currently 12 percent. You have the option to purchase the following bonds:

Three percent coupon with 12 years to maturity
Three percent coupon with 5 years to maturity
Fifteen percent coupon with 12 years to maturity
Fifteen percent coupon with 5 years to maturity

Which bond would give you the biggest percentage upswing in price should interest rates drop to, say, 10 percent? From your calculations, can you come up with a general rule about what kind of bond is most sensitive to interest rates in order to take the greatest advantage of interest rate swings (in terms of coupon rate and bond maturity)? Round your numbers to the nearest whole dollar.

III. PREFERRED STOCK VALUATION

Preferred stock is similar to common stock and resembles a bond. Hence, we refer to preferred stock as a hybrid security. Preferred stock is similar to common stock in that it pays dividends and typically does not mature (i.e., pays dividends in perpetuity). Preferred stock resembles a bond in that preferred stockholders, like bondholders, are not owners of the firm. In addition, preferred stock typically has a par value of $100 and the dividend is set as a percentage of its par value. This is the same fixed rate characteristic found in bonds, making preferred stock a fixed income security.

As we did with bonds, we value preferred stock by finding the discounted value of all the cash inflows. We know in advance what that level of cash inflows is going to be (a stated percentage of par) and we also know how long the cash inflows continue (typically forever). Let's see how this works.

Suppose you own a share of preferred stock that pays a fixed dividend of 6.5 percent. If the market rate of interest on similar securities is 8 percent, how much is your share of preferred stock worth? First, solve for the amount of the annual cash inflows. Your preferred stock pays an annual fixed dividend of 6.5 percent or $6.50 (0.065 × $100). Second, discount these cash inflows by the current 8 percent market rate of interest. Finally, add up the present value of these inflows to determine the price or value of your share of preferred stock.

$$\text{Preferred Stock Value} = \frac{\$6.50}{(1.08)^1} + \frac{\$6.50}{(1.08)^2} + \frac{\$6.50}{(1.08)^3} + \ldots + \frac{\$6.50}{(1.08)^{50}} + \ldots + \frac{\$6.50}{(1.08)^{100}} + \ldots + \frac{\$6.50}{(1.08)^\infty}$$

$$\text{Preferred Stock Value} = \$6.02 + \$5.57 + \$5.16 + \ldots + \$0.14 + \ldots + \$0.003 + \ldots + \$0.0000$$

Notice that as we get further out in time to, say, 50 or 100 years, the present value of the dividends approaches zero. Because the cash inflows are constant and last forever, you can solve the value as a discounted perpetuity.

$$\text{Perpetuity Value} = \frac{\text{Cash flow}}{\text{Discount rate}} = \text{Preferred Stock Value} = \frac{\$6.50}{0.08} = \$81.25$$

Why isn't this share of preferred stock selling for its par value of $100 dollars? Remember from our bond valuation discussion that anytime we are dealing with a fixed income security, a movement in interest rates causes an opposing movement in the price of the security. In this case, when the preferred shares were issued, the firm would have set the fixed dividend rate equal to the market rate so the shares would sell for their par value ($100).

Since these preferred shares were issued, the market rate of interest has increased from 6.5 to 8 percent. Thus, new shares of preferred stock offer $8.00 every year instead of $6.50. Everyone would rather receive $8 instead of a mere $6.50. So the only way you can sell your 6.5 percent preferred stock in a market made up of 8 percent securities is to lower your price until...your share of preferred stock offers the same rate of return as new (8 percent) preferred stock. Does this have a familiar ring to it?

How much will the preferred share sell for next year? Assuming the market rate of interest remains at 8 percent, the preferred share of stock will still sell for $81.25. As long as the market rate of interest *stays* at 8 percent, the preferred share will *continue* to sell for $81.25.

What if your share of preferred stock had a maturity date? You would have to find the present value of all the expected dividends and then add them together to find the discounted value.

In reality, preferred stock and the common stock we investigate next pay dividends on a quarterly basis. We ignored this timing element of the cash inflows because the difference between values is negligible.

IV. COMMON STOCK VALUATION

As with bonds and preferred stock, a common stock's value is the present value of all the cash inflows associated with that financial security. Common stock is similar to preferred stock in that it never matures. Thus, theoretically at least, a stock's cash inflows (i.e., dividends) continue forever.

To find the value of a share of stock our investor must estimate what the expected dividends are going to be and what interest rate to use to discount the stock's inflows.[2] Let's assume our investor, using the capital asset pricing model, finds she requires a 13 percent return on this investment. She can find the value for her share of stock as follows:

$$\text{Common stock value} = \frac{\text{Dividend}_{\text{year1}}}{(1.13)^1} + ... + \frac{\text{Dividend}_{\text{year50}}}{(1.13)^{50}} + ... + \frac{\text{Dividend}_{\text{year100}}}{(1.13)^{100}} + ... + \frac{\text{Dividend}_{\text{year}\infty}}{(1.13)^{\infty}}$$

There are some special cases where valuation is much easier, such as the case of zero growth, constant growth, and nonconstant growth followed by constant growth. We hear you ask, "What exactly is growth?" When we think of growth, we think of how much a company's business grows each year. Some firms have fairly predictable growth rates because they are long-established companies or are in an industry that has been around a long time. A public utility is a good example of a constant growth company. A public utility, such as your local power company, will probably find they can only grow as fast as the economy grows. We can measure economic growth using growth in gross domestic product (GDP).

A firm could have *zero* growth; a special case of constant growth. A zero-growth firm has peaked out and doesn't expect to be able to grow anymore. An example of a zero-growth firm is an apple producer that has limited resources (there is only so much land). Management found that it was not cost effective to get any bigger. The firm is profitable, but market analysts don't expect those profits to grow.

A firm could even have constant *negative* growth. Perhaps a firm is slowly, albeit predictably, experiencing constant negative growth. An example would be a coal mine operation whose costs increase as they dig deeper into the earth. The firm is profitable, but market analysts expect those profits to decline at a constant rate.

Many firms experience nonconstant growth followed by constant growth. For example, suppose a drug company discovers the cure for the common cold. The firm's subsequent growth would likely be phenomenal. Eventually, even with patent protection, other firms would successfully create

---

[2] Remember that dividends derive from earnings. When we say that dividends grow by a particular rate, be it constant growth, zero growth, etc., we are assuming that firms follow a constant dividend policy where dividends are paid out as a constant percentage of earnings.

acceptable substitutes, causing profits to decline as competition forces prices down. These are the models we'll explore to determine value. We'll look at each special case in turn.

A. Zero-Growth Model

If an investor owns a zero-growth stock she may logically assume that this firm would pay a constant dividend. In this case, she can use the same valuation equation she used for valuing preferred stock. That is, because the dividends are always the same (i.e., $Dividend_{year1}$ = $Dividend_{year50}$ = $Dividend_{year100}$ = $Dividend_{year\infty}$) she owns a perpetuity. If our investor's stock pays a $0.75 dividend, has a zero-growth rate, and her required rate of return is 13 percent, the value or price of her stock would be $5.77

$$\text{Common stock value} = \frac{\$0.75}{0.13} = \$5.77$$

What if her stock had an ever-changing dividend? How would she determine the value of such a share? She would have to find the present value of *all* cash inflows! But remember, in some cases, although the dividend is not the same each period, the dividends and stock price may have a constant predictable growth that makes valuation much easier than finding the present value of an infinite number of cash inflows. We call this the constant growth model.

B. Constant Growth Model

Frequently a stock's dividend and price grow at a steady rate. Thus, while the individual dividends differ (i.e., $Dividend_{year1} \neq Dividend_{year2} \neq Dividend_{year3}$), they grow at a constant rate. For example:

$$Dividend_{year1} = Dividend_{year0} [1+\text{growth rate}]$$
$$Dividend_{year2} = Dividend_{year1} [1+\text{growth rate}]$$
$$Dividend_{year3} = Dividend_{year2} [1+\text{growth rate}]$$

Do you detect a pattern? Let's assume that our investor received a dividend payment today of $0.75. She expects that dividend to grow at a constant rate of 6 percent. Then we would have the following.

$$Dividend_{year1} = \$0.75[1.06] = \$0.80$$
$$Dividend_{year2} = \$0.80[1.06] = \$0.85$$
$$Dividend_{year3} = \$0.85[1.06] = \$0.90$$

We could literally go on forever, but you get the idea. The thing to note is that the original dividend of $0.75 was a known value (i.e., she had already cashed the check). The dividends that followed for the next year (year1), and the next year (year2), and the year after that (year3) are all expected values. To account for this constant growth we adjust our valuation model as follows[3]:

$$\text{Common stock value} = \frac{Dividend_{year1}}{\text{Required rate of return} - \text{Growth rate}}$$

---

[3] This model was developed by Myron J. Gordon and is frequently called the Gordon Growth model.

If our investor had a 13 percent required rate of return, the value of her stock would be

$$\text{Common stock value} = \frac{\$0.75(1.06)}{0.13-0.06} = \frac{\$0.80}{0.07} = \$11.43$$

Remember, an investor doesn't value a security based on payments she has already received, but on the payments she *expects* to receive in the future. The constant growth model uses the dividend in year one as the numerator because it is the investor's first *expected* dividend.

Notice that with a 6 percent growth rate, the value of the stock increased from $5.77 using the zero-growth model to $11.43 with the constant growth model. From a mathematical standpoint this had to happen. The model accounts for the growth rate by reducing the amount by which the dividends are discounted. Instead of discounting the dividends by 13 percent, as the zero-growth model did, the constant growth model took out the 6 percent growth rate and discounted the dividends by only 7 percent. Remember from our present value calculations, the smaller the discount rate the larger present value. Therefore, the higher the growth rate, the smaller the discount rate applied to the dividend cash inflows, the greater the present value and hence the higher the stock price.

There are two necessary conditions for the constant growth model to work. First, the required rate of return must be greater than the growth rate or you will get a meaningless negative number. We'll show you what we mean. Suppose instead of a 6 percent growth rate, the expected rate of growth had been 15 percent. Think about this! We are saying that the firm has a growth rate of 15 percent while at the same time investors are requiring only a 13 percent return. That makes no sense at all!

$$\text{Common stock value} = \frac{\$0.75(1.15)}{0.13-0.15} = \frac{\$0.86}{-0.02} = -\$43.13$$

Literally, we would interpret this to mean that *you* would pay someone $43.13 to take this stock off your hands. This is not the way to get rich! The second necessary condition for the constant growth model to work is that the growth rate must remain constant. If the growth rate does not remain constant then we don't have a predictable set of cash inflows and we could not use the constant growth model to find the stock's value.

How do we go about finding the value of a stock that has constant negative growth? We use the same constant growth model only we recognize that the dividends are steadily declining. Let's look at an example. Suppose a manufacturing firm is operating in a declining market and analysts predict that their earnings and hence dividends will decline at a constant rate for the foreseeable future. This firm recently paid a dividend of $0.50 and the expected growth rate is a steady 5 percent. If an investor requires a 12 percent rate of return, what is the value of this stock?

$$\text{Common stock value} = \frac{\text{Dividend}_{year1}}{\text{Required rate of return} - \text{Growth rate}}$$

$$\text{Dividend}_{year1} = \text{Dividend}_{year0}\,[1+\text{growth rate}]$$

Because the growth rate is negative when we add it to 1, we get only 0.95.

$$\text{Dividend}_{year1} = \$0.50[0.95] = \$0.48$$

$$\text{Common stock value} = \frac{\$0.48}{0.12 - (0.05)} = \frac{\$0.48}{0.17} = \$28.23$$

Because the growth rate is negative we *add* the two components of the denominator to get a discount rate of 17 percent. Our final stock price for a company that has constant negative growth is $28.23.

C. Expected Rate of Return on a Constant Growth Stock

The annual cash inflow from our investor's stock investment consists of the dividend payment received and any increase in the stock's value. The two together give us our old friend:

$$\text{Annual cash inflow} \div \text{Investment} = \text{ROR}$$

Our investor can only harbor expectations about how much she will receive in her dividend payment and how much the stock's value will increase so we need to confine our vocabulary to the term expected values. Recall from our risk and return section that a stock whose expected rate of return is greater (lower) than its required rate of return is a must buy (sell). A stock whose required return equals its expected return is fairly priced (in equilibrium) and plots on the security market line.

The shareholder's expected annual cash inflow comes from two places: dividends and price appreciation (capital gains).

$$\begin{matrix} \text{Expected} \\ \text{rate} \\ \text{of return} \end{matrix} = \begin{matrix} \text{Expected} \\ \text{dividend} \\ \text{yield} \end{matrix} + \begin{matrix} \text{Expected} \\ \text{capital} \\ \text{gains yield} \end{matrix}$$

We begin with our constant growth model to solve for the expected rate of return.

$$\text{Common stock value} = \frac{\text{Dividend}_{\text{year1}}}{\begin{matrix}\text{Required rate} \\ \text{of return}\end{matrix} - \text{Growth rate}}$$

We then rewrite our constant growth model to solve for the expected rate of return.

The first thing you probably noticed when we rearranged our equation was a semantics change from *required* rate of return to *expected* rate of return. If an investment is fairly priced, the expected will equal the required and the semantics game is all for naught. We make this change in wording for an important reason. Remember, it is the investor's analysis of the security's risk that determines her *required* return. But her expected returns are based on expectations of future cash inflows. She *expects* to receive a certain size dividend payment and she *expects* to sell the stock for a certain percentage more than she paid for it.

Returning to our investor's constant growth stock investment we get the following values:

$$\text{Expected rate of return} = \frac{\$0.80}{\$11.43} + 6\% = 13\%$$

$$\text{Expected rate of return} = \underbrace{7\%}_{\substack{\text{Expected} \\ \text{dividend} \\ \text{yield}}} + \underbrace{6\%}_{\substack{\text{Expected} \\ \text{capital gains} \\ \text{yield}}} = 13\%$$

Thus, if she buys a share of stock for $11.43 *and* if she expects the stock to pay a dividend of $0.80 one year from now *and* she expects dividends—and hence stock price—to grow at a constant rate of 6 percent in the future, then she has an expected rate of return of 13 percent. Notice our stock price is in equilibrium. The expected rate of return (13 percent) is equal to the required rate of return (13 percent).

You may still be asking yourself, "How do we know the stock price will grow at a constant rate of six percent?" Let's calculate the stock price one year from now and see if the price grew by 6 percent. If the stock price ($11.43) grows by 6 percent we should get $11.43(1.06)= $12.12 as a price one year from now.

$$\text{Common stock value one year from today} = \frac{\text{Dividend}_{year2}}{\text{Required rate of return} - \text{Growth rate}}$$

We are still using the next expected dividend. When we solve for the stock's value one year from today, Dividend$_{year1}$ has already been paid. If our investor wants to know the value of her stock one year from now, she will use the first *expected* dividend which in this case is Dividend$_{year2}$. We solve for this value as follows: for Dividend$_{year2}$ we multiply Dividend$_{year1}$ by one plus the growth rate (six percent in this case).

$$\text{Dividend}_{Year2} = \text{Dividend}_{Year1} [1+\text{growth rate}] = \$0.80 [1.06] = \$0.85$$

$$\text{Common stock value one year from today} = \frac{\$0.85}{0.13-0.06} = \$12.12$$

Notice that the new stock price of $12.12 is 6 percent greater than the stock price one year ago. Thus, our investor expects to make a capital gain of $12.12 − $11.43 = $0.69.

Below is our old equation:

$$\text{Annual cash inflow} \div \text{Investment} = \text{ROR}$$

Rather than lump all the inflows together, we'll break our investor's annual cash inflows into two parts: cash inflow from dividends and cash inflow from stock price appreciation.

$$\text{Annual cash inflow} = \left.\begin{cases}\text{Dividends received} = \$0.80 \\ + \\ \text{Stock price appreciation} = \$0.69\end{cases}\right\} = \$1.49$$

We compare the annual cash inflow ($1.49) relative to her investment ($11.43) to determine her total rate of return.

$$\$1.49 \div \$11.43 = 13\%$$

We could also calculate our investor's expected dividend yield and the expected capital gain yield for the next year and again they would be 6 and 7 percent, respectively. The reason we are so confident without providing additional proof is that the steady growth rate ensures that this will be true as we demonstrated above. Thus, for a constant growth stock these conditions will *always* hold.

1. Investors expect earnings and therefore dividends to grow at a constant rate.

2. Investors expect the stock price to grow at this same rate.

3. The expected dividend yield is a constant.

4. The expected capital gains yield is also a constant, and it is equal to growth rate.

5. The expected total rate of return is equal to the expected dividend yield plus the expected capital gain yield (growth rate).

Practice Set B is on the next page and will give you some experience calculating the value or price of various stocks.

PRACTICE SET B
COMMON STOCK VALUATION

1. Records Inc. is a firm that archives computer records of numerous business firms to save them computer space and yet allow easy retrieval. The firm has 1 million common shares outstanding. The growth rate for Records Inc. is 6 percent and analysts expect it to remain constant for the foreseeable future. The last dividend paid ($Dividend_{year0}$) was $0.80. Investors require a 14 percent rate of return.

a. What is the current value or price of Record's stock?

b. What is the expected dividend yield?

c. What is the expected capital gain yield?

d. What is the expected total rate of return?

e. Why do we refer to each of the components in parts b, c, and d as <u>expected</u> values?

f. What is the common stock price one year from now?

g. What is the expected dividend yield one year from now?

h. What is the expected capital gain yield one year from now?

i. What is the expected total rate of return one year from now?

j. If the growth rate was 8 instead of 6 percent, what would be the value of Record's stock?

k. If the growth rate were as originally stated (6 percent) but the required rate of return increased from 14 to 16 percent, what would be the value of Record's stock?

l. Assume the required rate of return is back to its original value of 14 percent and the growth rate is still constant at 6 percent. If the last dividend paid (Dividend$_{year0}$) had been $1.00 instead of $0.80 what would be the value of Record's stock?

m. What are the two necessary conditions for the constant growth model to work?

2. Mysteries Press Incorporated has preferred stock outstanding that pays a stated rate of 9.3 percent. Investors' required rate of return is 7 percent.

a. What is the value of Mysteries' preferred stock?

b. Explain why the value is above (below) the par value?

3. **Challenge Problem:** Pendulum Mining Company's ore reserves are being depleted, so its sales are falling. Also, its pit is getting deeper each year, so its costs are increasing. As a result, the company's earnings and dividends are declining at the constant rate of 10 percent per year. If the last dividend paid was $6 and investors' required rate of return was 15 percent, what is the value of Pendulum Mining's stock?

D. Supernormal, or Nonconstant, Growth

Firms and their products typically go through a life cycle. During the early part of the cycle their growth is much faster than the economy's. Eventually, however, competition and market saturation cause this supergrowth to decline to a constant rate. As a demonstration we'll use Mouse Trap, Inc. as our example of a supergrowth company.

Mouse Trap, Inc., has built a better mouse trap and the world is currently beating a path to their door. Analysts expect their dividends to grow at a rate of 20 percent for the next two years. After two years, business analysts expect competitors will be able to successfully copy Mouse Trap's ingenious invention. The resulting competition and saturation of the market place (there are only so many doomed mice out there) make analysts believe the growth rate will decline to 8 percent and remain constant. The dividend just paid was $1.00.

Nothing's changed. The stock's value is still the present value of its expected future cash inflows (dividends).

To determine the value of Mouse Trap's stock, we first find the present value of the dividends that occur during the supergrowth period. Next, we find the price of Mouse Trap's stock once the supergrowth period is over. We then discount this price back to the present time. Finally, we add the present values of the dividends during the supergrowth period to the present value of the stock following the supergrowth period to solve for the value or price an investor would be willing to pay for Mouse Trap's stock today.

Below is the summarized information for Mouse Trap, Inc.:

Stockholders' required rate of return = 14%
Years of supernormal growth = 2
Rate of dividend growth during supernormal growth period = 20%
Constant rate of growth after supernormal period = 8%
Last dividend the company paid = $1.00

FIRST: Find the present value of Mouse Trap's dividends that occur during the supergrowth period.

$Dividend_{year1}$ = $1.00(1.20) = $1.20   Present value of $Dividend_{year1}$ = $1.05[4]
$Dividend_{year2}$ = $1.20 (1.20) = $1.44   Present value of $Dividend_{year2}$ = $1.11[5]
  Sum of PVs of supergrowth dividends = $2.16

SECOND: Find the price of the supergrowth stock once the super growth period is over – at the end of the second year. The first normal (constant) growth dividend the investor expects to receive is $Dividend_{year3}$. We use the constant growth rate of 8 percent to solve for $Dividend_{year3}$ as follows:

$Dividend_{year3}$ = $Dividend_{year2}$ [1+ *constant* growth rate]
$Dividend_{year3}$ = $1.44 [1.08] = $1.56

$$\begin{matrix} \textit{Common} \\ \textit{stock value} \\ \textit{after super} \\ \textit{growth period} \end{matrix} = \frac{Dividend_{year3}}{\begin{matrix} \text{Required rate} \\ \text{of return} \end{matrix} - \text{Growth rate}} = \frac{\$1.44(1.08)}{0.14 - 0.08} = \frac{\$1.56}{0.06} = \$26.00$$

---

[4] $\$1.20\dfrac{1}{(1.14)^1} = \$1.05$

[5] $\$1.44\dfrac{1}{(1.14)^2} = \$1.11$

__THIRD__: Discount Mouse Trap's price back to the present time

 Present value of common stock price at the end of second year = $20.01[6]

__FINALLY:__ Add the present values of the dividends during the supergrowth period to the present value of the stock following the supergrowth period. This gives us the price an investor would be willing to pay for Mouse Trap's stock today.

Common stock value = $2.16 + $20.01 = $22.17

Simple, right? It always looks so easy when someone else does it, so we'll work one more example before letting you loose with a practice set.

Tell Me Or Die Investigations (TMODI) is a detective franchise that has caught on extremely well in large metropolitan areas. Analysts project the firm will enjoy three years of 30 percent growth followed by two years of 20 percent growth before competition forces a long-term growth rate of 10 percent. The last dividend paid ($Dividend_{year0}$) was $1.40. Investors require a 15 percent rate of return. What is the value of TMODI's stock?

__FIRST:__ Find the present value of the dividends that occur during TMODI's supergrowth period.

__Three years at 30 percent__

D_1 = $1.40(1.30) = $1.82 Present value of $Dividend_{year1}$ = $1.60[7]

D_2 = $1.82(1.30) = $2.37 Present value of $Dividend_{year 2}$ = $1.79[8]

D_3 = $2.37(1.30) = $3.08 Present value of $Dividend_{year 3}$ = $2.03[9]

__Two years at 20 percent__

D_4 = $3.08(1.20) = $3.70 Present value of $Dividend_{year 4}$ = $2.12[10]

D_5 = $3.70(1.20) = $4.44 Present value of $Dividend_{year 5}$ = $2.21[11]

Sum of PVs of supergrowth dividends = $9.75

__SECOND:__ Find the price of TMODI's stock once the super growth period is over. The supergrowth period is over at the end of the fifth year. The first normal (constant) growth dividend the investor expects to receive is $Dividend_{year6}$. We use the normal growth rate of 10 percent to solve for $Dividend_{year6}$ as follows:

$Dividend_{year6}$ = $Dividend_{Year5}$ [1+ *constant* growth rate]

$Dividend_{year6}$ = $4.44 [1.10] = $4.88

---

[6] $26.00 $\dfrac{1}{(1.14)^2}$ = $20.01

[7] $1.82 $\dfrac{1}{(1.15)^1}$ = $1.58

[8] $2.37 $\dfrac{1}{(1.15)^2}$ = $1.79

[9] $3.08 $\dfrac{1}{(1.15)^3}$ = $2.02

[10] $3.69 $\dfrac{1}{(1.15)^4}$ = $2.11

[11] $4.43 $\dfrac{1}{(1.15)^5}$ = $2.20

Common stock value after super growth period $= \dfrac{\text{Dividend}_{\text{year6}}}{\begin{array}{c}\text{Required rate}\\ \text{of return}\end{array} - \text{Growth rate}} = \dfrac{\$4.88}{0.15 - 0.10} = \dfrac{\$4.88}{0.05} = \$97.60$

THIRD: Discount TMODI's stock price back to the present time:

Present value of common stock value at the end of fifth year[12] $= \$48.52$

FINALLY: Add the present values of the dividends during the supergrowth period to the present value of the stock following the supergrowth period. This gives us the price an investor would be willing to pay for TMODI's stock today.

Common stock value $= \$9.75 + \$48.52 = \$58.27$

A piece of cake! Now you're ready for Practice Set C.

NOTES:

_____

_____

_____

_____

_____

_____

_____

_____

_____

_____

_____

_____

_____

_____

_____

_____

_____

_____

---

[12] $\$97.60 \dfrac{1}{(1.15)^5} = \$48.52$

PRACTICE SET C
NONCONSTANT GROWTH
STOCK VALUATION

1. Analysts expect Kraitos Cable Corporation to grow by 25 percent for the next three years. Industry experts believe that their new cable system will boost Internet speeds by more than 30 percent. Fierce competition is expected to force their growth rate to a constant 6 percent thereafter. Kraitos just paid a dividend (Dividend$_{year0}$) of $1.50. Investors' required rate of return is 17 percent. What is the value of Kraitos stock today?

2. Silver Fish Aluminum Siding has found a new method for attaching aluminum siding that guarantees no leakage, mold, or mildew when installed by a qualified contractor. This breakthrough in quality should make their company grow at a phenomenal rate of 35 percent for two years before competitors find a way to circumvent the company's patent. Wall Street expects their growth to drop to a constant 8 percent thereafter. Silver Fish just paid a dividend (Dividend$_{year0}$) of $1.00. Investors require a 15 percent rate of return. What would a rational investor be willing to pay for a share of Silver Fish stock?

3. Bells and Bows Baby Corporation expects their new self-cleaning baby bottle to be a big hit with parents. Bells and Bows expects their dividend to grow at a rate of 35 percent for the first four years, then to drop to a growth rate of 15 percent for two more years, and then settle down to a 10 percent growth rate thereafter. Bells and Bows just paid a dividend (Dividend$_{year0}$) of $2.50. Investors' required rate of return is 12 percent. What would an investor be willing to pay for their stock?

4. Stunt Inc. expects their mass-produced android (affectionately known as Datum) to be a big hit with the major movie studios. Datum can perform any stunt with no liability worries, thereby drastically reducing insurance costs. Stunt Inc. expects dividends to grow at a rate of 20 percent for the first five years, and then drop to 15 percent for the next two years, and then to fall to a steady growth rate of 12 percent. The last dividend (Dividend$_{year0}$) was $3.00. The investors' required rate of return is 16 percent. What would an investor be willing to pay for this stock?

5. **Challenge Problem:** Canton Ohio Company is experiencing a severe slump in sales. They expect their dividends to decline at a rate of 7 percent for three years. After three years Canton expects their new plant to be complete and the efficiencies of the new plant will significantly reduce costs. Canton anticipates the new plant will cause their dividends to increase at a constant rate of 8 percent into the foreseeable future. Canton just paid a dividend (Dividend$_{year0}$) of $4.00. Investors' required rate of return is 12 percent. What would an investor be willing to pay for this stock?

6. **Challenge Problem:** The Uranana Corporation has fallen on hard times. Its management expects to pay no dividends for the next two years. However, the dividend for year 3 (Dividend$_{year3}$) will be $1.00 per share and it is expected to grow at a rate of 3 percent in year 4, 6 percent in year 5, and 10 percent in year 6 and thereafter. If the required return for Uranana Corporation is 20 percent, what is the price of the stock today?

7. **<u>Challenge Problem</u>:** Dr. Watson owns and operates the Carolina Pines Kennel and she has decided to incorporate and go public. As her trusted investment banker, you are to determine the selling price for Carolina's common stock. Carolina expects the first dividend ($\text{Dividend}_{\text{year0}}$) to be \$5.00 and grow at a constant rate of 6 percent for the foreseeable future. Given Carolina's financial structure and asset investment, investors are requiring a 5 percent rate of return on their investment. Given this information, what is the value or price for Carolina's common stock?

8. **<u>Challenge Problem</u>:** The B/Slash/B Corporation has been experiencing some tough times lately. They predict their growth rate will decline by 10 percent for the next two years, then decline by 5 percent in the following two years. After that the owners are confident their new line of products will cause their growth rate to increase to 16 percent for two years and then level off to 5 percent for the foreseeable future. Investors' required rate of return is 15 percent and the last dividend paid ($\text{Dividend}_{\text{year0}}$) was \$1.50. What would an investor be willing to pay for this stock today?

SOLUTIONS
PRACTICE SET A: Bond Valuation

1. DragonFly Robotics, Inc. issued 15 percent coupon bonds that have five years left until maturity. Market interest rates have fallen to 12 percent. What is the current value or price of a DragonFly Robotics bond?

$$\text{Bond Value} = \$75\left(\frac{1}{0.06} - \frac{1}{0.06(1.06)^{10}}\right) + \$1,000\left(\frac{1}{(1.06)^{10}}\right) = \$1,110.40$$

2. Bullseye Game Corporation issued 11 percent coupon bonds that have 15 years until they mature. Market interest rates have increased to 13 percent. What is the current value or price of a Bullseye bond?

$$\text{Bond Value} = \$55\left(\frac{1}{0.065} - \frac{1}{0.065(1.065)^{30}}\right) + \$1,000\left(\frac{1}{(1.065)^{30}}\right) = \$869.42$$

3. The present value of the interest payments doesn't decline by the amount of the cash payments made to the investor because the value of the remaining interest payments are all greater because they are all five years closer. The other offsetting amount is the value of the principal that is higher because it is also five years closer.

4. Contrarian Investments Corporation issued 18 percent junk bonds 3 years ago. The bonds have 17 years remaining until they mature. The current market rate of interest for this type of speculative debt remains at 18 percent. What is the current value or price of a Contrarian bond?

$$\text{Bond Value} = \$90\left(\frac{1}{0.09} - \frac{1}{0.09(1.09)^{34}}\right) + \$1,000\left(\frac{1}{(1.09)^{34}}\right) = \$1,000$$

5. NightOwl Corporation issued twenty thousand $1,000 par value, 13 percent, coupon bonds. The market rate of interest on similar debt instruments is 11 percent. The bonds have ten years until maturity. At what price will an investor be indifferent to the NightOwl bond and any new (equivalent) bond being issued? Please prove your argument numerically by showing interest and capital yields. Now assume that the market rate of interest on similar debt instruments is 15 percent instead of 11 percent. At what price will an investor be indifferent between the NightOwl bond and any new (equivalent) bond being issued? Please prove your argument numerically by showing interest and capital yields.

Solution when interest rates on similar debt instruments is 11%

Value of the bond with 20 periods left until maturity = $1,119.50
Value of the bond with 18 periods left until maturity = $1,112.46
Dollar drop in value of bond = -$7.04

Interest yield $130÷$1,119.50 =	0.116123
Capital yield –$7.04÷$1,119.50 =	–0.006289
Total rate of return $122.96÷$1,119.50 =	11%

Solution when interest rates on similar debt instruments is 15%

Value of the bond with 20 periods left until maturity = $898.05
Value of the bond with 18 periods left until maturity = $902.94
Dollar increase in value of bond = $4.89

Interest yield $130÷$898.05 = 0.144758
Capital yield $4.89÷$898.05 = 0.005445
Total rate of return $134.89÷$898.05 = 15%

6. Genetic Engineering, Inc. issued two hundred $1,000 par value bonds on September 30, 1998. The bonds mature in 20 years and have an 8 percent coupon.

a. What is the value of the bond on September 30, 1999, if the market interest rate on comparable debt is 8 percent?

$$\text{Bond Value} = \$40\left(\frac{1}{0.04} - \frac{1}{0.04(1.04)^{38}}\right) + \$1,000\left(\frac{1}{(1.04)^{38}}\right) = \$1,000$$

b. What is the value of the bond on September 30, 1999, if the market interest on comparable debt is 12 percent?

$$\text{Bond Value} = \$40\left(\frac{1}{0.06} - \frac{1}{0.06(1.06)^{38}}\right) + \$1,000\left(\frac{1}{(1.06)^{38}}\right) = \$703.08$$

c . What is the value of the bond on September 30, 1999, if the market interest on comparable debt is 5 percent?

$$\text{Bond Value} = \$40\left(\frac{1}{0.025} - \frac{1}{0.025(1.025)^{38}}\right) + \$1,000\left(\frac{1}{(1.025)^{38}}\right) = \$1,365.23$$

d. Track the path of value of an 8 percent coupon, $1,000 par value bond when market interest rates are 5, 8, and 12 percent.

TRACKING BOND VALUES

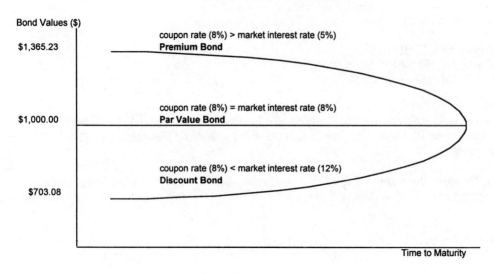

7. You purchased an18-year, 12 percent coupon bond for $1,165.47. What is your current yield? What is your yield to maturity?

Current yield = $\dfrac{\text{Coupon rate}}{\text{Price}}$ = $\dfrac{\$120}{\$1,165.47}$ = 10.3%

8. Your marginal tax rate is 28 percent and you are looking into purchasing a municipal bond that has a coupon rate of 7 percent. What would a corporate bond have to offer you as a coupon rate to make you indifferent between the two bonds?

$\dfrac{\text{Bond Equivalent}}{\text{Yield}}$ = $\dfrac{\text{Yield on Municipal Bond}}{(1 - \text{margin tax rate})}$ = $\dfrac{0.07}{(1 - .28)}$ = 9.72%

	Municipal Bond	Corporate Bond
Annual interest payment	$70	$97.20
Less: taxes on income	($0)	($27.22)
After-tax cash flows	$70	$70

9. Graphics Art Products, Inc. issued two thousand 20-year, zero-coupon bonds. The market interest rate is 12 percent. What is the value or price of a Graphic Art's bond?

$$\text{Bond Value} = +\$1,000\left(\frac{1}{(1.06)^{40}}\right) = \$97.22$$

10. **Challenge Problem:** 13,277

11. **Challenge Problem:** Three percent coupon with 12 years to maturity. The lower the coupon rate and the longer the term to maturity, the greater the resultant price movements

SOLUTIONS
PRACTICE SET B: Common Stock Valuation

1. Records Inc. is a firm that archives computer records of numerous business firms to save them computer space and yet allow easy retrieval. The firm has one million common shares outstanding. The growth rate for Records Inc. is 6 percent and analysts expect it to remain constant for the foreseeable future. The last dividend paid (Dividend$_{year0}$) was $0.80. Investors require a 14 percent rate of return.

a. What is the current value or price of Record's stock?

$$\text{Common stock value} = \frac{\$0.80(1.06)}{0.14 - 0.06} = \$10.60$$

b. What is the expected dividend yield?

$$\frac{\$0.848}{\$10.60} = 8\%$$

c. What is the expected capital gain yield?

growth rate of 6%

d. What is the expected total rate of return?

$$\frac{\$0.848}{\$10.60} + 6\% = 14\%$$

e. Why do we refer to each of the components in parts b, c, and d as <u>expected</u> values?

We are dealing with expected values not known quantities.

f. What is the stock price one year from now?

$$\frac{\$0.848(1.06)}{0.14 - 0.06} = \$11.24$$

g. What is the expected dividend yield one year from now?

$$\frac{\$0.8989}{\$11.24} = 8\%$$

h. What is the expected capital gain yield one year from now?

Growth rate of 6%

i. What is the expected total rate of return one year from now?

$$\frac{\$0.8989}{\$11.24} + 6\% = 14\%$$

j. If the growth rate were 8 instead of 6 percent, what would be the value of Record's stock?

$$\frac{\$0.80(1.08)}{0.14 - 0.08} = \$14.40$$

k. If the growth rate were as originally stated (6 percent), but the required rate of return increased from 14 to 16 percent what would be the value of Record's stock?

$$\frac{\$0.80(1.06)}{0.16 - 0.06} = \$8.48$$

l. Assume the required rate of return is back to its original value of 14 percent and the growth rate is still constant at 6 percent. If the last dividend paid (Dividend$_{year0}$) had been $1.00 instead of $0.80 what would be the value of Record's stock?

$$\frac{\$1.00(1.06)}{0.14 - 0.06} = \$13.25$$

m. What are the two necessary conditions for the constant growth model to work?

1. The required rate of return must be greater than the growth rate or you would get a meaningless negative number.
2. The growth rate must be constant.

2. Mysteries Press Incorporated has preferred stock outstanding that pays a stated rate of 9.3 percent. Investors' required rate of return on preferred stock is 7 percent.

a. What is the value of Mysteries preferred stock?

$$\frac{\$9.30}{0.07} = \$132.86$$

b. Explain why the value is above (below) the par value.

Just as with bonds (and other fixed income securities) there is an inverse relationship between prices and interest rates. Since this preferred share of stock was issued, interest rates have declined resulting in a preferred stock that is selling above its par value.

3. **Challenge Problem:**

$$\frac{\$6.00[1 + (-0.10)]}{0.15 - (-0.10)} = \frac{\$6.00(0.90)}{0.15 + 0.10} = \frac{\$5.40}{0.25} = \$21.60$$

SOLUTIONS
PRACTICE SET C: Nonconstant Stock Valuation

1. Analysts expect Kraitos Cable Corporation to grow by 25 percent for the next three years. Industry experts believe that their new cable system will boost Internet speeds by more than 30 percent. Fierce competition is expected to force their growth rate to a constant 6 percent thereafter. Kraitos just paid a dividend (Dividend$_{year0}$) of $1.50. Investors' required rate of return is 17 percent. What is the value of Kraitos stock today?

Three years at 25 percent

$D_1 = \$1.50(1.25) = \$1.87$ Present value of Dividend$_{year\ 1} = \$1.60$[13]

$D_2 = \$1.87(1.25) = \$2.34$ Present value of Dividend$_{year2} = \$1.71$[14]

$D_3 = \$2.34(1.25) = \$2.92$ Present value of Dividend$_{year3} = \underline{\$2.83}$[15]

Sum of PVs of supergrowth dividends $= \underline{\$6.14}$

Dividend$_{Year4} = \$2.92\ [1.06] = \$3.10$

$$\begin{array}{l}\textit{Common} \\ \textit{stock value} \\ \textit{after super} \\ \textit{growth period}\end{array} = \frac{\text{Dividend}_{year4}}{\begin{array}{l}\text{Required rate} \\ \text{of return}\end{array} - \text{G rowth rate}} = \frac{\$3.10}{0.17-0.06} = \frac{\$3.10}{0.11} = \$28.18$$

Present value of common stock value at the end of fourth year $= \$15.04$[16]

Common stock value $= \$6.14 + \$15.04 = \$21.18$

---

[13] $\$1.87\dfrac{1}{(1.17)^1} = \$1.60$

[14] $\$2.34\dfrac{1}{(1.17)^2} = \$1.71$

[15] $\$2.92\dfrac{1}{(1.17)^3} = \$2.83$

[16] $\$28.18\dfrac{1}{(1.17)^4} = \$15.04$

2. Silver Fish Aluminum Siding has found a new method for attaching aluminum siding that guarantees no leakage, mold or mildew when installed by a qualified contractor. This breakthrough in quality should make their company grow at a phenomenal rate of 35 percent for two years before competitors find a way to circumvent the company's patent. Wall Street expects their growth to drop to a constant 8 percent thereafter. Silver Fish just paid a dividend (Dividend$_{year0}$) of $1.00. Investors require a 15 percent rate of return. What would a rational investor be willing to pay for a share of Silver Fish stock?

Three years at 35 percent

$D_1 = \$1.00(1.25) = \$1.25$ Present value of Dividend$_{year1}$ = \$1.09[17]

$D_2 = \$1.25(1.25) = \$1.56$ Present value of Dividend$_{year2}$ = $\underline{\$1.18}$[18]

Sum of PVs of supergrowth dividends = $\underline{\$2.27}$

Dividend$_{year3} = \$1.56\,[1.08] = \$1.68$

$$\begin{array}{l}\text{Common} \\ \text{stock value} \\ \text{after super} \\ \text{growth period}\end{array} = \frac{\text{Dividend}_{year4}}{\begin{array}{l}\text{Required rate} \\ \text{of return}\end{array} - \text{Growth rate}} = \frac{\$1.68}{0.15-0.08} = \frac{\$1.68}{0.07} = \$24.00$$

Present value of common stock value at the end of fourth year = \$18.15[19]

Common stock value = \$2.27 + \$18.15 = \$20.42

---

[17] $\$1.25\dfrac{1}{(1.15)^1} = \$1.09$

[18] $\$1.56\dfrac{1}{(1.15)^2} = \$1.18$

[19] $\$24.00\dfrac{1}{(1.15)^2} = \$18.15$

3. Bells and Bows Baby Corporation expects their new self-cleaning baby bottle to be a big hit with parents. Bells and Bows expects their dividend to grow at a rate of 35 percent for the first four years, then to drop to a growth rate of 15 percent for two more years, and then settle down to a 10 percent growth rate thereafter. Bells and Bows just paid a dividend ($Dividend_{year0}$) of $2.50. Investors' required rate of return is 12 percent. What would an investor be willing to pay for their stock?

Four years at 35 percent
$D_1 = \$2.50(1.35) = \$3.38$ Present value of $Dividend_{year1} = \$3.02$[20]
$D_2 = \$3.38(1.35) = \$4.56$ Present value of $Dividend_{year2} = \$3.64$[21]
$D_3 = \$4.56(1.35) = \$6.16$ Present value of $Dividend_{year3} = \$4.38$[22]
$D_4 = \$6.16(1.35) = \$8.32$ Present value of $Dividend_{year4} = \$5.29$[23]
Two years at 15 percent
$D_5 = \$8.32(1.15) = \$9.56$ Present value of $Dividend_{year5} = \$5.42$[24]
$D_6 = \$9.56(1.15) = \$10.99$ Present value of $Dividend_{year6} = \$5.57$[25]
Sum of PVs of supergrowth dividends = $\underline{\$27.32}$

$Dividend_{year3} = \$10.99\,[1.10] = \$12.09$

$$\begin{array}{l}\textit{Common}\\\textit{stock value}\\\textit{after super}\\\textit{growth period}\end{array} = \frac{Dividend_{year4}}{\begin{array}{c}\text{Required rate}\\\text{of return}\end{array} - \text{Growth rate}} = \frac{\$12.09}{0.12-0.10} = \frac{\$12.09}{0.02} = \$604.50$$

Present value of common stock value at the end of fourth year = $306.26[26]

Common stock value = $27.32 + $306.26= $333.58

---

[20] $\$3.38\dfrac{1}{(1.12)^1} = \$3.02$

[21] $\$4.56\dfrac{1}{(1.12)^2} = \$3.64$

[22] $\$6.16\dfrac{1}{(1.12)^3} = \$4.38$

[23] $\$8.32\dfrac{1}{(1.12)^4} = \$5.29$

[24] $\$9.56\dfrac{1}{(1.12)^5} = \$5.42$

[25] $\$10.99\dfrac{1}{(1.12)^6} = \$5.57$

[26] $\$604.50\dfrac{1}{(1.12)^6} = \$306.26$

4. Stunt Inc. expects their mass-produced android (affectionately known as Datum) to be a big hit with the major movie studios. Datum can perform any stunt with no liability worries, thereby drastically reducing insurance costs. Stunt Inc. expects dividends to grow at a rate of 20 percent for the first five years, and then drop to 15 percent for the next two years, and then to fall to a steady growth rate of 12 percent. The last dividend (Dividend$_{year0}$) was $3.00. The investors' required rate of return is 16 percent. What would an investor be willing to pay for this stock?

Four years at 20 percent

D_1 = $3.00(1.20) = $3.60 Present value of Dividend$_{year1}$ = $3.10[27]

D_2 = $3.60(1.20) = $4.32 Present value of Dividend$_{year2}$ = $3.21[28]

D_3 = $4.32(1.20) = $5.18 Present value of Dividend$_{year3}$ = $3.32[29]

D_4 = $5.18(1.20) = $6.22 Present value of Dividend$_{year4}$ = $3.44[30]

D_5 = $6.22(1.20) = $7.46 Present value of Dividend$_{year5}$ = $3.55[31]

Two years at 15 percent

D_6 = $7.46(1.15) = $8.58 Present value of Dividend$_{year6}$ = $3.52[32]

D_7 = $8.58(1.15) = $9.87 Present value of Dividend$_{year7}$ = $3.50[33]

Sum of PVs of super growth dividends = $23.64

$$\text{Dividend}_{year8} = \$9.88\ [1.12] = \$11.07$$

$$\begin{array}{l}\textit{Common}\\ \textit{stock value}\\ \textit{after super}\\ \textit{growth period}\end{array} = \frac{\text{Dividend}_{year4}}{\substack{\text{Required rate} \\ \text{of return}} - \text{Growth rate}} = \frac{\$11.07}{0.16 - 0.12} = \frac{\$11.07}{0.04} = \$276.75$$

Present value of common stock value at the end of fourth year = $97.92[34]

Common stock value = $23.64 + $97.92= $121.56

5. **Challenge Problem:** $70.30

---

[27] $\$3.60\ \dfrac{1}{(1.16)^1} = \$3.10$

[28] $\$4.32\ \dfrac{1}{(1.16)^2} = \$3.21$

[29] $\$5.18\ \dfrac{1}{(1.16)^3} = \$3.32$

[30] $\$6.22\ \dfrac{1}{(1.16)^4} = \$3.44$

[31] $\$7.46\ \dfrac{1}{(1.16)^5} = \$3.55$

[32] $\$8.58\ \dfrac{1}{(1.16)^6} = \$3.52$

[33] $\$9.88\ \dfrac{1}{(1.16)^7} = \$3.50$

[34] $\$276.75\ \dfrac{1}{(1.16)^7} = \$97.92$

6. **Challenge Problem:** $6.34

7. **Challenge Problem:**   Problem can't be solved because the necessary
                                 condition that k > g does not hold.

8. **Challenge Problem:** $11.45

SECTION 5:
Capital Budgeting

I. COST OF CAPITAL

As if managers did not have enough to think about, we now introduce one of the most, if not *the* most important topic in finance – cost of capital. Cost of capital is the number that decides which projects the firm will take on and hence what profits the firm will generate. This ultimately impacts the size of our manager's compensation package so don't underestimate the motivational power of self-interest. Because the cost of capital impacts shareholders as well as our manager's personal wealth, everyone has a keen interest in its derivation and usage.

Management can only judge the value of a project by comparing the project's costs to the present value of its anticipated cash inflows. The first question our manager will ask when she tries to put this into practice is "What discount rate do I use to find the present value of the cash inflows?" The discount rate used should be whatever investors require as compensation for the use of their money.

By now we are familiar with the term *investor's required rate of return*. Now we examine the other side of that coin and recognize that an investor's required rate of return is the firm's cost of financing. If the firm uses only equity to finance their projects, then their cost of financing is shareholders' required rate of return. If investors demand 15 percent as their required return then the firm's cost of financing is 15 percent. "One woman's required return is another woman's cost of capital."

Of course, it's not quite that simple. What if our firm also uses debt or preferred stock to raise funds for capital projects? Your first thought may be to use the required rate of return for whatever funds you raise at the moment. To ignore our firm's target capital structure, however, is to make non-value-maximizing decisions (a.k.a. bad decisions). We must keep in mind that firms use a variety of financing sources and each has a different cost. The next section examines the logic behind using a weighted average of financing to determine the firm's true cost of raising capital.

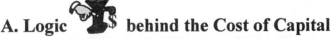

A. Logic behind the Cost of Capital

In the long run, firms tend to maintain a target capital structure (i.e., how much financing with debt relative to equity). The target capital structure typically relates to the degree of business risk and financial risk. The composition of capital (debt versus equity) tends to be consistent within an industry. In other words, industries that have high business risk tend to take on less financial risk (i.e., use less debt financing). In determining their cost of funds, firms keep in mind that, in the long run, they will maintain their target capital structure. Thus, it is irrelevant whether the firm plans to finance their next project with all debt or all equity because the firm constructs their cost of capital to reflect their long-run target capital structure that includes both debt and equity. Let's look at an example of a firm that ignores this sage advice.

Assume that Short-Term Thinking, Inc., has a target capital structure composed of 30 percent debt and 70 percent equity. Suppose further that Short-Term Thinking has an opportunity to invest in a project that offers a 12 percent rate of return. Let's assume that the firm plans to issue debt because of favorable bond market conditions. The firm's after-tax cost of debt is 8 percent. From a discounted cash flow perspective they should take the project because their cost of funds (debt at 8 percent) is well below the 12 percent rate of return offered by the project. Later the firm has the option to invest in a project that offers a 14 percent rate of return. Market conditions as well as capital structure targets now favor the issuance of common stock. The cost of equity is 15 percent. So even though this project offers a better rate of return than the 12 percent return project, they cannot accept it because their cost of funds is above the rate of return of the project.

Houston, we have a problem! By ignoring the firm's long-term objectives to maintain their target capital structure, they have accepted the inferior (lower rate of return) project. What's a firm to do? Use the weighted average cost of capital approach. Weighted average cost of capital recognizes the firm's target capital structure and weights the component costs accordingly. If Short-Term Thinking, Inc. had used the weighted average cost of capital they would have accepted the 14 percent project and rejected the 12 percent project.[1]

B. Calculating  the Cost of Capital

The first step to calculate the cost of capital is to determine the weight of each component in the firm's target capital structure. In the second step we calculate the cost of each component. Finally, we multiply each component's cost by its weight in the firm's target capital structure to get the weighted average cost of capital.

The components may include debt, preferred stock, and equity. Firms use long-term debt to finance projects in an effort to match the liabilities with the assets for repayment purposes. Some (but not all) firms use preferred stock as a permanent component in their capital structure. Equity may be either retained earnings (internal equity) or common stock (external equity). Because of the cost to issue new common stock, firms use the "cheaper" retained earnings first. If they raise enough new dollars of capital and exhaust (use up) retained earnings, they will have to start issuing the more expensive new common stock. To

---

[1] 30% debt (8%) + 70% equity (15%) = 12.90% cost of capital. The firm's cost of financing (12.9%) is greater than the first project's expected rate of return (12%) and thus acceptance of this project would cause the firm to suffer a loss. When we compare the cost of financing (12.9%) to the second project's return (14%) we see that acceptance of this project would be profitable. Thus, by ignoring their target capital structure the firm erroneously accepted the wrong project and rejected the project that would have made them money! This is not the way to make shareholders happy.

identify the sources of financing a firm's uses, we examine its balance sheet. Be sure to convert these numbers from book value to market values. We use the current *market* price for their common and preferred stock times the number of shares outstanding to solve for market value of common and preferred.[2] We solve for the market value of debt by finding the current price of any outstanding bond issue(s) and multiplying by the number of bonds the firm has outstanding. If necessary, please consult your textbook for the mechanics of solving for market values.

Examination of the Cyclops' financial statements and market data reveals the following target capital structure:

Debt = 40 percent
Preferred Stock = 10 percent
Equity = 50 percent

Thus for every dollar of new capital raised by Cyclops, 40 cents comes from borrowed funds, preferred stockholders provide 10 cents, and the firm's owners furnish 50 cents of every dollar.

C. Cost of Debt

Let's suppose Cyclops' investment bankers tell them that their before-tax cost of debt is 12 percent. The interest component of debt is a tax-deductible expense. Because the U.S. government subsidizes the cost of borrowed funds this makes the firm's after-tax cost less than 12 percent. Cyclops' marginal tax rate is 40 percent.

After-tax cost of debt = coupon rate(1 – marginal tax rate)

Cyclops' after-tax cost of debt = 0.12(1 – 0.40) = 0.072 or 7.2%

D. Cost of Preferred Stock

We saw in the valuation section how to calculate the cost of preferred stock. We want to solve for the discount rate so we have to rearrange our perpetuity value equation as follows:

$$\text{Perpetuity value} = \frac{\text{Cash flow}}{\text{Discount rate}} = \text{Discount rate} = \frac{\text{Cash flow}}{\text{Perpetuity value}}$$

Cyclops can issue 13 percent preferred. Thus, their preferred stock has a dividend of $13 (13 percent of the $100 par value). For calculating the cost of capital they have to take into account flotation costs. Investment bankers earn their fees by purchasing the preferred shares for something less than their par value. The spread between the par value ($100) and the amount the firm receives we call flotation costs and that's what pays the investment bank's underwriting fees. Let's say Cyclops has flotation costs of $3 per share. Thus, Cyclops nets $97 for each share of preferred stock that it sells to the underwriters, who in turn sell

---

[2] We do not include retained earnings because the value of these dollars is already impounded in the value of the firm's common stock.

to investors for $100. Now let's calculate the cost of preferred when we include flotation costs.

$$\text{Discount rate} = \frac{\text{Cash flow}}{\text{Perpetuity value}} = \frac{\$13.00}{\$97} = 13.40\%$$

Cyclops' cost for preferred stock is 13.40 percent. Preferred dividends, like common dividends, are not a tax-deductible expense. Thus, the government does not subsidize the firm's preferred stock costs and Cyclops has to pay the full price of issuance.

E. Cost of Retained Earnings

The cost of retained earnings is the required rate of return on the firm's common stock. Why is there a cost to retained earnings? Remember that retained earnings are the portion of net income that belongs to shareholders but is reinvested in the firm (i.e., internally generated cash inflows). Shareholders still require a return. As a matter of fact, shareholders require the same rate of return they would earn if they used this money to purchase new shares of the company. We look at retained earnings first because it is cheaper to raise money internally than have to issue new common stock because of flotation costs. To keep costs to a minimum we *always* assume that the firm uses the less expensive form of funds (retained earnings) before raising funds in the stock market (issuing new shares). The big thing to keep firmly in mind is that retained earnings are not a "free" source of cash.

Recall that the investor's required rate of return is the firm's cost of financing. We saw in the valuation section how to calculate the required rate of return for constant growth common stock as follows:

$$\frac{\text{Required rate of return}}{} = \frac{\text{Dividend}_{\text{year1}}}{\text{Stock price}} + \text{Growth rate}$$

If we assume the firm's stock price is $15, the growth rate is a constant 6 percent, and the last dividend paid (Dividend$_{\text{year0}}$) was $1.20, then the cost of retained earnings is:

$$\frac{\text{Required rate of return}}{} = \frac{\$1.20(1.06)}{\$15} + 0.06 = 14.48\%$$

Thus the firm's cost of using internally generated cash flows is 14.48 percent.

F. Cost of New Common Stock

Remember that once the firm has exhausted retained earnings they must issue new common stock that is more expensive because of flotation costs. Why didn't Cyclops include flotation costs when calculating their cost of debt? The selling syndicate of investment bankers only has to place one bond to raise $1,000, but they would have to place about 67 shares of stock ($1,000/$15) to raise the same amount of cash. So yes, there are flotation costs for bonds, but they are negligible and in the interest of simplicity we ignored them.

Now, let's get back to the business at hand. Let's assume the flotation cost for common stock is $1.00 per share. We recast the firm's stock valuation equation to take into account these flotation costs:

$$\text{Required rate of return} = \frac{\text{Dividend}_{year1}}{\text{Stock price} - \text{Flotation}} + \text{Growth rate}$$

$$\text{Required rate of return} = \frac{\$1.20(1.06)}{(\$15 - \$1)} + 0.06 = 15.09\%$$

Our cost of externally generated equity funding is 15.09 percent. When we use up retained earnings and have to issue new common stock, flotation costs increased the firm's price of owner-supplied financing by 0.61 percent from 14.48 to 15.09 percent. Now that we have all the pieces—the components used in the weighted average cost of capital and the cost of those components—let's put it all together to determine the firm's cost of raising new capital.

G. Nailing Down the Cost of Capital

Now that Cyclops has the cost and weight of each component they can put everything together and get their weighted average cost of capital. To get the weighted average, we multiply the percentage of each component in the firm's cost of capital times the after-tax cost of each component.

$$\text{Weighted average cost of capital} = \text{Percentage of debt}\left[\text{Cost of debt}\right] + \text{Percentage of preferred}\left[\text{Cost of preferred}\right] + \text{Percentage of equity}\left[\text{Cost of equity}\right]$$

$$\text{Weighted average cost of capital} = 0.40[0.072] + 0.10[0.134] + 0.50[0.1448]$$

$$= 0.0288 + 0.0134 + 0.0724 = 0.1146 \text{ or } 11.46\%$$

The firm's weighted average cost of capital is 11.46 percent. What does this mean? Well, let's say Cyclops wanted to raise $50,000 in new capital. The firm would get 40 percent or $20,000 from its creditors, 10 percent or $5,000 from preferred shareholders, and the remaining 50 percent or $25,000 from the firm's owners at a weighted average cost of 11.46 percent. You'll notice they used the cost of retained earnings for the equity component because it is the least expensive form of equity. The next obvious questions seems to be what happens when the firm runs out of the less expensive retained earnings and has to start issuing new shares of common stock? You can probably take an educated guess that the firm's cost of financing will increase. The two more interesting questions are how much can Cyclops raise in new funds before it uses up their retained earnings and what will be the new cost of raising funds once this happens?

H. Break Points in the Cost of Capital Schedule

Let's say Cyclops wants to raise $100,000 dollars. Remember they want to maintain their capital structure so 40 percent comes from debt, 10 percent from preferred stock, and 50 percent from equity. Thus, their dollar amounts would be as follows:

Debt $100,000(0.40) = $40,000
Preferred Stock $100,000(0.10) = $10,000
Equity $100,000(0.50) = $50,000
$100,000

Eventually, Cyclops will use up their retained earnings and have to issue the more expensive new common stock. When that happens, their cost of capital will increase as follows:

$$\text{Weighted average cost of capital} = \text{Percentage of debt} \begin{bmatrix} \text{Cost} \\ \text{of debt} \end{bmatrix} + \text{Percentage of preferred} \begin{bmatrix} \text{Cost of} \\ \text{preferred} \end{bmatrix} + \text{Percentage of equity} \begin{bmatrix} \text{Cost of} \\ \text{equity} \end{bmatrix}$$

$$\text{Weighted average cost of capital} = 0.40[0.072] + 0.10[0.134] + 0.50[0.1509]$$

$$= 0.0288 + 0.0134 + 0.0755 = 0.1177 \text{ or } 11.77\%$$

Notice that the component cost of equity is now 15.09 percent to reflect the higher cost of issuing new stock. Thus, when the firm exhausts their retained earnings and has to start issuing common stock, their marginal cost of capital (the cost of raising the next dollar) increases from 11.46 to 11.77 percent. This reflects the higher cost of external equity due to flotation costs.

When does this break point occur? That is, at what dollar amount does the firm run out of retained earnings and have to start issuing new common stock?

$$\text{Break point} = \frac{\text{Dollar amount of lower cost capital available}}{\text{Portion that component represents in the firm's capital structure}}$$

Let's suppose that Cyclops has $300,000 available in retained earnings. We already know that retained earnings (i.e., internal equity) represents 50 percent of the firm's target capital structure.

$$\text{Break point} = \frac{\$300,000}{0.50} = \$600,000$$

Thus, Cyclops can raise up to $600,000 in new capital before they exhaust retained earnings. So if the firm wanted to raise $600,000 in new capital it would do so accordingly:

Debt $600,000(0.40) =	$240,000
Preferred Stock $600,000(0.10) =	$60,000
Retained Earnings $600,000 (0.50) =	$300,000
Total New Capital Raised =	$600,000

We can see that at a level of $600,000 in new capital Cyclops will have exhausted their $300,000 in retained earnings. If they want to raise one dollar more ($600,001) of new capital they will have to start issuing new common stock for the equity component and the cost of capital goes up to 11.77 percent. Can there be other break points where the cost of capital increases? As we demonstrate next, the answer is yes.

I. Other Break Points in the Cost of Capital Schedule

Other break points in the marginal cost of capital schedule can also occur. What happens when Cyclops runs out of the relatively inexpensive debt? At some point in time, as they issue more and more debt, new creditors may start to demand a higher rate of return to compensate them for the perceived increase in financial risk. We'll assume that Cyclops can issue $400,000 of 12 percent debt (0.072 after tax) and after this their before-tax cost of debt will increase to 14 percent (0.084 after tax). Assuming they have already run out of retained earnings, this will cause their cost of capital to increase to:

$$\text{Weighted average cost of capital} = \text{Percentage of debt}\begin{bmatrix}\text{Cost of debt}\end{bmatrix} + \text{Percentage of preferred}\begin{bmatrix}\text{Cost of preferred}\end{bmatrix} + \text{Percentage of equity}\begin{bmatrix}\text{Cost of equity}\end{bmatrix}$$

$$\text{Weighted average cost of capital} = 0.40[0.084] + 0.10[0.134] + 0.50[0.1509]$$

$$= 0.0336 + 0.0134 + 0.0754 = 0.1224 \text{ or } 12.24\%$$

When does this break point occur? That is, at what dollar amount does the firm run out of 12 percent debt and have to start issuing 14 percent debt?

$$\text{Break point} = \frac{\text{Dollar amount of lower cost capital available}}{\text{Portion that component represents in the firm's capital structure}}$$

Remember that Cyclops can issue up to $400,000 in 12 percent debt before issuing 14 percent debt. We already know that debt represents 40 percent of their target capital structure.

$$\text{Break point} = \frac{\$400,000}{0.40} = \$1,000,000$$

Thus, Cyclops can raise up to $1,000,000 in new capital before they exhaust the lower cost debt. So if the firm wanted to raise $1,000,000 in new capital it would do so accordingly:

Debt $1,000,000(0.40) =	$400,000
Preferred Stock $1,000,000 (0.10) =	$100,000
Equity $1,000,000 (0.50) =	$500,000
Total New Capital Raised =	$1,000,000

We can see that at a level of $1,000,000 in new capital they will have exhausted their $400,000 in lower cost debt. If they want to raise one dollar more ($1,000,001) of new capital they will have to start issuing the more expensive (14 percent) bonds for the debt component and the cost of capital goes up to 12.24 percent.

J. Marginal versus Weighted Average Cost of Capital

We used the target capital structure weights multiplied by the cost of the capital structure components to calculate the weighted average cost of capital. How does the weighted average cost of capital differ from the marginal cost of capital? Sometimes the weighted average cost of capital is the marginal cost of capital, but sometimes it's not. Marginal cost, as we're sure you remember from your economics courses, means the cost of the next item or as in this case the cost of the next dollar of new capital. Let's put together the marginal cost of capital schedule for Cyclops. We have developed three costs of capital:

1. 11.46 percent before they exhaust retained earnings or lower cost debt.

2. 11.77 percent after they run out of retained earnings but before they have used up their lower cost debt.

3. 12.24 percent after they use up their retained earnings and their lower cost debt.

And, they have two break points:

1. when they run out of retained earnings ($600,000), and

2. when use up their lower cost (12 percent) debt ($1,000,000).

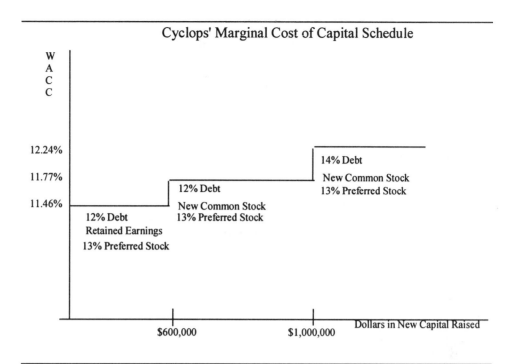

Cyclops' Marginal Cost of Capital Schedule

Notice that when Cyclops ran out of retained earnings their cost of capital for the next (marginal) dollar increased to 11.77 percent. So while 11.46 percent is still a weighted average cost of capital, 11.77 percent is the marginal cost of capital – the cost of raising the next dollar. Once the firm raises $1,000,000 dollars they exhaust their supply of 12 percent debt. Their weighted average cost of capital is 11.77 percent, but their marginal cost (i.e., the cost of raising the next dollar) is now 12.24 percent.

So we now have the marginal cost of capital schedule showing the marginal cost of capital and the break points. We now need to construct the investment opportunity schedule to see what projects the firm has available for possible investment and rank order these in terms of their rate of return.

K. Investment Opportunity Schedule

Cyclops has the following investment opportunities:

Project	Cost	Rate of Return
A	$500,000	16%
B	$100,000	14%
C	$700,000	12%
D	$300,000	10%

Now we'll construct Cyclops' investment opportunity schedule where we note the dollars of new capital needed for each project on the horizontal axis and the rate of return offered by each project on the vertical axis.

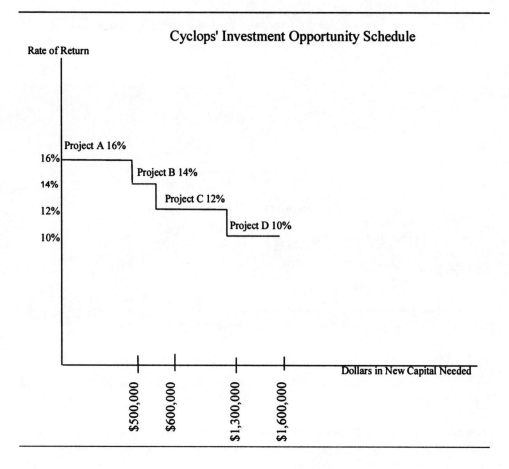

Cyclops' Investment Opportunity Schedule

L. Optimal Capital Budget

We can now combine Cyclops' marginal cost of capital schedule with their investment opportunity schedule. Where the two schedules intersect is Cyclops' optimal capital budget.

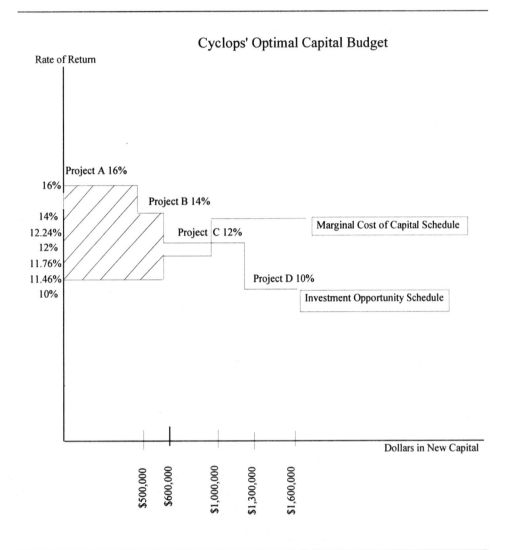

Cyclops' Optimal Capital Budget

Cyclops should accept projects A and B because their promised rate of return is greater than the firm's cost of capital. Cyclops should reject projects C and D because their promised rate of return is below the firm's cost of capital. The optimal capital budget for Cyclops is $600,000 (the required investment for projects A and B).   The highlighted area represents Cyclops' profits from accepting projects A and B.

Practice Set A is on the next page. Be sure to identify each of the components, calculate each component's cost, and then multiply the component's cost by their weights in the capital structure.

PRACTICE SET A
COST OF CAPITAL

1. Below is the balance sheet for Fire Dragon Corporation. Assume that Dragon's current stock price is $23. Dragon has 9 percent coupon mortgage bonds with 15 years left until maturity. The market interest on comparable mortgage bonds is now 8 percent. Dragon also has 13 percent coupon debentures with 10 years left until maturity. The market interest rate on comparable debentures is now 11 percent.[3] What is Dragon's capital structure?

 FIRE DRAGON CORPORATION
BALANCE SHEET
FOR THE YEAR ENDED DECEMBER 31, 2000
(Thousands of Dollars, Except Per Share Data)

ASSETS		LIABILITIES	
Cash	$3,000	Accounts Payable	$1,800
Marketable Securities	$3,000	Accrued Salaries & Wages	$1,200
Accounts Receivable	$8,000	Accrued Taxes	$2,000
Inventory	$10,000	Total Current Liabilities	$5,000
Total Current Assets	$24,000	Mortgage Bonds	$37,000
Gross Fixed Assets	$98,000	Debentures	$15,000
Accumulated Depreciation	$14,000	Total Long-Term Debt	$52,000
Net Fixed Assets	$84,000	Total Liabilities	$57,000
		SHAREHOLDER'S EQUITY	
		Common Stock (par value)	$1,000
		Additional Paid-In Capital	$15,000
		Retained Earnings	$35,000
		Total Shareholders' Equity	$51,000
Total Assets	$108,000	Total Claims	$108,000

1 Million Shares Outstanding
Current market value per share = $23

---

[3] You will need to solve for the value of these bonds as we did in the security valuation section. If you do not remember how to value bonds, please refer back to this section for a review.

2. Assume that Fire Dragon Corporation's marginal tax rate is 34 percent. Further assume that Fire Dragon maintains its current long-term capital structure that you calculated in Problem 1. If Fire Dragon can issue additional debt at a cost of 12 percent and investors require a 15 percent rate of return on their equity investment, what is Fire Dragon's weighted average cost of capital? (HINT: Fire Dragon only uses internal equity financing.)

3. Fire Dragon can issue $100,000 of 12 percent debt after which they must issue 13 percent debt. When will Fire Dragon use up their 12 percent debt? What is Fire Dragon's weighted average cost of capital once they have to issue the 13 percent debt?

 # Griffin Company

4. Griffin Company has a target capital structure of 30 percent debt and 70 percent equity. They have $250,000 in retained earnings. Investors require a 16 percent return on their equity investment. Griffin's investment banking firm has advised them they can issue $400,000 of 10 percent secured debt after which they will have to issue 12 percent debt. The beta coefficient for Griffin is 1.5, the return on treasury securities is 5 percent, while the return on the S&P 500 is 13 percent. Flotation costs for new common stock is $1 per share. The last dividend paid was $0.75 and analysts expect their constant growth rate of 6 percent to continue into the foreseeable future. Flotation cost for debt is negligible and ignored. Griffin's marginal tax rate is 40 percent.

a.   What is Griffin Company's weighted average cost of capital?

b.   Where does the break point for equity occur?

c. What is the weighted average cost of capital after the first break point?

d. Where does the break point for debt occur?

e. What is the weighted average cost of capital after the second break point?

f.   Draw Griffin's marginal cost of capital schedule.

5. **Challenge Problem:**Gargoyle Corporation has a target capital structure of 80 percent debt, 5 percent preferred stock, and 15 percent equity. Gargoyle expects earnings to be $1 million next year. The firm has traditionally paid out 70 percent of its earnings as dividends.

Gargoyle Corporation can raise $1.5 million in debt by issuing 12 percent mortgage bonds and then must issue debentures at a cost of 14 percent. Preferred stock has a fixed 13 percent dividend rate. The firm can sell their preferred stock for par value minus a 5 percent flotation cost.

The firm paid a common stock dividend of $2.50 last year (Dividend$_{year0}$) and has a constant growth rate of 8 percent. Analysts estimate the firm's beta to be 2.0. The rate of return for the market index is currently 16 percent while the return on Treasury bonds is 9 percent. Flotation costs for debt are negligible and are ignored. Flotation costs for common stock are 15 percent. Gargoyle has a 40 percent tax rate applied to all income. (*Hint*: You will need to use the CAPM to solve for the cost of retained earnings.)

a. What is the current marginal cost of capital (i.e., what is the cost of capital before the first break point)?

b. Where does the first break point occur?

c. What is the marginal cost of capital after the first break point?

d. Where does the second break point occur?

e. What is the marginal cost of capital after the second break point?

f. In the space below, draw the marginal cost of capital schedule for Gargoyle
    Corporation.

g.   Gargoyle has the following investment opportunities:

Project	Cost	Rate of Return
A	$1,000,000	14%
B	$500,000	13%
C	$700,000	12%
D	$300,000	10%

In the space below construct the investment opportunity schedule for Gargoyle.

h. In the space below combine the marginal cost of capital schedule and the investment opportunity schedule for Gargoyle and determine which projects they should accept. What is the dollar amount of Gargoyle's optimal capital budget?

M. Additional Complications

Now let's add an additional complication. (Just what you were hoping for!) What if Cyclops Corporation could only raise $400,000 of new common stock with a flotation cost of $1 and any amount after that had a flotation cost of $2 per share? Redraw the marginal cost of capital schedule with this new piece of information. Remember you'll have to find the new break point and the cost of capital after the new break point for Cyclops.

When does this break point occur? That is, at what dollar amount does the firm run out of lower cost new common stock and have to start issuing higher cost new common stock?

$$\text{Break point} = \frac{\text{Dollar amount of lower cost capital available}}{\text{Portion that component represents in the firm's capital structure}}$$

Recall that Cyclops has $300,000 available in retained earnings plus an additional $400,000 of lower cost new common stock. They have to use up *both* the retained earnings and the lower cost new common stock before issuing the higher cost common stock. We already know that equity represents 50 percent of the firm's target capital structure.

$$\text{Break point} = \frac{\$300,000 + \$400,000}{0.50} = \$1,400,000$$

Thus, Cyclops can raise up to $1,400,000 in new capital before exhausting its retained earnings and lower cost new common stock. Now let's calculate the firm's cost of capital taking into account the higher cost new common stock.

Flotation costs for common stock after the first $400,000 is $2 per share. We recast the firm's stock valuation equation to take into account these new flotation costs.

$$\begin{aligned}\text{Required rate of return} &= \frac{\text{Dividend}_{year1}}{\text{Stock price} - \text{Flotation costs}_2} + \text{Growth rate}\end{aligned}$$

$$= \frac{\$1.10(1.06)}{(\$15 - \$2)} + 6\% = 15.78\%$$

$$\begin{aligned}\text{Weighted average cost of capital} &= \text{Percentage of debt}\begin{bmatrix}\text{Cost of debt}\end{bmatrix} + \text{Percentage of preferred}\begin{bmatrix}\text{Cost of preferred}\end{bmatrix} + \text{Percentage of equity}\begin{bmatrix}\text{Cost of equity}\end{bmatrix}\end{aligned}$$

$$\begin{aligned}\text{Weighted average cost of capital} &= 0.40[0.084] + 0.10[0.134] + 0.50[0.1578]\\ &= 0.0336 + 0.0134 + 0.0789 = 0.1259 \text{ or } 12.59\%\end{aligned}$$

Remember that once the firm has raised $1,400,000 in new capital the firm has already used up retained earnings, lower cost new common stock, and its lower cost (12 percent) debt. So to raise the next dollar ($1,400,001) the firm will have to issue the higher cost new common stock ($2 flotation cost) and higher cost (14 percent) debt.

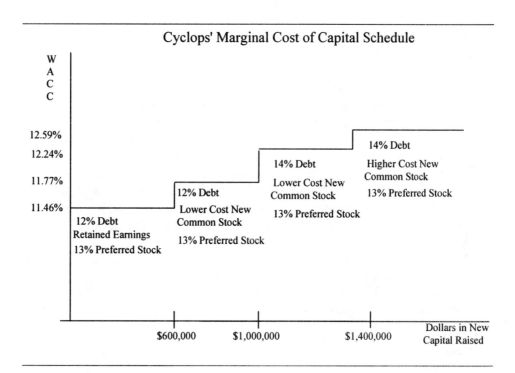

Cyclops' Marginal Cost of Capital Schedule

Time for another practice set to get this additional complication solidified in your mind. Practice Set B is on the next page.

NOTES:

PRACTICE SET B
COST OF CAPITAL WITH
ADDITIONAL COMPLICATIONS

1.   Barking Dog Industries has a capital structure of 40 percent debt and 60 percent equity. Their current stock price is $20 per share. Their investment bankers advise them that their before-tax cost of debt is 9 percent. They can raise $400,000 of 9 percent debt and after that amount they will have to offer their bond investors a 12 percent rate of return. Flotation costs for common stock are 15 percent for the first $350,000 of common stock issued. Flotation costs for common stock increases to 20 percent if they have to issue more than $350,000. The last dividend paid (Dividend$_{year1}$) was $1.30 and Barking Dog has a constant growth rate of 8 percent. Retained earnings for the year amounted to $180,000. Barking Dog is in a 40 percent tax bracket.

In the space below, calculate the firm's marginal cost of capital before and after each break point. Then on the next page construct the firm's marginal cost of capital schedule. Be sure to show *all* calculations and *meticulously* label the marginal cost of capital schedule.

BARKING DOG INDUSTRIES
MARGINAL COST OF CAPITAL SCHEDULE

2.   Snarling Cat Enterprises has a capital structure of 30 percent debt and 70 percent equity. Their current stock price is $25 per share. Their investment bankers advise them that their before-tax cost of debt is 10 percent. They can raise $100,000 of 10 percent debt and after that amount they will have to offer their bond investors a 13 percent rate of return. Flotation costs for common stock are 10 percent for the first $200,000 of common stock issued. Flotation costs for common stock increases to 15 percent if they have to issue more than $200,000. The last dividend paid (Dividend$_{year1}$) was $2.12 and Snarling Cat has a constant growth rate of 6 percent. Retained earnings for the year amounted to $150,000. Snarling Cat is in a 40 percent tax bracket.

In the space below, calculate the firm's marginal cost of capital before and after each break point. Then on the next page construct the firm's marginal cost of capital schedule. Be sure to show *all* calculations and *meticulously* label the marginal cost of capital schedule.

SNARLING CAT ENTERPRISES
MARGINAL COST OF CAPITAL SCHEDULE

3. Challenge Problem: Explain how the firm's choice of a target capital structure (i.e., the weights of debt relative to equity) might influence the firm's cost of capital.

4. Challenge Problem: Explain how the firm's dividend policy (i.e., the amount of earnings they retain) might influence the firm's cost of capital.

II. CAPITAL BUDGETING TECHNIQUES

Capital budgeting is the process of evaluating proposals for expenditures on plant and equipment. Each capital budgeting project under consideration by a particular firm will produce a series of cash flows (inflows and outflows). There will generally be an initial cash outflow, and perhaps additional cash outflows in subsequent years if the firm envisions a long start-up or construction period. In later years the project will generate cash inflows as the result of increased sales, labor savings, decreased materials waste, etc.

Suppose a manufacturing firm has the following projects under consideration for inclusion in the capital budget for next year. Both projects have an initial cost of $100,000. Project A has $0 cash inflows in the first two years followed by a $40,000 inflow in year 3, $70,000 in year 4, and $100,000 in year 5. Project B, on the other hand, has $100,000 inflow in year 1, $70,000 in year 2, $40,000 in year 3, and $0 cash inflows in years 4 and 5.

Year	Project A	Project B
0	($100,000)	($100,000)
1	$0	$100,000
2	$0	$70,000
3	$40,000	$40,000
4	$70,000	$0
5	$100,000	$0

Should the firm accept these projects? The inflows of $210,000 outweigh the $100,000 outflow for both projects. Such a simple comparison ignores the timing of cash flows. In the following sections we will examine various methods used by firms to select projects. These methods not only provide an accept–reject decision, but also provide a means for project ranking.

A. Payback

Payback measures the length of time required to recover the initial cash investment. In our example with projects A and B, payback measures how long it would take to recoup the initial $100,000 investment made at time 0. A firm may set an arbitrary number of years as the maximum acceptable payback period. In general, the decision rules state that the firm would accept all projects with payback less than or equal to the maximum acceptable payback.

What if the projects are mutually exclusive? This doesn't mean they are swank uptown projects with an attitude. Projects are mutually exclusive if acceptance of one project necessarily excludes acceptance of another. For example, let's say a manufacturing firm has two alternatives to transport their work-in-progress between operations. They could buy a conveyor belt system or use a robotic carrier. Acceptance of one method of transportation rules out selection of another (i.e., they only need one mode of transport).

If the projects are mutually exclusive, the firm will choose the project that has the lowest payback period (provided it is less than or equal to the maximum acceptable payback).

One of the problems with payback is that it favors projects with early cash flows. Thus, the firm would choose project B with a payback of 1-year over project A with a payback of 3.86 years. We compute project A's payback by figuring the cumulative cash inflows. When the cash inflows equal the initial outflow ($100,000 in this case) that gives us the payback period. For example, with project B the first year's cash inflow is equal to $100,000 so the company recoups the initial investment in the first year. For project A there are no cash inflows in the first two years, the third year produces an inflow of $40,000 leaving the firm with $60,000 left to recoup. The fourth year the firm receives an inflow of $70,000. Therefore, at some point during the fourth year the firm recoups the remaining $60,000.

Year	Inflow	Cumulative Inflow
1	$0	$0
2	$0	$0
3	$40,000	$40,000
4	$70,000	$110,000

As we see from the chart above, the firm only needs $60,000 of the $70,000 cash flow from year 4 to bring the cumulative cash inflows equal to the cash outflow. We divide $60,000 by $70,000 to find out at what point during the fourth year the firm achieves payback.

$60,000/$70,000 = 0.86. Thus, the payback period is 3.86 years.

If the maximum acceptable payback is two years then the firm will reject project A and accept project B. If the maximum acceptable payback is four years they will accept both projects unless the projects are mutually exclusive. If the projects are mutually exclusive, the firm would only accept project B because it has the lower payback signifying that the firm recovers their initial investment sooner.

Payback is easy to use, but has some inherent flaws. Projects C, D, and E below have significantly different cash flow patterns yet each project has the same two-year payback period.

Year	Project C	Project D	Project E
0	($50,000)	($50,000)	($50,000)
1	$40,000	$10,000	$10,000
2	$10,000	$40,000	$40,000
3	$10,000	$10,000	$300,000

When we compare projects C and D, the payback method is indifferent between the two projects despite the deferral of $30,000 in cash flow from year 1 to year 2. The timing of cash flows is irrelevant to the calculation of the payback. Unlike payback, the time value of money concept would clearly prefer project C to project D.

In considering project E, the payback method completely ignores the $300,000 cash flow in the third year. In fact, the payback method ignores any cash flow beyond the payback period. Despite these flaws in the payback method, firms often use it to evaluate small capital projects (i.e., $100,000 or less initial cost) and as a secondary evaluation measure that emphasizes liquidity. A project that has a payback of seven years would be less liquid than a project with a payback period of two years. Payback can also provide a crude measure of risk. For example, the project with a payback of seven years would be inherently more risky than the project with a payback of two years. Nearer term cash flows are typically easier to estimate with accuracy than cash flows that occur much further in the future. Payback is most popular with smaller, less financially sophisticated businesses.

More refined methods of project selection are net present value, internal rate of return and adjusted internal rate of return. Each of these methods bases its calculations on the time value of money concept.

B. Net Present Value

With the net present value (NPV) method the firm discounts all cash flows associated with the project back to time 0–the time of the initial cash outflow. A summation of the positive and negative present values produces the net present value.

In general, the decision rules are to accept all projects with net present value greater than or equal to 0. If the projects were mutually exclusive, the firm would choose the project that has the highest net present value (provided it is greater than or equal to zero).

In the calculation of NPV the firm must specify a required rate of return for use as a discount rate. Generally, this rate is the firm's marginal cost of capital.[4]

A positive NPV indicates that the project provides a return that is higher than the firm's cost of capital (the firm's required rate of return). An NPV of 0 indicates that the project's rate of return equals the firm's cost of capital. A project with a negative NPV provides a return that is lower than the firm's cost of capital. The NPV is a dollar measure of the change in firm value provided by the project.

In practice, firms often require that NPV be significantly greater than 0 for project acceptance. A firm would be unwilling to accept a $30 million project that the capital budgeting committee estimates will add only $50 to firm value (an NPV of $50). This is particularly reasonable considering the uncertainties surrounding cash flow estimates. A low positive NPV estimate may well turn out to be negative when the firm encounters unanticipated snags in the project.

---

[4] This is based on the assumption that any project the firm might evaluate for possible investment has the same risk as the firm. If a project's risk is higher than the average project in which the firm invests, the firm would have to adjust their cost of capital to reflect this significant difference in risk.

Let's return to our example. If our firm's marginal cost of capital is 10 percent, what is the NPV for projects C, D, and E?

$$NPV\,(C) = \frac{(\$50,000)}{(1.10)^0} + \frac{\$40,000}{(1.10)^1} + \frac{\$10,000}{(1.10)^2} + \frac{\$10,000}{(1.10)^3}$$

$$= (\$50,000) + \$36,364 + \$8,264 + \$7,513 = \$2,141$$

$$NPV\,(D) = \frac{(\$50,000)}{(1.10)^0} + \frac{\$10,000}{(1.10)^1} + \frac{\$40,000}{(1.10)^2} + \frac{\$10,000}{(1.10)^3}$$

$$= (\$50,000) + \$9,090 + \$33,058 + \$7,513 = (\$339)$$

$$NPV\,(E) = \frac{(\$50,000)}{(1.10)^0} + \frac{\$10,000}{(1.10)^1} + \frac{\$40,000}{(1.10)^2} + \frac{\$300,000}{(1.10)^3}$$

$$= (\$50,000) + \$9,090 + \$33,058 + \$225,394 = \$217,542$$

Recall that Projects C, D, and E had identical paybacks. Clearly, project E has the best NPV. Project C's NPV is also acceptable (>0) provided the projects are independent (i.e., not mutually exclusive). Net present value properly accounts for the time value of money as evidenced by the effect on NPV from reversing the first two years of cash inflows in projects C and D. Net present value also considers all cash flows (witness project E). Before we move on to the internal rate of return and adjusted internal rate of return methods, let's work a practice set to make sure we have mastered the concept and mathematics of payback and net present value.

NOTES:

_____

_____

_____

_____

_____

_____

_____

PRACTICE SET C
PAYBACK AND NET PRESENT VALUE

1. Sony expects the following cash flows from their new line of robotic animals (cash flows are in millions of dollars):

Year	Cash Flow
0	($100,000)
1	$35,000
2	$65,000
3	$40,000

a. What is the payback period?

b. What is the net present value for this project if the required rate of return (i.e., marginal cost of capital) is 18 percent?

2. Farmer Smith would like to buy a new egg incubator. The incubator would cost $48,000 and would lead to increased cash inflows of $12,000 per year over its five-year life.

a. What is the payback period for the incubator? Should Farmer Smith purchase the incubator if she wants a payback of three years or better?

b. What is the net present value of the incubator if Farmer Smith's marginal cost of capital is 12 percent? Should Farmer Smith accept the project? (*Hint:* Recognize that the cash inflows are an annuity.)

3. Keith's Rock Shop, Inc., is considering a move to a new location. Moving costs would be $120,000 (rocks are heavy and don't always roll). The more visible location should lead to an increase in sales and hence larger cash inflows. Even considering the higher rent, after-tax cash flows should be $25,000 more than in the old location in each of the next seven years. Keith believes that competition will saturate the rock market after seven years. At that time, he plans to sell his rock store and invest in a Rolling Rock beer distributorship.

a. What is the payback period for this move?

b. If Keith's marginal cost of capital is 10 percent, what is the NPV?

4. One step on the production line at Murray's Cookies is sealing cookie packages. The production supervisor has submitted a capital budgeting proposal for a new gluing machine. This machine will cost $20,000 and will produce more reliable seals, reducing product waste. Cost savings, over the five-year expected life of the machine, are as follows:

Year	Savings (Inflows)
1	$4,000
2	$4,000
3	$6,000
4	$6,000
5	$7,000

a. If Murray's marginal cost of capital is 9 percent, what is the NPV?

b. What is the NPV if the marginal cost of capital is 14 percent?

5. **Challenge Problem:** Memorial Hospital is considering the purchase of a magnetic resonance imaging machine. Memorial could obtain a used MRI machine from Discount Medical Equipment for only $19,000,000. The hospital's marginal cost of capital is 8 percent. Cash flows over the life of the machine are as follows:

Year	Cash Flow
0	($19,000,000)
1	($500,000)
2	$3,000,000
3	$12,000,000
4	$14,000,000

What is the net present value of the MRI machine?

C. Internal Rate of Return

The internal rate of return indicates what rate the firm will earn if they invest in a particular project. Technically, the internal rate of return (IRR) is the discount rate that results in a net present value equal to zero.

Recall that an NPV of zero indicates the project's rate of return equals the firm's marginal cost of capital. In general, the decision rules for IRR are to accept all projects with an internal rate of return greater than or equal to the firm's marginal cost of capital. If, however, the projects are mutually exclusive, the firm would choose the project that has the highest internal rate of return provided it is greater than or equal to the marginal cost of capital.

Let's revisit project C. Earlier our manufacturing firm found that project C had an NPV of $2,141.

Year	Project C
0	($50,000)
1	$40,000
2	$10,000
3	$10,000

What is project C's IRR? We need to find the discount rate that will cause the NPV to equal zero.

$$\frac{(\$50,000)}{(1+\text{Internal rate})^0} - \left(\frac{\$40,000}{(1+\text{Internal rate})^1} + \frac{\$10,000}{(1+\text{Internal rate})^2} + \frac{\$10,000}{(1+\text{Internal rate})^3} \right) = \$0$$

One approach to solve for IRR would be trial and error.[5] Try a particular value for IRR, see if it's too high (a negative result) or too low (a positive result). Then keep searching until you have bracketed the IRR they need. For instance, if 4 percent is too high and 3 percent is too low, they would interpolate to estimate IRR more exactly. Before when we calculated project C's NPV using a 10 percent discount rate, we got an NPV equal to $2,141.

$$\frac{(\$50,000)}{(1.10)^0} - \left(\frac{\$40,000}{(1.10)^1} + \frac{\$10,000}{(1.10)^2} + \frac{\$10,000}{(1.10)^3} \right) = \$2,141$$

This is not equal to zero. To reduce the present value of the cash flows toward zero we need to use a bigger discount rate. Using a 15 percent discount rate gives us an NPV equal to –$1,081.

$$\frac{(\$50,000)}{(1.15)^0} - \left(\frac{\$40,000}{(1.15)^1} + \frac{\$10,000}{(1.15)^2} + \frac{\$10,000}{(1.15)^3} \right) = (\$1,081)$$

---

[5] Your financial calculator will no doubt be able to solve for IRR in a more convenient fashion. We work through the mathematics so you have an appreciation for how it all comes together rather than remembering which buttons to push.

This is also not equal to zero because we used a discount rate that was too large. Let's try 13 percent.

$$\frac{(\$50,000)}{(1.13)^0} - \left(\frac{\$40,000}{(1.13)^1} + \frac{\$10,000}{(1.13)^2} + \frac{\$10,000}{(1.13)^3} \right) = \$318$$

We get an NPV equal to \$318. Still not equal to zero, but a heck of a lot closer than we were. If we stayed with it we would eventually arrive at the correct solution of 13.25 percent. We can verify the answer in the IRR calculation.

$$\frac{(\$50,000)}{(1.1325)^0} - \left(\frac{\$40,000}{(1.1325)^1} + \frac{\$10,000}{(1.1325)^2} + \frac{\$10,000}{(1.1325)^3} \right) = \$0$$

We could also solve for IRR using the net present value profile. This is a graphical representation of the net present value of a project at various discount rates. We start with a discount rate of zero and keep increasing (typically by increments of five) until the NPV crosses the horizontal axis at which point NPV equals zero. Below is the NPV profile for project C.

NET PRESENT VALUE PROFILE
FOR PROJECT C

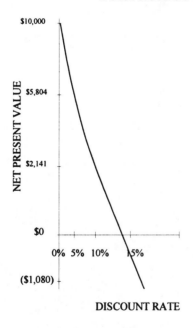

Before we turn you loose on a practice set, let's work through an example of calculating both NPV and IRR.

Lieutenant Electric (a less famous competitor of General Electric) is considering the construction of a new plant to build air conditioners. The firm has estimated the cash flows as follows:

Year	Cash Flow (in millions)
0	($400)
1	($200)
2	$0
3	$5
4-20	$120

Assume the firm has a 12 percent marginal cost of capital. Find the NPV and IRR of this project.

$$NPV = \frac{(\$400)}{(1.12)^0} + \frac{(\$200)}{(1.12)^1} + \frac{\$0}{(1.12)^2} + \frac{\$5}{(1.12)^3} +$$

$$\$120 \left(\frac{1}{0.12} - \frac{1}{0.12(1.12)^{17}} \right) \times \left(\frac{1}{(1.12)^3} \right) = \$33,100,955.40 [6]$$

Trial and error, with the help of the NPV profile, produces an internal rate of return of 12.69%.

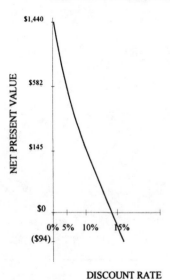

NET PRESENT VALUE PROFILE FOR AIR CONDITIONER PLANT

NET PRESENT VALUE

$1,440

$582

$145

$0

($94)

0% 5% 10% 15%

DISCOUNT RATE

Practice Set D is on the next page.

---

[6] Recall from our uneven cash flow analysis in Section 2 that we first find the present value of the annuity and then have to discount it back to time 0.

PRACTICE SET D
NET PRESENT VALUE AND
INTERNAL RATE OF RETURN

1. Prototype Industries expects the following cash flows from their new line of robotic helpmates (cash flows are in millions of dollars):

Year	Cash Flow
0	($115,000)
1	$45,000
2	$55,000
3	$65,000

Assuming their marginal cost of capital is 16 percent, find the NPV and IRR for this new project.

2. eSing is considering investment in opera arias produced specifically for the military. Sales are estimated to produce the following cash flows:

Year	Cash Flow
0	($12,000)
1	$5,000
2	$6,000
3	$7,000

Assuming their marginal cost of capital is 17 percent, find the project's NPV and IRR.

3. **Challenge Problem:** A collectible manufacturing firm is considering a new line of collectibles entitled "flying pigs." The investment will require an initial outflow of $500,000 at the beginning of the project's life and $50,000 per year for each new edition. They plan on introducing a total of five editions, one each year over the next five years. The firm's marginal cost of capital is 8 percent. The firm expects sales to generate $200,000 each year over the five years of the project's life. Use NPV and IRR to determine whether this is a good investment.

D. NPV versus IRR

Businesses widely use both NPV and IRR as capital budget evaluation criteria. Of the two, IRR is more popular. Managers prefer to compare investments on the basis of a rate of return. IRR and NPV can at times, however, provide conflicting answers. When the two methods differ, NPV gives the correct answer.

Among the projects Texas Tuba is considering is a metal polishing machine and a brass shaper. The CFO has provided the projected cash flows (in thousands) associated with the projects below:

Year	Polisher	Shaper
0	($250)	($250)
1	$100	$160
2	$100	$150
3	$250	$115

The IRRs are 29.97 and 34.23 percent for the polisher and shaper, respectively. If Texas Tuba's cost of capital is 10 percent, the NPVs are $111,382 and $105,823 for the polisher and shaper, respectively. Thus, IRR ranks the shaper higher and NPV favors the polishing machine.

One reason the difference arises is because of the assumptions implicit in the IRR and NPV calculations regarding the reinvestment of cash flows from a project. The IRR calculation assumes the firm will be able to reinvest the cash flows from the project at the IRR. Thus if the IRR is 29.97 percent as in our example, IRR assumes the firm will be able to reinvest all cash flows at 29.97 percent for the life of the project. NPV, however, assumes the firm can reinvest all cash flows at the marginal cost of capital for the life of the project.

The NPV assumption is generally felt to be more realistic. A firm that seeks to maximize its shareholders' wealth should accept all projects with positive NPVs. Thus, the marginal projects accepted would have rates of return essentially at the firm's marginal cost of capital. This makes it likely that firms would reinvest funds at the firm's marginal cost of capital.

A given set of cash flows from a project could produce a wide range of net present values depending on the discount rate (marginal cost of capital) used. If the marginal cost of capital is high, the cash flows are more heavily discounted and the NPV is lower. Remember we can construct a project's NPV profile by graphing the project's NPV as a function of the discount rate. The point at which the NPV profile crosses the x-axis (NPV = 0) is the IRR. Thus, if the NPV profile crosses the x-axis at a return of 29.97 percent, then 29.97 percent is the IRR.

The NPV profile for the polishing machine is given on the next page.

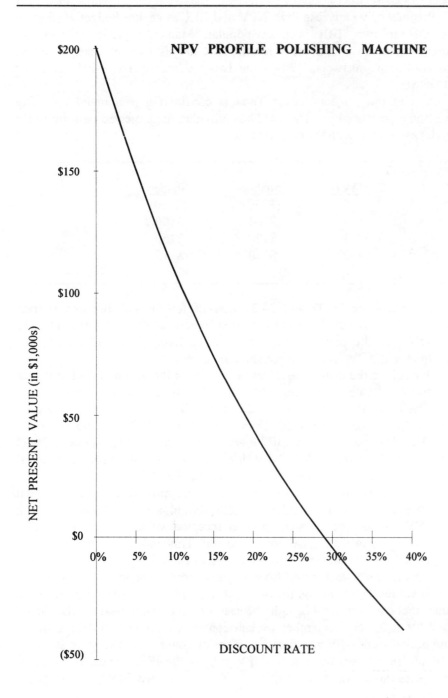

Combining two NPV profiles on one graph will reveal the *conflict zone*. The conflict zone is the range of discount rates under which NPV and IRR provide different rankings. The graph on the next page combines the NPV profiles for the polisher and the shaper. The conflict occurs because either the sizes of the projects, as measured by the initial investment, are significantly different or the timing of the cash flows is significantly different. The timing of the cash flows is the reason for the conflict between the two projects for Texas Tuba. The polisher's largest cash flows come at the end of the project's life whereas the shaper's larger cash flows come at the beginning. We see this illustrated in the graph below.

NPV PROFILES FOR POLISHING AND SHAPING MACHINES

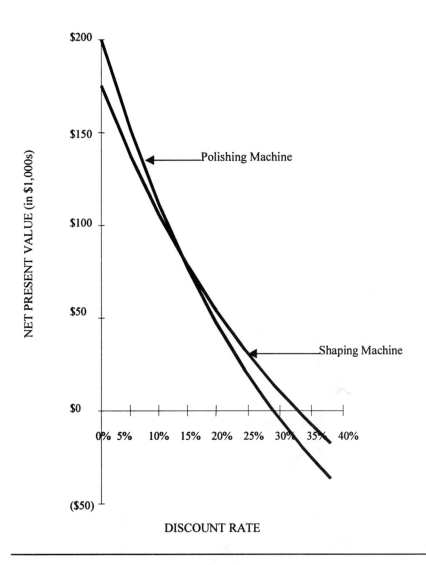

The steepness of the slope is an indication of how sensitive the project's cash flows are to changes in the discount rate (marginal cost of capital). The polishing machine has the steeper slope and thus is more sensitive to changes in the discount rate. This makes sense because the polisher's largest cash flows come at the end of the project's life, whereas the shaper's larger cash flows come at the beginning. The zone of conflict occurs when the two NPV profiles cross each other. The point of contact between the two NPV profiles is called the crossover rate. The crossover rate for the polisher and the shaper is 12.49 percent. At a discount rate of 12.49 percent the two projects have the same NPV.

We want to emphasize here that this conflict would be a moot point if these projects were independent of one another. If they were independent Texas Tuba would choose both projects because both have a positive net present value and both have an internal rate of return larger than the firm's cost of capital. The problem arises because we have to rank these projects and choose the one that is deemed the most profitable to the firm. When we rank these we have a conflict between the two ranking methods (NPV and IRR).

On the graph below notice the zone of conflict. At any discount rate below the crossover rate the NPV and IRR give different accept–reject decisions. For example, as we reported earlier the NPV and IRR for the polisher and shaper are:

	NPV	IRR
Polisher	$111,382	29.97%
Shaper	$105,823	34.23%

Thus, IRR ranks the shaper higher and NPV favors the polishing machine.

NPV PROFILES FOR POLISHING AND SHAPING MACHINES

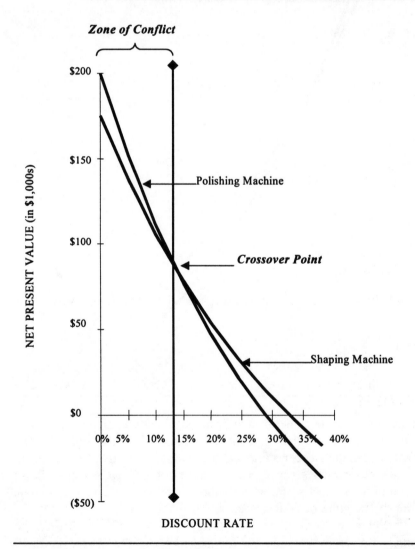

To reduce the possibility of this conflict and to incorporate the more reasonable assumption of reinvested project cash flows, we can modify the internal rate of return evaluation method to incorporate the more rational supposition that project cash inflows are reinvested at the firm's marginal cost of capital. To make this modification, we recalculate IRR with the cash flows invested at the firm's marginal cost of capital.

E. Adjusted Internal Rate of Return

The adjusted internal rate of return (AIRR) assumes reinvestment at the firm's cost of capital, yet still provides a rate of return for ranking. Usually AIRR and NPV will provide identical rankings, but they can differ if the size or timing of the cash flows of two projects is significantly different. Let's use the adjusted internal rate of return to evaluate Texas Tuba's polisher project. Remember that Texas Tuba's marginal cost of capital is 10 percent. We first have to find the future value of the inflows invested at 10 percent.

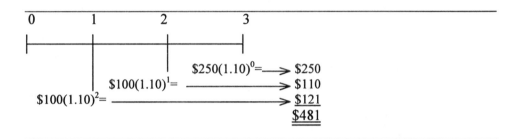

All AIRR does is find the rate of return that causes the present value of the outflows ($250) minus the future value of the reinvested inflows ($481) to be equal to zero (i.e., the discount rate that makes net present value equal to zero). Yeah, right, that's easy for us to say!

$$\frac{\$250}{(1 + \text{Modified internal rate})^0} - \frac{\$481}{(1 + \text{Modified internal rate})^3} = \$0$$

Because we only have one outflow at time zero we can simplify this a bit.

$$\$250 - \frac{\$481}{(1 + \text{Modified internal rate})^3} = \$0$$

What AIRR would equate the present value costs ($250) to the future value of cash inflows ($481)? We can rearrange our equation and solve for the AIRR as follows:

$$\frac{\$250}{\$481} = \frac{1}{(1 + \text{Modified internal rate})^3} = 0.52$$

When we look across three years (the life of the polisher project) on the present value table we find 0.52 under the 24 percent column. The adjusted internal rate of return is, therefore, equal to about 24 percent (24.38 percent to be precise).

$$\$250 - \frac{\$481}{(1.2438)^3} = \$0$$

The IRR decision rules state that the IRR of any *acceptable* project is above the firm's marginal cost of capital. Thus we can also say that the AIRR of any *acceptable* project will always be below the IRR. This is true because for any *acceptable* project, the AIRR always assumes investment at the lower marginal cost of capital rate. This is proven in our example by the fact that the AIRR of 24 percent is below the polisher's IRR of 29.97 percent. Before we move on to Practice Set E, let's work through one more example using Texas Tuba's shaper project.

We still assume that the required rate of return is 10 percent (i.e., the marginal cost of capital is 10 percent). The cash flows for the shaper machine are as follows:

Year	Shaper
0	($250)
1	$160
2	$150
3	$115

We first have to find the future value of the inflows invested at 10 percent.

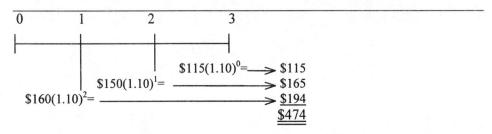

Remember that AIRR finds the rate of return that makes the present value of the outflows ($250) minus the future value of the inflows ($474) equal to zero (i.e., the discount rate that makes net present value equal to zero).

$$\frac{\$250}{(1+\text{Modified internal rate})^0} - \frac{\$474}{(1+\text{Modified internal rate})^3} = \$0$$

Because we only have one outflow at time 0 we can simplify.

$$\$250 - \frac{\$474}{(1+\text{Modified internal rate})^3} = \$0$$

What AIRR would equate the present value costs ($250) to the future value of cash inflows ($474)? We can rearrange our equation and solve for the AIRR as follows:

$$\frac{\$250}{\$474} = \frac{1}{(1+\text{Modified internal rate})^3} = 0.52$$

Look across three years (the life of the shaper project) on the present value table where we find 0.52 under the 24 percent column. The adjusted internal rate of return is, therefore, equal to about 24 percent (23.73 percent to be precise).

$$\$250 - \frac{\$474}{(1.2373)^3} = \$0$$

Now the NPV and AIRR give us the same accept–reject decision. As observed below, NPV and AIRR both favor the polisher machine over the shaper.

	NPV	**AIRR**
Polisher	$111,382	24.38%
Shaper	$105,823	23.72%

As long as the projects are independent, each method (NPV, IRR and AIRR) gives the correct response—invest in the project. We run into difficulty if the projects are mutually exclusive and the projects must be ranked. When a firm must rank projects, IRR could give the wrong selection.

The internal rate of return method of project evaluation can also give faulty answers if the cash flows change signs (e.g., change from outflows to inflows and back to outflows again).[7] Practice Set E is on the next page.

NOTES:

_____

_____

_____

_____

_____

_____

_____

_____

_____

_____

_____

_____

_____

_____

_____

_____

---

[7] Consult your textbook for more discussion of this phenomenon.

PRACTICE SET E
ADJUSTED INTERNAL RATE OF RETURN

1. Medieval Travels has a marginal cost of capital of 12 percent. They are considering an investment in another private train car that would allow them to double their capacity. The cash flows from the proposed project are given below.

Year	Cash Flows
0	($25,000)
1	$12,000
2	$15,000
3	$11,000

a. What is the project's net present value (NPV)?

b. What is the project's internal rate of return (IRR)?

c. What is the project's adjusted internal rate of return (AIRR)?

2. Viking Enterprises specializes in unique antiquities. The firm has the opportunity to bid for a rare artifact that the firm would then "rent out" to museums around the world. The initial investment will be $12 million. The anticipated cash flows (in millions of dollars) from this job, if their bid is successful, are given below. Assume that the cost of capital for Viking is 11 percent.

YEAR	CASH FLOWS
0	($12,000)
1	$5,200
2	$5,200
3	$5,200

a.   What is the project's payback?

b.   What is the project's net present value (NPV)?

c. What is the project's internal rate of return (IRR)?

d. What is the project's adjusted internal rate of return (AIRR)?

3. Assume that Viking has another investment opportunity that also requires a cash investment of $12 million and has the following cash inflows (in millions of dollars): year 1, $0; year 2, $1,200; years 3 and 4, $2,200; year 5, $3,200; and years 6 and 7, $4,200. Assume that the cost of capital for Viking remains at 11 percent.

a.   What is the project's net present value (NPV)?

b.   What is the project's internal rate of return (IRR)?

c.   What is the project's adjusted internal rate of return (AIRR)?

4. **Challenge Problem:** Collegiate OnLine is a new venture from eTeach. The project requires an initial investment of $75,000. The cash inflows are estimated to be $20,000 each year of the project's four-year life. eTeach's marginal cost of capital is 15 percent. What is the project's net present value, internal rate of return and adjusted internal rate of return? Explain your answer in terms of the AIRR's fit relative to the project's NPV and IRR.

5. **<u>Challenge Problem:</u>** Columbia Books plans to begin a new product line making entire novels available on their book-shaped computers. The computers fold like a book and the reader simply downloads the latest best seller at a greatly reduced price over hardback editions. The start-up costs include an initial price tag of $275,000. The firm estimates it will have to upgrade its hardware spending an additional $225,000 in the fourth year of the project's seven-year life. The firm expects that the project will generate $150,000 in each of the project's seven years. Columbia's marginal cost of capital is 12 percent. What is the project's adjusted internal rate of return?

F.   One More Thing!

We have told you that for a firm to accept a project, the internal rate of return must be equal to or greater than the cost of capital. We've also told you that the internal rate of return is that point at which net present value is equal to zero. This is all true. Remember when we discussed stocks that were overpriced and underpriced? We said that when a stock's expected rate of return is greater than the required rate of return the stock was in disequilibrium because it is underpriced and the investor should purchase such a security. The parallel argument for capital budgeting is to invest in projects whose internal rate of return is greater than the firm's marginal cost of capital. When the internal rate of return is above the firm's marginal cost of capital the project is in disequilibrium because the project is underpriced and the firm should make the investment. When a project's internal rate of return is below the firm's marginal cost of capital the project is in disequilibrium because it is overpriced and the firm should not make the investment.

What is interesting to note is the required disequilibrium. How does a firm get projects that are underpriced? If a project is underpriced there is certainly reason for other firms to enter the playing field and bid up the price (and hence lower the possible return) of the project in question. How does a firm keep other players out so as not to instigate a bidding war? One way is to have access to resources that others do not. For example, perhaps your firm is the only one that has the raw materials to manufacture the project (e.g., only a few companies have access to Indiana limestone). You can garner government protection via a patent that guarantees you to be the only company on the playing field for a specific period of time such as a drug company that patents the cure for the common cold. You may be the only firm that has the production facilities to take advantage of a project opportunity. For example, to build a new car may take relatively fewer dollar resources for an existing car company than for anyone else. Millions of dollars are spent in industrial espionage to pry company secrets out of competitor's hands. The best way to keep others out of the bidding war is through silence. Your competitors can't bid for a project if they don't know it exists. Of course, a company can't keep silent forever because once the firm announces the project, competitors may enter the game at will. How many Beanie Baby imitations have you seen?

Thus the name of the game is to identify and take advantage of disequilibrium in the pricing of projects. Competition only serves to bid up the price and lower returns. That may be good for consumers, but does not maximize shareholder wealth.

III. CASH FLOW ESTIMATION

Evaluating a capital investment requires the financial manager to estimate expected cash flows and anticipate the project's impact on the firm's stock price. As we learned in the capital budgeting section, the value of the firm rises and falls with the acceptance of capital projects (i.e., with the expected increase or decrease in the firm's future cash inflows). Projects that produce a rate of return above the firm's marginal cost of capital increase firm value, and projects whose return falls below the firm's marginal cost of capital decrease firm value. Thus, you can see how the accuracy of cash flow estimation can have a significant impact on shareholder wealth. There are some simple rules and procedures to keep in mind when evaluating capital project cash flows.

A. Cardinal Rules of Capital Budgeting

First, you must base capital budgeting decisions on cash flows, not on accounting income. Remember the accountant may report profits even when there are no cash inflows. Capital budgeting is dependent on cash flows not paper profits. Second, we have an interest in only incremental cash flows. That is, the only relevant cash flows in capital budgeting are those directly attributable to the project. Incremental cash flows, therefore, represent the change in the firm's total cash flows that occur as a direct result of accepting or rejecting the project.

	CASH FLOWS OF THE COMPANY WITH THE PROJECT
MINUS −	CASH FLOWS OF THE COMPANY WITHOUT THE PROJECT
EQUALS =	INCREMENTAL CASH FLOWS

For example, suppose your firm has a market value of $12.5 million. You are currently evaluating whether to accept a project whose NPV is $1.2 million. The value of your firm, should you invest in this project, will be $13.7 million. The incremental cash flows are equal to the project's NPV. There are, of course, some unique considerations that we have to keep in mind when we estimate cash flows.

B. Special Considerations for Estimating Cash Flows

The greatest difficulty in capital budgeting is not the calculation of NPV, IRR, or AIRR, but the estimation of the project cash flows used to carry out the calculations. How much will the new plant cost to construct? If the firm modifies its production line, how much will these modifications reduce operating expenses and thus increase net cash inflows? If a firm replaces a piece of old equipment with a new and more modernized version, how much will the firm gain from the increased efficiency? These are but a few of the questions the financial manager must answer by consulting with the various departments including production, engineering, quality control, marketing, human resources, etc.

Some factors to consider when estimating cash flows include the recognition of sunk costs, the impact of new products on existing product lines, and the tax repercussions. Sunk costs, as you may remember from your accounting courses, are funds the firm has already spent on a particular project. These might include a marketing survey or cost of the time expended to collect information from various bidders for equipment, expert consulting advice, etc. These costs are irrelevant to the decision of project acceptance. Why? Because the firm has already spent this money. Regardless of whether the firm decides to invest in this project, the money is already gone. If the company should decide not to invest in this project they are not going to get these dollars back. If the company does invest in this project, the money is still gone. The relevant question is what return this project offers versus alternative investment opportunities. The fact that the firm has invested substantial sums in a particular project doesn't justify spending additional cash if the project has a low return. This is akin to throwing good money after bad. Let's look at a typical example.

Suppose Mr. Phelps is the manager at Queen of Hearts Casinos, Inc. He has found what he considers a good investment opportunity. Before taking his idea to the firm's Capital Budgeting Committee, he has a marketing survey done by Market Analyst, Inc. Mr. Phelps uses Market Analyst's estimate of potential cash flows to calculate the rate of return on the project. The return comes out to be only 10 percent. Queen of Hearts' marginal cost of capital is 10 percent. Mr. Phelps pays Market Analyst $25,000 for the market analysis. He goes before the Capital Budgeting Committee and argues that Queen of Hearts can only recoup this money if they make the required investment in his proposed project. As a member of the Capital Budgeting Committee what is your response?

You point out that the $25,000 paid to Market Analyst is a sunk cost. That is, Queen of Hearts must pay this $25,000 liability regardless of whether they accept the project proposed by Mr. Phelps. The $25,000 cash outflow associated with the market analysis is not a relevant cash flow specific to this project because . . . it is a sunk cost!

The firm should consider only incremental cash flows when evaluating projects. Thus, if the production department proposed replacing a piece of machinery, the firm should consider only the change in expenses, the change in sales, etc., in the analysis of whether to make the switch.

When considering a particular project we need to make sure that the associated cash inflows come from only that project. For example, suppose the powers that be at Soapers Incorporated are in the process of evaluating the introduction of a new laundry detergent called Scissors, "The soap that cuts the stains right out of your clothes." The firm already has several other detergent brands on the market. Suppose the company targets Scissors at the upper-middle class, a market niche in which the firm has not had much success. Unfortunately, Scissors only attracts the middle class away from the firm's already existing brand, Stone's Throw, "The detergent that made creek washing obsolete." What we find is that the introduction of Scissors has no incremental impact on the firm's cash inflows because all the inflows associated with Scissors come as the result of lower cash inflows for Stone's Throw. Besides sunk costs and the success of market niches and product placement there are *always* tax repercussions.

Clearly, tax policy toward a particular type of investment will have a major impact on cash flows. Thus the firm has an interest in only after-tax cash inflows. Accelerated depreciation can increase cash inflows in the early years of a project. Disposing of equipment can have an impact on depreciation recapture and hence on the firm's tax liability. When the federal government is in a particularly good mood and they want to spur capital investments, they often reinstate the Investment Tax Credit that can reduce project costs via tax credits. We'll examine the tax implications of new projects as well as the impact on taxes from equipment replacement decisions in more detail later in this section. One last proviso that needs scrutinizing is the emotional factors that become mixed in with the more quantifiable aspects of project analysis.

Every manager has his or her pet project. Time and emotional commitment may cause their cash flow estimates to be overly optimistic. Many more projects suffer cost overruns than come in under budget. After a project's completion, the firm should conduct a post-audit. The post-audit asks the tough questions: What were the actual cash outflows compared to original estimates? What were the actual cost savings, increased sales, quality improvements, etc.? What assumptions were made in determining the estimates? Did the project measure up to expectations? Holding managers accountable for their estimates through a rigorous post-audit will help ensure that estimates given for future projects will be more realistic. Everyone learns valuable lessons from their mistakes, but the faster we learn, the less costly our mistakes will be in the future.

C. Estimating Cash Outflows

Typically, the largest cash outflow is the purchase of the depreciable asset(s). Estimating the purchase price of a depreciable asset involves assessing the base price (including taxes on the purchase) plus inclusion of any shipping and installation charges. Because the investment in depreciable assets is usually the first cash outflow of the project we denote the time it occurs as time 0, the beginning of the project's expected life. Next we estimate the firm's need for working capital as a result of project acceptance.

Expanded sales will necessarily result in increased inventories, increased receivables, and perhaps more cash for daily transactions—all of which the firm must finance. Part of the financing will come from spontaneously generated liabilities (e.g., increases in accounts payable). The difference between the change in current assets and the change in current liabilities we define as the change in net working capital.

$$\Delta\text{Net working capital} = \Delta\text{Current assets} - \Delta\text{Current liabilities}$$

Because management could use working capital funds to invest in other capital projects, it is only right that they consider these funds when estimating project investment costs.

As the project approaches termination, inventories are sold off and not replaced and the firm converts the remaining receivables into cash. This produces an end-of-project cash inflow that, if all goes well, equals the net working capital investment requirement when the project began. Let's look at an example of changes in net working capital.

Northwest Clothiers, Inc., produces apparel for the well-groomed canine. The firm is considering investment in a new line of doggie sport sweaters. Management's best estimate of the additional inventory needed for the new line is $65,000. Many of the sweater sales will be made on credit and the firm's accountant expects accounts receivable to increase by $43,000. Northwest will rely on trade credit (accounts payable) to finance part of the inventory. As a result, the firm expects accounts payable to increase by $15,000. Under these conditions the increase in net working capital is $93,000.

Change in current assets:	
Increase in accounts receivable	$43,000
Increase in inventory	$65,000
Change in current liabilities:	
Increase in accounts payable	($15,000)
Change in net working capital:	$93,000

The increase in net working capital is part of the investment cash outflow at the start of the project's life. Thus, the initial investment cash outflow (cash outflow at time 0) consists of expenditures for depreciable assets and the change in net working capital.

D. Estimating Operating Cash Inflows

Capital budgeting requires the estimation of annual operating cash inflows during the estimated life of a proposed project. After-tax operating cash flows, not earnings after taxes, are the dollar amounts used to evaluate proposed capital investments. Operating cash flows typically occur over several years, where the amount in each year may differ because of varying sales revenue, production and distribution costs, materials costs, and depreciation expense.

E. Disposal Cash Flows

At this point we only need to estimate one more cash inflow, the expected cash inflow arising from the termination of the project (a.k.a. disposal or terminal cash inflow). Because capital projects have a finite life, capital budgeting analysis includes the cash inflows associated with project termination. The project's disposal cash flow consists of two parts: (1) the sale of depreciable assets and (2) the recapture of net working capital.

The cash flow from disposal of depreciable assets equals the liquidation price adjusted for any tax consequences. Recall that when a firm sells an asset for more than its book value the IRS treats the gain on the sale as taxable income. When a firm sells an asset for less than its book value, the IRS allows the firm to deduct the loss as an ordinary expense, thereby producing a tax saving for the firm. Let's look at an example to determine the cash flows from the disposal of an asset.[8]

---

[8] This topic is covered in greater detail in Section One.

Northwest Corporation sold a depreciable asset for $40,000 that they originally acquired two years ago. The company used MACRS depreciation resulting in a book value of $30,000. The company pays marginal income taxes at a rate of 34 percent.

Tax Gain: Selling the asset for more than its book value.

Selling Price	$40,000
Less Book Value	($30,000)
Taxable Gain	$10,000
Tax Rate	× 0.34
Tax Liability	$3,400

Northwest's net cash flow from disposal of the asset is the difference between cash inflows and outflows.

Cash Inflow (selling price)	$40,000
Less: Cash Outflow (taxes)	($3,400)
Net Cash Flow from Disposal of Asset	$36,600

What if they had sold the asset for only $26,000, creating a loss?

Tax Loss: Selling the asset for less than its book value.

Selling Price	$26,000
Less Book Value	($30,000)
Amount of Loss	($4,000)
Tax Rate	× 0.34
Tax Saving[9]	$1,360

Northwest's net cash flow from disposal of the asset is the difference between cash inflows and outflows

Cash Inflow (selling price)	$26,000
Add: Tax Saving	$1,360
Net Cash Flow from Disposal of Asset	$27,360

Remember we said that part of the investment in a capital project consists of any increases in net working capital such as larger receivables and bigger inventory holdings minus any incremental increase in current liabilities. At the end of a project's life, the company liquidates the current assets linked with the project and pays the current liabilities associated with the project. The difference between the current assets and the current liabilities affiliated with a

---

[9] From an income statement viewpoint, the loss has a tax savings because we can deduct the loss from taxable income. Let's assume our firm has $50,000 in taxable operating income, producing a tax liability of $17,000 ($50,000 × 0.34). Now what if our firm experiences a loss of $4,000 from the sale of a piece of equipment. Now our taxable income is $46,000 ($50,000 – $4,000 loss). Now our tax liability is $15,640 ($46,000 × 0.34). Thus, while we suffered a $4,000 loss we gained $1,360 in the form of a tax savings making the after-tax loss equal to $2,640 ($4,000 – $1,360 tax savings). While you would go broke losing a dollar to save $0.34, the tax savings does takes some of the sting out of suffering a loss.

particular project is the recognized cash flow from disposal (all handled at book values). Let's look at an example of recouping working capital.

Our canine clothier, Northwest Corporation, invested $43,000 in inventory and $65,000 in receivables as part of its investment in a proposed capital project. The company used trade credit (accounts payable) to finance $15,000 of their increase in current assets. At the end of the project, the firm will finish collecting the remaining receivables and will stop replacing inventory. Assuming that all this is done at book value and the firm is able to recoup all cash flows (i.e., all receivables pay up and all inventory is sold at book value) then the firm would have liquidated current assets in the amount of $108,000. The firm must then repay their own creditors (accounts payable) presumably at book value in the amount of $15,000. This would leave a $93,000 inflow at the end of the project's life (a disposal cash inflow).

Liquidated current assets	$108,000
Less: Amount paid to short-term creditors	($15,000)
Cash flow from disposal of net working capital	$93,000

This is the same amount as the initial investment required at the beginning of the project's life. The firm may or may not recoup all of these costs. If not, then the firm will have to make adjustments accordingly. For example, what if Northwest only expects to recoup 80 percent of their receivables while at the same time past experience has shown that 10 percent inventory is unusable due to damage and losses.

Recoupment of accounts receivable ($43,000 × 0.80)	$34,400
Recoupment of inventory ($65,000 × 0.90)	$58,500
Total liquidated current assets	$92,900
Less: Amount paid to short-term creditors	($15,000)
Cash flow from disposal of net working capital	$77,900

In this case, the firm was able to recoup only $77,900 of their initial $93,000 investment in net working capital. Before we work through a full-blown example, let's briefly review the finer points of estimating cash flows.

F. Review of Capital Cash Flows Estimation

Cash Required to Initiate the Capital Project (Outflows)

- Purchase price of depreciable asset including sales taxes, delivery, and installation charges necessary to put the asset in working order.
- Investment in net working capital.

Wait! There's More!

Operating and Disposal Cash Flows (Inflows)
- Estimate the expected operating cash inflow for each year of the proposed project's life.
- Estimate the disposal cash flows expected at the end of the project's life.
  - √ Cash flows from disposal of the depreciable asset
  - √ Cash flows from recoupment of net working capital

We next analyze the inflows and outflows from a new capital project and then we'll examine how to handle replacement analysis. In Part G, we consider a proposed project for Natasha Lighting. Our job is to decide if this is a worthwhile investment.

G. New Project Analysis Example

Natasha Lighting, Inc., is thinking of investing in a light designed for the college crowd called SeeEver. The project has the following information available:

Selling price per unit	$14.60	
Cost per unit		
Variable labor	$2.60	
Variable materials	$4.20	
Variable selling & admin.	$3.80	
Total Variable Costs	$10.60	

Equipment purchased for production of this project will cost $380,000 (including sales tax) with an additional expense of $20,000 for delivery and installation. The equipment has a MACRS five-year life. Annual fixed costs are $53,000.

According to the marketing department, the three-year project will result in sales of 200,000 units annually. The firm expects to have to purchase $400,000 more in inventory and will need $100,000 more in accounts receivable. The firm's accountant expects accounts payable to increase by $300,000 as a result of accepting this project. At the end of the project's life, the company will be able to sell the machinery for $250,000. The firm's marginal tax rate is 40 percent. The required rate of return (marginal cost of capital) used by Natasha to determine which capital projects to accept is 14 percent. Using the various evaluation techniques we learned in capital budgeting (e.g., NPV, IRR, and AIRR) determine whether the firm should accept this project. (CF = cash flows.)

Let's begin with the cash required to make the initial investment (i.e., purchase of depreciable asset and working capital investment). The fixed asset investment consists of the $380,000 purchase price plus the $20,000 for delivery and installation for a total investment in depreciable asset of $400,000. This is also the number we'll use as the depreciable base when we estimate cash flows. In addition to the depreciable asset investment the firm must also increase their net working capital as follows.

Change in current assets:

Increase in accounts receivable	$100,000
Increase in inventory	$400,000
Change in current liabilities:	
Increase in accounts payable	($300,000)
Change in net working capital	$200,000

Thus, the initial investment cash outflow at time 0 consists of expenditures for the depreciable asset and the changes in net working capital. The project has a three-year life as depicted on the time line. At the end of three years the project will produce a disposal cash flow. The time line below shows the initial cash requirements.

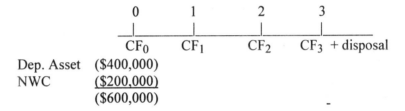

Next we use the expected number of unit sales to develop Natasha's series of cash inflows resulting from this project. To determine the cash flows, we need to calculate the asset's depreciation expense because this works as a tax shield resulting in larger cash flows. The depreciation schedule for a five-year asset is given below.

YEAR MACRS 5-YEAR CLASS LIFE

1	20%	4	12%
2	32%	5	11%
3	19%	6	6%

NEW PROJECT ANALYSIS
NATASHA LIGHTING, INC

	Year 1	Year 2	Year 3
Sales	$2,920,000	$2,920,000	$2,920,000
Less Variable Costs	$2,120,000	$2,120,000	$2,120,000
Less Fixed Costs	$53,000	$53,000	$53,000
Less Depreciation	$80,000	$128,000	$76,000
EBIT	$667,000	$619,000	$671,000
Less Taxes @ 40%	$266,800	$247,600	$268,400
Earnings After Taxes	$400,200	$371,400	$402,600
Plus Depreciation	$80,000	$128,000	$76,000
After-Tax Cash Flows	$480,200	$499,400	$478,600

Notice that we added the depreciation expense back before finding cash flows. Remember that depreciation is a noncash charge and as such works only as a tax shield and should be added back to determine cash flows. We've added the cash inflows for the three-year project to our time line below.

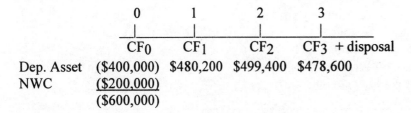

	0	1	2	3
	CF$_0$	CF$_1$	CF$_2$	CF$_3$ + disposal
Dep. Asset	($400,000)	$480,200	$499,400	$478,600
NWC	($200,000)			
	($600,000)			

Finally, we need to consider the disposal cash flows at the end of the third year. We were told that Natasha would be able to sell the depreciable asset for $250,000. To see what tax consequences there may be, we have to determine the asset's book value at the end of the third year (remember the asset has a five-year class life so the asset has not been fully depreciated). We use the book value as a means to determine if there are any taxes owed from the sale or if there are any tax savings. The book value is the amount of depreciation taken to date subtracted from the depreciable base.

	Depreciation Expense
Year 1	$80,000
Year 2	$128,000
Year 3	$76,000
Total	$284,000

Depreciable base – Depreciation expense = Book value
$400,000 – $284,000 = $116,000

- *Sale of Depreciable Asset*

Selling Price	$250,000
Less Book Value	($116,000)
Taxable Gain	$134,000
Tax Rate	× 0.40
Tax Liability	$53,600

The net cash flow from disposal of the asset is the difference between cash inflows and outflows.

Cash Inflow (selling price)	$250,000
Less: Cash Outflow (taxes)	($53,600)
Net Cash Flow from Disposal of Asset	$196,400

- *Recoupment of net working capital*

Sell off of remaining inventory	$400,000
Collection of accounts receivable	$100,000
Repayment of accounts payable	($300,000)
Recoupment of net working capital	$200,000

Thus our disposal cash flows consist of $196,400 from the sale of the depreciable asset and $200,000 from the recoupment of net working capital. We now add these cash inflows to our time line.

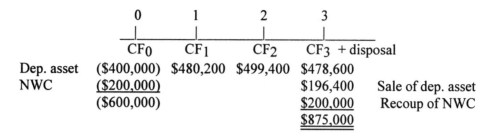

	0	1	2	3	
	CF$_0$	CF$_1$	CF$_2$	CF$_3$ + disposal	
Dep. asset	($400,000)	$480,200	$499,400	$478,600	
NWC	($200,000)			$196,400	Sale of dep. asset
	($600,000)			$200,000	Recoup of NWC
				$875,000	

Now we use the techniques from the capital budgeting section to determine if this is a project in which the firm should invest. Remember the firm's marginal cost of capital is 14 percent.

NPV = $796,100
IRR = 75.12%
AIRR = 51.06%

Needless to say, this is a profitable project. Time for a practice set before we forget everything. Work the first problem in Practice Set F and, if you feel up to it, work the challenge problem as well.

NOTES:

_____

_____

_____

_____

_____

_____

_____

_____

_____

_____

_____

PRACTICE SET F
CASH FLOW ESTIMATION: NEW PROJECT ANALYSIS

1. Spice Gingerale is considering a proposal to add a new "Red Hot" variety to their line of soft drinks. The new assets needed include a new bottling machine and a new conveyor system. The bottling machine costs $80,000 plus $10,000 for delivery and installation. The new conveyor system will cost $40,000 plus $5,000 for delivery and installation. Both machines have a three-year class life. The company will have to increase its inventory holdings by $20,000 and their accountant expects accounts receivable to increase by $35,000 if the company accepts the project. Spice Gingerale expects their current suppliers to extend additional trade credit in the amount of $15,000. Spice Gingerale expects to sell the bottling machine for $30,000 at the end of the three-year project and also expects to recover 90 percent of net working capital. Spice Gingerale anticipates keeping the conveyor for future projects.

All income is taxed at a rate of 40 percent. Project management estimates that labor and materials required to produce each case (24 bottles) of Spice Gingerale's "Red Hot" variety will be $5.00. The marketing manager expects to spend $50,000 each year for advertising the new variety. The human resource department anticipates that hiring additional personnel to run and maintain the new equipment will cost $120,000 annually. Each case of "Red Hot" Spice Gingerale will sell for $25. Spice Gingerale's cost of capital is 12 percent. Calculate all incremental cash flows associated with this project and place your results on a time line to summarize your findings. For ease of calculation and readability, round your cash flows to the nearest whole dollar. Using net present value, internal rate of return, and adjusted internal rate of return, decide whether the firm should accept this project.

Price and Cost Information

Unit selling price	$25.00	
Variable labor		$2.00
Variable materials		$3.00
Total variable costs		$5.00

Estimated Unit Sales (number of cases)

Year 1	Year 2	Year 3
70,000	90,000	110,000

Incremental Annual Fixed Costs

Salaries	$120,000	Advertising	$50,000

Depreciation Schedule: Year 3-Year Life

1	33%
2	45%
3	15%
4	7%

SPICE GINGERALE
NEW PROJECT ANALYSIS

2. Challenge Problem: The financial manager of Beagle Corporation is considering a proposal for the company to develop a new line of dry dog food. The company had previously only sold canned dog food. The new dog food will not only be nutritious but shaped in the form of little beagles. The depreciable assets needed include a new machine to make the little beagle shapes and another machine to bag the dry dog food. The shaper machine will cost $135,000 and the bagging machine will cost $85,000. Beagle will purchase both of these machines from Dog Maniacs Supply Company. The delivery and installation charges for the machines are $10,000 for the shaper and $7,000 for the bagger.

Beagle's tax experts have indicated that the sharper and the bagger will have a useful life of five years and three years, respectively. The financial manager expects the company to carry an inventory of $75,000 and to have accounts receivable of $85,000 associated with the proposed project. Beagle expects their suppliers to extend trade credit to finance $65,000 of the increase in current assets. The financial manager also expects to be able to dispose of the shaper machine for $15,000 at the end of the four-year life of the project and to recover all the net working capital in the project. Beagle expects to sell the bagger for $5,000 at the end of the project's life. Beagle's cost of capital is 13 percent.

The company uses accelerated depreciation. The company is in the 40 percent tax range. The company's cost accountant informs the financial manager that the labor and materials required to produce each bag will be $3.90 per bag, consisting of $2.40 in labor and materials and $1.50 in additional variable overhead costs. The marketing manager expects to spend $25,000 annually for advertising the new dog food. Each bag will sell for $10. The demand for the dog food is expected to vary over the project's four-year life. Personnel anticipates hiring an additional machine expert at a salary of $45,000 annually. The following table summarizes the cost and sales information.

Price and Cost Information

Unit selling price	$10.00
Unit production costs:	
Labor and material	$2.40
Variable overhead	$1.50
Total variable costs	$3.90

Estimated Unit Sales

Year 1	Year 2	Year 3	Year 4
40,000	70,000	100,000	100,000

Incremental Annual Fixed Costs

Salaries	$45,000	Advertising	$25,000

Depreciation Schedules Year	3-Year Life	5-Year Life
1	33%	20%
2	45%	32%
3	15%	19%
4	7%	12%
5		11%
6		6%

a. What are the cash flows for this project? For ease of calculation and readability, round your cash flows to the nearest whole dollar. Put your cash flows on a time line. Be sure to show your calculations so you can backtrack for checking errors.

b. Should the company accept this project (i.e., calculate the project's net present value, internal rate of return, and adjusted internal rate of return)?

H. Replacement Analysis

With replacement analysis we examine a firm's decision to replace a piece of equipment typically with a new and improved model designed to save the firm money on labor and/or operating expenses. Management needs to know the initial cash outflow taking into account the resale of the old piece of equipment and the tax implications from its removal. Management's main interest is in the after-tax cash flows produced by the purported savings on labor and/or operating expenses. Finally, management needs to recognize the difference in depreciation expense (i.e., tax shelters) between the two pieces of equipment. Remember, it's incremental cash flows that count. So, if the old machine already produces $100,000 in depreciation and management expects the new machine to generate $150,000 in depreciation, then management should account for only the difference in depreciation ($50,000) between the old and new machine.

The general method for dealing with replacement analysis is to first determine what the cash outflow is for the initial investment including the sale of the old piece of equipment and the tax consequences from the sale. Next we measure the annual cash flows on an after-tax basis and add the tax benefit or loss from the annual change in depreciation expenses. Finally, we take into account any disposal cash flows. Let's work through an example.

Stella's House of Beauty purchased a bank of hair dryers eight years ago at a cost of $10,000. The dryers had an expected life of ten years at the time of purchase and they have a disposal value of zero at the end of their lives. The company uses straight-line depreciation generating an annual depreciation charge of $1,000. The dryers' current book value is $2,000.

There is a new line of dryers out that the firm can purchase for $15,000 (including all freight and installation charges). Over their five-year life the dryers will reduce labor, repairs, and operating expenses from $9,000 down to $5,000 per year. This will cause before-tax profits for Stella's to increase by $4,000 ($9,000 – $5,000). Stella's accountant estimates they will be able to sell the new machines for $5,000 at the end of five years. Blind Man's House of Scissors, a salon across town, has offered to purchase the old dryers for $2,500. Stella's marginal tax rate is 40 percent. The firm will have to increase net working capital by $1,500 at the time of replacement. The new dryers are in a five-year MACRS class. The project's cost of capital is 12 percent. Below we show Stella's initial investment for the new dryers.

Investment Cash Outflow at Time 0

• *Purchase of Depreciable Asset*	
Cost of new equipment	$15,000
Minus market value of old equipment	($2,500)
Tax effect of sale of old equipment	$200*
Total net investment in depreciable asset	<u>$12,700</u>
• *Investment in New Working Capital*	
Increase in net working capital	$1,500

*Selling price – Book value = Gain on sale (Tax rate) = Tax liability
$2,500 – $2,000 = $500(0.40) = $200

Thus the initial investment cash outflow (cash flow at time zero) consists of the expenditure to purchase the new piece of equipment less the selling price of the old equipment, while taking into account the tax consequences of the sale (i.e., that the old piece of equipment was sold for more than its book value creating a tax liability). The net investment for the equipment is $14,200 and we show this on the project time line below.

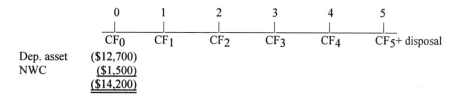

Next we determine the cash inflows for the five years of the project's life. This project generates cash flows that management must convert to an after-tax basis. To that annual amount management must add the annual change in the tax shield generated by depreciation expense. To determine the annual change in depreciation, we calculate the depreciation on the old machine and subtract the new machine's depreciation.

Year	Depreciation Old Machine	Depreciation New Machine	Δ Dep
1	$1,000	($15,000)(.20)$3,000	$2,000
2	$1,000	($15,000)(.32)$4,800	$3,800
3	$0	($15,000)(.19)$2,850	$2,850
4	$0	($15,000)(.12)$1,800	$1,800
5	$0	($15,000)(.11)$1,650	$1,650

The first annual cash flow is $4,000 (in the form of lower expenses) multiplied by one minus the tax rate to convert to an after-tax basis. To this we add the change in depreciation between the old and new machines. We can see from the chart above that the change in depreciation in the first year is $2,000. We multiply this times the tax rate to find the value of the tax shield.[10]

$$CashFlow_{year1} = (\$4,000)(1 - 0.40) + \$2,000(0.40) = \$3,200$$

Thus the after-tax cash flow for the first year is $3,200. We continue this process for the remaining years of the project's life.

$$CashFlow_{year2} = (\$4,000)(1 - 0.40) + \$3,800 (0.40) = \$3,920$$
$$CashFlow_{year3} = (\$4,000)(1 - 0.40) + \$2,850 (0.40) = \$3,540$$
$$CashFlow_{year4} = (\$4,000)(1 - 0.40) + \$1,800 (0.40) = \$3,120$$
$$CashFlow_{year5} = (\$4,000)(1 - 0.40) + \$1,650 (0.40) = \$3,060$$

We now put these project cash inflows on a time line.

---

[10] We calculate the value of the tax shield as depreciation multiplied by the tax rate. To see this from an income statement point of view, consider the following. If the depreciation expense is $2,000 and the income before depreciation is $10,000 then the firm is taxed on only $8,000. The tax without depreciation (the full $10,000) at a rate of 40 percent is $4,000 ($10,000 × 0.40). Alternatively, income with depreciation is $8,000 and the tax is $3,200 ($8,000 × 0.40). Thus the tax shield provided by depreciation is $800 or the depreciation multiplied by the tax rate ($2,000 × 0.40).

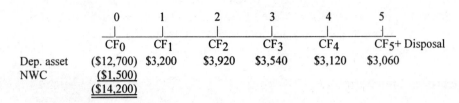

Last, we need to add disposal cash flow to the cash inflow in year 5. The firm will recoup all $1,500 in working capital and expects to sell the new dryers for $5,000. At the end of the project's life, the new dryers will have a book value of $900.

Disposal Cash Inflow
- *Sale of Depreciable Asset*

Estimated sale price of new equipment	$5,000
Tax effect of sale of new equipment	($1,640)*
Net cash inflow from disposal of depreciable asset	$3,360

- *Recoupment of Net Working Capital*

Recovery of net working capital	$1,500

---

*Selling price – Book value = Gain on sale (Tax rate) = Tax liability
$5,000 – $900 = $4,100(0.40) = $1,640

We now add the disposal cash flow to the cash flows at the end of the project's life to the time line.

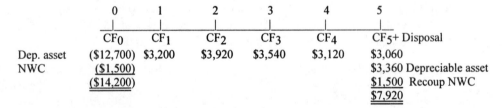

To determine whether Stella's should make this investment, we need to calculate the net present value, internal rate of return, and adjusted internal rate of return using the information from the time line above.

NPV = $778.68
IRR = 13.93%
AIRR = 13.20%

Practice Set G is on the next page.

PRACTICE SET G
CASH FLOW ESTIMATION:
REPLACEMENT ANALYSIS

1. Troll Inc. is considering replacing an old, relatively inefficient Troll injection-mold machine that was purchased three years ago with a new, more efficient model. The cost of the old machine was $7,500 and had an expected MACRS life of three years. If they sell the old machine now they would receive $1,000. However, at the end of five years the old machine is worthless. The cost of the new machine is $12,000 and would require an increase in inventory of $1,500. Suppliers would grant the firm an additional $500 in trade credit for the new level of inventory. The expected life of the new machine is three years and will reduce annual labor expenses from $10,000 to $4,000. At the end of the project the firm will be able to sell the new machine for $3,000 and recoup their investment in working capital. The firm has a marginal tax rate of 40 percent. Troll's marginal cost of capital is 12 percent, and they depreciate all equipment using MACRS. For ease of calculation and readability, round your cash flows to the nearest whole dollar. Using net present value, internal rate of return, and adjusted internal rate of return decide whether they should accept this project.

YEAR MACRS 3-YEAR
YEAR	MACRS 3-YEAR
1	33%
2	45%
3	15%
4	7%

2. **Challenge Problem**: Toucan Industries is thinking about replacing one of its machines with a more efficient model. The old machine has a book value of $32,000 and a remaining life of four years. The firm is depreciating the old machine by $8,000 per year using the straight-line method. Toucan doesn't expect to receive anything for the old machine when they scrap it in four years. If they sold the old machine now, however, to another firm in the industry Toucan would receive $40,000.  The new machine would cost $70,000 and has an expected resale value of 12,000 at the end of the fifth year. The new machine falls into the MACRS five-year class life (see chart below). The new machine uses less power, thus reducing electrical costs, and a more efficient cooling system to reduce labor costs. The annual before-tax savings are $7,500 per year. Toucan Industries is in a 40 percent marginal tax bracket. The firm's marginal cost of capital is 12 percent. For ease of calculation and readability, round your cash flows to the nearest whole dollar.

YEAR MACRS 5-YEAR

YEAR	MACRS 5-YEAR
1	20%
2	32%
3	19%
4	12%
5	11%
6	6%

a. What are the cash flows for this project? Put your cash flows on a time line.

b. Should the company accept this project (i.e., calculate the project's net present value, internal rate of return, and adjusted internal rate of return)?

SOLUTIONS
PRACTICE SET A: Cost of Capital

1. Refer to the balance sheet for Fire Dragon Corporation on page 236. Assume that Dragon's current stock price is $23. Dragon has 9 percent coupon mortgage bonds with 15 years left until maturity. The market interest on comparable mortgage bonds is now 8 percent. Dragon also has 13 percent coupon debentures with 10 years left until maturity. The market interest rate on comparable debentures is now 11 percent. What is Dragon's capital structure?

Market value of equity
Stock price × number of shares outstanding
= $23(1,000,000) = $23,000,000

Market value of debt
     Market value of mortgage bonds
     Bond price × number of bonds outstanding
         = $1,086.46(37,000,000) = $40,199,020

plus
     Market value of debenture bonds
     Bond price × number of bonds outstanding
         = $1,119.50(15,000,000) = $16,792,500
                                   $56,991,520

Total capitalization = equity + debt
          = $23,000,000 + $56,991,520 = $79,991,520

Equity portion of capital structure = $\dfrac{\$23,000,000}{\$79,991,520}$ = 29%

Debt portion of capital structure = $\dfrac{\$56,991,520}{\$79,991,520}$ = 71%

2. Assume that Fire Dragon Corporation's marginal tax rate is 34 percent. Further assume that Fire Dragon maintains its current long-term capital structure that you calculated in Problem 1. If Fire Dragon can issue additional debt at a cost of 12 percent and investors require a 15 percent rate of return on their equity investment, what is Fire Dragon's weighted average cost of capital? (Hint: Fire Dragon only uses internal equity financing.)

After-tax cost = Coupon (1 − Marginal tax rate) = 0.12(1 − 0.34) = 0.079 or 7.9%
of 12% debt   rate

Weighted average = 0.71[0.079] + 0.29[0.15] = 9.96%
cost of capital

3. Fire Dragon can issue $100,000 of 12 percent debt after which they must issue 13 percent debt. When will Fire Dragon use up their 12 percent debt? What is Fire Dragon's weighted average cost of capital once they have to issue the 13 percent debt?

$$\text{Break point} = \frac{\text{Dollar amount of lower cost capital available}}{\text{Portion that component represents in the firm's capital structure}} = \frac{\$100,000}{0.71} = \$140,845$$

for 12% debt

After-tax cost = Coupon (1 – Marginal tax rate) = 0.13(1 – 0.34) = 0.086 or 8.6%
of 12% debt   rate

Weighted average = 0.71[0.086] + 0.29[0.15] = 10.46%
cost of capital

4. Griffin Company has a target capital structure of 30 percent debt and 70 percent equity. They have $250,000 in retained earnings. Investors require a 16 percent return on their equity investment. Griffin's investment banking firm has advised them they can issue $400,000 of 10 percent secured debt after which they will have to issue 12 percent debt. The beta coefficient for Griffin is 1.5, the return on treasury securities is 5 percent, while the return on the S&P 500 is 13 percent. Flotation costs for new common stock is $1 per share. The last dividend paid was $0.75 and analysts expect their constant growth rate of 6 percent to continue into the foreseeable future. Flotation cost for debt is negligible and ignored. Griffin's marginal tax rate is 40 percent.

a. What is Griffin Company's weighted average cost of capital?

After-tax cost = Coupon (1 – Marginal tax rate) = 0.10(1 – 0.40) = 0.06 or 6%
of 10% debt   rate

Cost of retained earnings:
 Solve for required rate of return using CAPM.

$$\text{Required rate of return} = \text{Risk-free rate} + \left[\text{Return on the market} - \text{Risk-free rate} \right] \text{Quantity of risk}$$

$$= 0.05 + [0.13 - 0.05]1.5 = 17\%$$

WACC before first break point

$$\text{WACC}_1 = 0.3[0.06] + 0.7[0.17] = 13.70\%$$

b. Where does the break point for equity occur?

$$\text{Retained earnings} \atop \text{break point (BP}_1) = \frac{\$250,000}{0.7} = \$357,143$$

c. What is the weighted average cost of capital after the first break point?

Cost of equity after using up retained earnings

Solve for the stock price

$$\text{Stock price} = \frac{\text{Dividend}_{\text{year1}}}{\text{Require rate} \atop \text{of return} - \text{Growth} \atop \text{rate}} = \frac{\$0.75(1.06)}{0.17 - 0.06} = \frac{\$0.80}{0.11} = \$7.27$$

Solve for the required rate of return on new common stock

$$\text{Required rate of return} = \frac{\text{Dividend}_{\text{year1}}}{\text{Stock price}(1-\text{Flotation}_2)} + \text{Growth rate}$$

$$= \frac{\$0.75(1.06)}{\$7.27 - \$1} + 6\% = 18.76\%$$

$$WACC_2 = 0.3[0.06] + 0.7[0.1876] = 14.93\%$$

d. Where does the break point for debt occur?

$$\text{10\% debt} \atop \text{break point (BP}_2) = \frac{\$400,000}{0.3} = \$1,333,333$$

e. What is the weighted average cost of capital after the second break point?

$$\text{After-tax cost} \atop \text{of 12\% debt} = \text{Coupon} \atop \text{rate} (1 - \text{Marginal tax rate}) = 0.12(1 - 0.40) = 0.072 \text{ or } 7.2\%$$

$$WACC_3 = 0.3[0.072] + 0.7[0.1876] = 15.29\%$$

f. Draw Griffin's marginal cost of capital schedule.

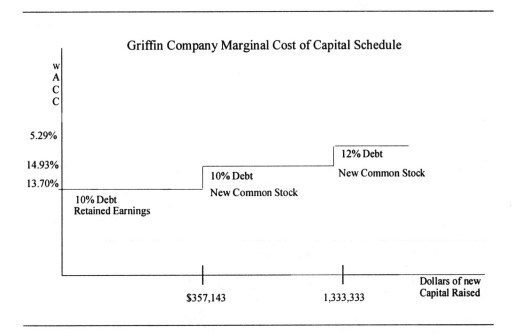

Griffin Company Marginal Cost of Capital Schedule

5. **Challenge Problem:** Accept A, B, C
                          Reject D

SOLUTIONS
PRACTICE SET B: Cost of Capital With Additional Complications

1. Barking Dog Industries has a capital structure of 40 percent debt and 60 percent equity. Their current stock price is $20 per share. Their investment bankers advise them that their before-tax cost of debt is 9 percent. They can raise $400,000 of 9 percent debt and after that amount they will have to offer their bond investors a 12 percent rate of return. Flotation costs for common stock are 15 percent for the first $350,000 of common stock issued. Flotation costs for common stock increases to 20 percent if they have to issue more than $350,000. The last dividend paid (Dividend$_{year1}$) was $1.30 and Barking Dog has a constant growth rate of 8 percent. Retained earnings for the year amounted to $180,000. Barking Dog is in a 40 percent tax bracket.

Barking Dog break points and the cost of each component

After-tax cost = Coupon (1 – Marginal tax rate) = 0.09(1 – 0.40) = 0.054 or 5.4%
of 9% debt   rate

After-tax cost = Coupon (1 – Marginal tax rate) = 0.12(1 – 0.40) = 0.072 or 7.2%
of 12% debt   rate

Cost of retained earnings:

$$\text{Required rate of return} = \frac{\text{Dividend}_{year1}}{\text{Stock price}} + \text{Growth rate}$$

$$= \frac{\$1.30(1.08)}{\$20} + 8\% = 15.02\%$$

$$\text{Retained earnings break point (BP}_1) = \frac{\$180,000}{0.6} = \$300,000$$

Cost of equity after using up retained earnings

$$\text{Required rate of return} = \frac{\text{Dividend}_{year1}}{\text{Stock price}(1-\text{Flotation}_1)} + \text{Growth rate}$$

$$= \frac{\$1.30(1.08)}{\$20(1-0.15)} + 8\% = 16.26\%$$

$$\text{15\% flotation cost break point (BP}_2) = \frac{\$180,000 + \$350,000}{0.6} = \$883,333$$

Cost of equity after using up lower flotation costs

$$\text{Required rate of return} = \frac{\text{Dividend}_{year1}}{\text{Stock price}(1 - \text{Flotation}_2)} + \text{Growth rate}$$

$$= \frac{\$1.30(1.08)}{\$20\,(1 - 0.20)} + 8\% = 16.78\%$$

9 percent debt break point (BP$_3$) $= \dfrac{\$400,000}{0.4} = \$1,000,000$

WACC before using up retained earnings

$$\text{WACC}_1 = 0.4[0.054] + 0.6[0.1502] = 11.17\%$$

WACC after using up retained earnings (at the BP$_1$ = $300,000)

$$\text{WACC}_2 = 0.4[0.054] + 0.6\,[\mathbf{0.1626}] = 11.92\%$$

WACC after using up 15 percent flotation equity (at the BP$_2$ = $883,333)

$$\text{WACC}_3 = 0.4[0.054] + 0.6[\mathbf{0.1678}] = 12.23\%$$

WACC after using up 9 percent debt (at the BP$_3$=$1,000,000)

$$\text{WACC}_4 = 0.4[\mathbf{0.072}] + 0.6[0.1678] = 12.95\%$$

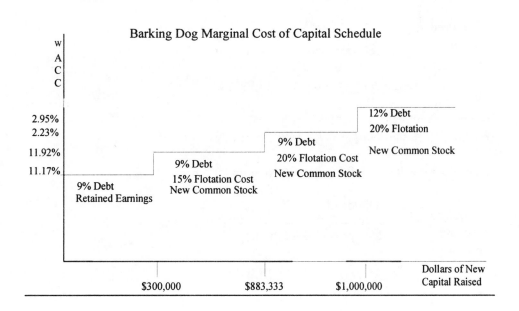

Barking Dog Marginal Cost of Capital Schedule

2.   Snarling Cat Enterprises has a capital structure of 30 percent debt and 70 percent equity. Their current stock price is $25 per share. Their investment bankers advise them that their before-tax cost of debt is 10 percent. They can raise $100,000 of 10 percent debt and after that amount they will have to offer their bond investors a 13 percent rate of return. Flotation costs for common stock are 10 percent for the first $200,000 of common stock issued. Flotation costs for common stock increases to 15 percent if they have to issue more than $200,000. The last dividend paid (Dividend$_{year1}$) was $2.12 and Snarling Cat has a constant growth rate of 6 percent. Retained earnings for the year amounted to $150,000. Snarling Cat is in a 40 percent tax bracket.

Snarling Cat break points and the cost of each component

After-tax cost = Coupon $(1 - $ Marginal tax rate$) = 0.09(1 - 0.40) = 0.054$ or 5.4%
of 10% debt   rate

After-tax cost = Coupon $(1 - $ Marginal tax rate$) = 0.12(1 - 0.40) = 0.072$ or 7.2%
of 13% debt   rate

Break point for $= \dfrac{\$150,000}{0.7} = \$214,286$
retained earnings (BP$_1$)

Break point for $= \dfrac{\$100,000}{0.3} = \$333,333$
10 percent debt (BP$_2$)

Break point 10 % $= \dfrac{(\$150,000 + \$200,000)}{0.7} = \$500,000$
flotation costs(BP$_3$)

WACC before using up retained earnings

$$\text{Required rate of return} = \frac{\text{Dividend}_{year1}}{\text{Stock price}} + \text{Growth rate}$$

$$= \frac{\$2.12(1.06)}{\$25} + 6\% = 14.99\%$$

WACC$_1$ $= 0.3[0.06] + 0.7[0.1499] = 12.29\%$

WACC after using up RE but before using up 10% percent debt

$$\text{Required rate of return} = \frac{\text{Dividend}_{year1}}{\text{Stock price}(1-\text{Flotation}_1)} + \text{Growth rate}$$

$$= \frac{\$2.12(1.06)}{\$25(1 - 0.10)} + 6\% = 15.99\%$$

WACC$_2$ $= 0.3[0.06] + 0.7[\mathbf{0.1599}] = 12.99\%$

WACC after using up RE and after using up 10 percent debt

$$WACC_3 = 0.3[\textbf{0.078}] + 0.7[0.1599] = 13.53\%$$

WACC after using up 10 percent flotation equity and after 10% debt

$$\text{Required rate of return} = \frac{\text{Dividend}_{year1}}{\text{Stock price}(1-\text{Flotation}_2)} + \text{Growth rate}$$

$$= \frac{\$2.12(1.06)}{\$25(1-0.15)} + 6\% = 16.58\%$$

$$WACC_4 = 0.3[0.078] + 0.7[\textbf{0.1658}] = 13.95\%$$

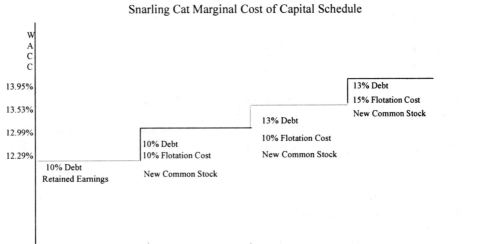

Snarling Cat Marginal Cost of Capital Schedule

SOLUTIONS
PRACTICE SET C: Payback and
Net Present Value

1. Sony expects the following cash flows from their new line of robotic animals (cash flows are in millions of dollars):

Year	Cash Flow
0	($100,000)
1	$35,000
2	$65,000
3	$40,000

a. What is the payback period?
Two years. $100,000 outflow at time 0 = $35,000 inflow in year 1 + $65,000 inflow in year 2.

b. What is the net present value for this project if the required rate of return (i.e., marginal cost of capital) is 18 percent?

$$\text{NPV} = \frac{(\$100,000)}{(1.18)^0} + \frac{\$35,000}{(1.18)^1} + \frac{\$65,000}{(1.18)^2} + \frac{\$40,000}{(1.18)^3} = \$688$$

2. Farmer Smith would like to buy a new egg incubator. The incubator would cost $48,000 and would lead to increased cash inflows of $12,000 per year over its five-year life.

a. What is the payback period for the incubator? Should Farmer Smith purchase the incubator if she wants a payback of three years or better?

Payback = 4 years. She should not purchase the incubator.

b. What is the net present value of the incubator if Farmer Smith's marginal cost of capital is 12 percent? Should Farmer Smith accept the project? (*Hint*: Recognize that the cash inflows are an annuity.)

$$\text{NPV} = \frac{(\$48,000)}{(1.12)^0} + \$12,000 \left[\frac{1}{0.12} - \frac{1}{0.12(1.12)^5} \right] = (\$4,743)$$

Farmer Smith would not accept the project because the net present value is less than $0. The value of her firm would *decline* by $4,743 if she accepts this project.

3. Keith's Rock Shop, Inc., is considering a move to a new location. Moving costs would be $120,000 (rocks are heavy and don't always roll). The more visible location should lead to an increase in sales and hence larger cash inflows. Even considering the higher rent, after-tax cash flows should be $25,000 more than in the old location in each of the next seven years. Keith believes that competition will saturate the rock market after seven years. At that time, he plans to sell his rock store and invest in a Rolling Rock beer distributorship.

a. What is the payback period for this move?

Payback = 4.8 years.
  $120,000 = $25,000 + $25,000 +$25,000 +$25,000 +$20,000/$25,000

b. If Keith's marginal cost of capital is 10 percent, what is the NPV?

$$NPV = \frac{(\$120,000)}{(1.10)^0} + \$25,000 \left[\frac{1}{0.10} - \frac{1}{0.10(1.10)^7} \right] = \$1,711$$

4. One step on the production line at Murray's Cookies is sealing cookie packages. The production supervisor has submitted a capital budgeting proposal for a new gluing machine. This machine will cost $20,000 and will produce more reliable seals, reducing product waste. Cost savings, over the five-year expected life of the machine, are as follows:

Year	Savings (Inflows)
1	$4,000
2	$4,000
3	$6,000
4	$6,000
5	$7,000

a. If Murray's marginal cost of capital is 9 percent, what is the NPV?

$$NPV = \frac{(\$20,000)}{(1.09)^0} + \frac{\$4,000}{(1.09)^1} + \frac{\$4,000}{(1.09)^2} + \frac{\$6,000}{(1.09)^3} + \frac{\$6,000}{(1.09)^4} + \frac{\$7,000}{(1.09)^5} = \$470$$

b. What is the NPV if the marginal cost of capital is 14 percent?

$$NPV = \frac{(\$20,000)}{(1.14)^0} + \frac{\$4,000}{(1.14)^1} + \frac{\$4,000}{(1.14)^2} + \frac{\$6,000}{(1.14)^3} + \frac{\$6,000}{(1.14)^4} + \frac{\$7,000}{(1.14)^5} = (\$2,175)$$

5. **Challenge Problem:** $2,925,458

SOLUTIONS
PRACTICE SET D: Net Present Value and
Internal Rate of Return

1. Prototype Industries expects the following cash flows from their new line of robotic helpmates (cash flows are in millions of dollars):

Year	Cash Flow
0	($115,000)
1	$45,000
2	$55,000
3	$65,000

Assuming their marginal cost of capital is 16 percent, find the NPV and IRR for this new project.

$$NPV = \frac{(\$115,000)}{(1.16)^0} + \frac{\$45,000}{(1.16)^1} + \frac{\$55,000}{(1.16)^2} + \frac{\$65,000}{(1.16)^3} = \$6,310$$

$$IRR = 19.12\% \quad \therefore \frac{(\$115,000)}{(1.1912)^0} - \left(\frac{\$45,000}{(1.1912)^1} + \frac{\$55,000}{(1.1912)^2} + \frac{\$65,000}{(1.1912)^3} \right) = \$0$$

2. eSing is considering investment in opera arias produced specifically for the military. Sales are estimated to produce the following cash flows:

Year	Cash Flow
0	($12,000)
1	$5,000
2	$6,000
3	$7,000

Assuming their marginal cost of capital is 17 percent, find the project's NPV and IRR.

$$NPV = \frac{(\$12,000)}{(1.17)^0} + \frac{\$5,000}{(1.17)^1} + \frac{\$6,000}{(1.17)^2} + \frac{\$7,000}{(1.17)^3} = \$1,027$$

$$IRR = 21.92\% \quad \therefore \frac{(\$12,000)}{(1.2192)^0} - \left(\frac{\$5,000}{(1.2192)^1} + \frac{\$6,000}{(1.2192)^2} + \frac{\$7,000}{(1.2192)^3} \right) = \$0$$

3. **Challenge Problem:** NPV = $98,915; IRR=14.60%.

SOLUTIONS
PRACTICE SET E: Adjusted Internal Rate of Return

1. Medieval Travels has a marginal cost of capital is 12 percent. They are considering an investment in another private train car that would allow them to double their capacity. The cash flows from the proposed project are given below.

Year	Cash Flows
0	($25,000)
1	$12,000
2	$15,000
3	$11,000
4	

a. What is the project's net present value (NPV)?

$$NPV = \frac{(\$25,000)}{(1.12)^0} + \frac{\$12,000}{(1.12)^1} + \frac{\$15,000}{(1.12)^2} + \frac{\$11,000}{(1.12)^3} = \$5,502$$

b. What is the project's internal rate of return (IRR)?

IRR=24.54%

c. What is the project's adjusted internal rate of return (AIRR)?

We first have to find the future value of the inflows invested at 12 percent.

$11,000 (1.12)^0 \rightarrow = \$11,000$

$15,000(1.12)^1 \rightarrow = \$16,800$

$12,000(1.12)^2 \rightarrow = \underline{\$15,053}$

$\underline{\$42,853}$

Remember that AIRR finds the rate of return that makes the present value of the outflows ($25,000) minus the present value of the reinvested inflows ($42,853) equal to zero.

$$\frac{\$25,000}{(1 + \text{Modified internal rate})^0} - \frac{\$42,853}{(1 + \text{Modified internal rate})^3} = \$0$$

Because we only have one outflow at time 0 we can simplify.

$$\$25,000 - \frac{\$42,853}{(1 + \text{Modified internal rate})^3} = \$0$$

What AIRR would equate the present value costs ($25,000) to the future value of cash inflows ($42,853)? We can rearrange our equation and solve for the AIRR as follows:

$$\frac{\$25,000}{\$42,853} = \frac{1}{\left(1 + \text{modified internal rate}\right)^3} = 0.58$$

When we look across three years (the life of the project) on the present value tables we find 0.58 under the 20 percent column. The adjusted internal rate of return is, therefore, equal to about 20 percent (19.67 percent to be precise).

$$\$25,000 - \frac{\$42,853}{\left(1.1967\right)^3} = \$0$$

2. Viking Enterprises specializes in unique antiquities. The firm has the opportunity to bid for a rare artifact that the firm would then "rent out" to museums around the world. The initial investment will be $12 million. The anticipated cash flows (in millions of dollars) from this job, if their bid is successful, are given below. Assume that the cost of capital for Viking is 11 percent.

YEAR	CASH FLOWS
0	($12,000)
1	$5,200
2	$5,200
3	$5,200

a. What is the project's payback?

Payback = 12,000/$5,200 = 2.31 years.

b. What is the project's net present value?

$$\text{NPV} = \frac{(\$12,000)}{(1.11)^0} + \frac{\$5,200}{(1.11)^1} + \frac{\$5,200}{(1.11)^2} + \frac{\$5,200}{(1.11)^3} = \$707$$

c. What is the project's internal rate of return (IRR)?

$$\text{IRR} = 14.36\% \quad \therefore \frac{(\$12,000)}{(1.1436)^0} - \left(\frac{\$5,200}{(1.1436)^1} + \frac{\$5,200}{(1.1436)^2} + \frac{\$5,200}{(1.1436)^3} \right) = \$0$$

d. What is the project's adjusted internal rate of return (AIRR)?

We first have to find the future value of the inflows invested at 12 percent. Because this is an annuity the future value can be found as:

$$\text{Future value of an annuity} = \text{Payment} \left[\frac{\left(1 + \text{Interest rate}\right)^{\# \text{of periods}} - 1}{\text{Interest rate}} \right]$$

$$\text{Future value of an annuity} = \$5,200 \left[\frac{(1.12)^3 - 1}{0.12}\right] = \$17,547$$

Remember that AIRR finds the rate of return that makes the present value of the outflows ($25,000) minus the present value of the reinvested inflows ($42,853) equal to zero.

$$\frac{\$12,000}{(1 + \text{modified internal rate})^0} - \frac{\$17,547}{(1 + \text{modified internal rate})^3} = \$0$$

Because we only have one outflow at time 0 we can simplify.

$$\$12,000 - \frac{\$17,547}{(1 + \text{modified internal rate})^3} = \$0$$

What AIRR would equate the present value costs ($12,000) to the future value of cash inflows ($17,547)? We can rearrange our equation and solve for the AIRR as follows:

$$\frac{\$12,000}{\$17,547} = \frac{1}{(1 + \text{modified internal rate})^3} = 0.68$$

When we look across three years (the life of the project) on the present value tables we find 0.68 under the 14 percent column. The adjusted internal rate of return is, therefore, equal to about 14 percent (13.50 percent to be precise).

$$\$12,000 - \frac{\$17,547}{(1.1350)^3} = \$0$$

3. Assume that Viking has another project opportunity that also requires a cash investment of $12,000 and has the following cash inflows (millions of dollars): year 1, $0; year 2, $1,200; years 3 and 4, $2,200; year 5, $3,200; and years 6 and 7, $4,200. Assume that the cost of capital for Viking remains at 11 percent

a. What is the project's net present value (NPV)?

$$NPV = \frac{(\$12,000)}{(1.11)^0} + \frac{\$0}{(1.11)^1} + \frac{\$1,200}{(1.11)^2} + \frac{\$2,200}{(1.11)^3} + \frac{\$2,200}{(1.11)^4} + \frac{\$3,200}{(1.11)^5} + \frac{\$4,200}{(1.11)^6} + \frac{\$4,200}{(1.11)^7} = (\$1,801)$$

b. What is the project's internal rate of return (IRR)?

IRR = 7.39%

$$\therefore \frac{(\$12,000)}{(1.0739)^0} + \frac{\$0}{(1.0739)^1} + \frac{\$1,200}{(1.0739)^2} + \frac{\$2,200}{(1.0739)^3} + \frac{\$2,200}{(1.0739)^4} + \frac{\$3,200}{(1.0739)^5} + \frac{\$4,200}{(1.0739)^6} + \frac{\$4,200}{(1.0739)^7}$$

c.   What is the project's adjusted internal rate of return (AIRR)?

We first have to find the future value of the reinvested cash inflows:

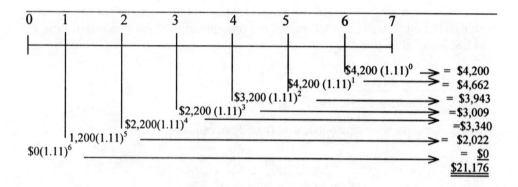

Find the rate of return that causes the present value of the outflows ($12,000) minus the future value of the reinvested inflows ($21,176) to be equal to zero (i.e., the discount rate that makes net present value equal to zero).

$$\frac{\$12,000}{(1+\text{Modified internal rate})^0} - \frac{\$21,176}{(1+\text{Modified internal rate})^7} = \$0$$

Simplify

$$\$12,000 - \frac{\$21,176}{(1+\text{Modified internal rate})^7} = \$0$$

What AIRR would equate the present value costs ($12,000) to the future value of cash inflows ($21,176)? We can rearrange our equation and solve for the AIRR as follows:

$$\frac{\$12,000}{\$21,176} = \frac{1}{(1+\text{Modified internal rate})^7} = 0.57$$

When we look across seven years (the life of the project) on the present value table we find 0.57 under the 8 percent column. The adjusted internal rate of return is, therefore, equal to about 8 percent (8.16 percent to be precise).

$$\$12,000 - \frac{\$21,176}{(1.0816)^3} = \$0$$

4. **Challenge Problem:**   NPV: −$26,800
                                                IRR: 2.63%
                                                AIRR: 7.42%

5. **Challenge Problem:**   AIRR: 20.18%

SOLUTIONS
PRACTICE SET F: Cash Flow Estimation
New Project Analysis

1. SPICE GINGERALE

Initial Cash Outflow

Depreciable Assets

Bottler	$90,000
Conveyer	$45,000
Depreciable asset investment	$135,000

New Working Capital

Change in current assets:

Increase in accounts receivable	$35,000
Increase in inventory	$20,000

Change in current liabilities:

Increase in accounts payable	($15,000)
Change in net working capital:	$40,000

Depreciation Expense

Bottler	Conveyor
$90,000(0.33) = $29,700	$45,000(0.33) = $14,850
$90,000(0.45) = $40,500	$45,000(0.45) = $20,250
$90,000(0.15) = $13,500	$45,000(0.15) = $6,750
$83,700	$41,850

Book Value of Bottler	Book Value of Conveyor
$90,000 − $83,700 = $6,300	$45,000 − $41,850 = $3,150

OPERATION CASH FLOWS

Revenues	1,750,000	2,250,000	2,750,000
Less Variable Costs	350,000	450,000	550,000
Less Fixed Costs	170,000	170,000	170,000
Less Depreciation	44,550	60,750	20,250
EBIT	1,185,450	1,569,250	2,009,750
Less Taxes (40%)	474,180	627,700	803,900
Earnings After Taxes	711,270	941,550	1,205,850
Add Depreciation	44,550	60,750	20,250
Operation Cash Flows	$755,820	$1,002,300	$1,226,100

SPICE GINGERALE (continued)

<u>Disposal Cash Flows</u>
Depreciable Assets

Selling Price of Bottler	$30,000
Less Book Value	($6,300)
Gain on Sale	$23,700
Tax rate	× 0.40
Tax Liability	$9,480
Selling price	$30,000
Less Tax Liability	($9,480)
Cash Flow from Depreciable Asset	$20,520

<u>Net Working Capital</u>

Increase in Inventory	$20,000
Increase in Accounts Receivable	$35,000
Less: Increase in Accounts Payable	($15,000)
Total Net Investment in Working Capital	$40,000
Percent of Working Capital Recoupment	×0.90
Recouped Working Capital (disposal value)	$36,000

```
              0          1          2            3
              |          |          |            |
              |          |          |            |
             CF0        CF1        CF2        CF3  + Disposal
Dep. asset ($135,000)  $755,820  $1,002,300  $1,226,100
NWC         ($40,000)                          $20,520 Sale of dep. asset
           ($175,000)                          $36,000 Recoup of NWC
                                             $1,282,620
```

NPV = $2,211,810
IRR = 458.06%
AIRR =167.59 %

2. **Challenge Problem:**

b.   NPV = $488,903
      IRR = 59.47%
      AIRR = 41.70%

SOLUTIONS
PRACTICE SET G: Cash Flow Estimation
Replacement Analysis

1. TROLL, INC.

Initial Cash Outflow	
Depreciable Assets	
Cost of new equipment	$12,000
Market value of old equipment	($1,000)
Tax effect of sale of old equipment	$190*
Depreciable asset investment	$11,190
New Working Capital	
Increase in net working capital	$1,000

*Selling price – Book value = Gain on sale (Tax rate) = Tax liability
$1,000 – $525 = $475(0.40) = $190

Year	Depreciation Old Machine	Depreciation New Machine	Δ Dep
1	$525	($12,000)(0.33)$3,960	$3,435
2	$0	($12,000)(0.45)$5,400	$5,400
3	$0	($12,000)(0.15)$1,800	$1,800

$CashFlow_{year1} = (\$6,000)(1 - 0.40) + \$3,435 \, (0.40) = \$4,974$
$CashFlow_{year2} = (\$6,000)(1 - 0.40) + \$5,400 \, (0.40) = \$5,760$
$CashFlow_{year3} = (\$6,000)(1 - 0.40) + \$1,800 \, (0.40) = \$4,320$

We need to add disposal cash flow to the cash flow in year five. Recall that at the end of the project's life the firm expects to sell the new injection molder for $3,000. At the end of the project's life the new injection molder will have a book value of $840.

Disposal Cash Inflow
• *Sale of Depreciable Asset*

Estimated sale price of new equipment	$3,000
Tax effect of sale of new equipment	($864)*
Net cash inflow from disposal of depreciable asset	$2,136
• *Recoupment of Net Working Capital*	
Recovery of net working capital	$1,000

*Selling price – Book value = Gain on sale (Tax rate) = Tax liability
$3,000 – $840 = $2,160(0.40) = $864

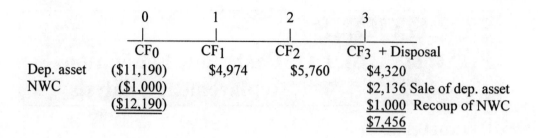

	0	1	2	3
	CF$_0$	CF$_1$	CF$_2$	CF$_3$ + Disposal
Dep. asset	($11,190)	$4,974	$5,760	$4,320
NWC	($1,000)			$2,136 Sale of dep. asset
	($12,190)			$1,000 Recoup of NWC
				$7,456

NPV = $2,150
IRR = 21.31%
AIRR = 18.23%

2. Challenge Problem: NPV = ($1,847)
IRR = 9.92%
AIRR = 10.73%